Reimagining Climate Change

T0304051

Responding to climate change has become an industry. Governments, corporations, activist groups, and others now devote billions of dollars to mitigation and adaptation, and their efforts represent one of the most significant policy measures ever dedicated to a global challenge. Despite its laudatory intent, the response industry, or "Climate Inc.", is failing.

Reimagining Climate Change questions established categories, routines, and practices that presently constitute accepted solutions to tackling climate change and offers alternative routes forward. It does so by unleashing the political imagination. The chapters grasp the larger arc of collective experience, interpret its meaning for the choices we face, and creatively visualize alternative trajectories that can help us cognitively and emotionally enter into alternative climate futures. They probe the meaning and effectiveness of climate protection "from below" – forms of community and practice that are emerging in various locales around the world and that hold promise for greater collective resonance. They also question climate protection "from above" in the form of industrial and modernist orientations and examine large-scale agribusinesses, as well as criticize the concept of resilience as it is presently being promoted as a response to climate change.

This book will be of great interest to students and scholars of climate change, global environmental politics, and environmental studies in general, as well as climate change activists.

Paul Wapner is Professor of Global Environmental Politics in the School of International Service at American University, USA.

Hilal Elver is the UN Special Rapporteur on the Right to Food, and Global Distinguished Fellow at the UCLA School of Law Resnick Food Law and Policy Program, USA.

Routledge Advances in Climate Change Research

Reimagining Climate Change
Edited by Paul Wapner and Hilal Elver

Climate Change and the Anthropos
Planet, people and places
Linda Connor

Reimagining Climate Change

Edited by Paul Wapner and Hilal Elver

LONDON AND NEW YORK

First published 2016
by Routledge
2 Park Square, Milton Park, Abingdon, Oxon OX14 4RN

and by Routledge
711 Third Avenue, New York, NY 10017

First issued in paperback 2017

Routledge is an imprint of the Taylor & Francis Group, an informa business

British Library Cataloguing-in-Publication Data
A catalogue record for this book is available from the British Library

Library of Congress Cataloging-in-Publication Data
Names: Wapner, Paul Kevin, editor. | Elver, Hilal, editor.
Title: Reimagining climate change / edited by Paul Wapner and Hilal Elver.
Description: Abingdon, Oxon : Routledge, Earthscan, 2016. | Includes bibliographical references and index.
Identifiers: LCCN 2015035192| ISBN 9781138944268 (hardback) | ISBN 9781315671468 (ebook)
Subjects: LCSH: Climatic changes. | Climate change mitigation. | Environmental policy
Classification: LCC QC903 .R45 2016 | DDC 363.738/74—dc23
LC record available at http://lccn.loc.gov/2015035192

ISBN 13: 978-1-138-30421-5 (pbk)
ISBN 13: 978-1-138-94426-8 (hbk)

Typeset in Sabon
by FiSH Books Ltd, Enfield

Contents

Contributors

Simon Dalby is CIGI Chair in the Political Economy of Climate Change at the Balsillie School of International Affairs, and Professor of Geography and Environmental Studies at Wilfrid Laurier University, Waterloo, Ontario. He is the author of *Environmental Security* (2002) and *Security and Environmental Change* (2009), and recently coedited (with Shannon O'Lear at the University of Kansas) *Reframing Climate Change: Constructing Ecological Geopolitics* (Routledge 2016).

Hilal Elver is the United Nations Special Rapporteur on Right to Food since June 2014, and Global Distinguished Fellow at Resnick Food Law and Policy Program at the UCLA Law School. Since 2009, she has been co-director of the Climate Change, Human Security and Democracy Project at the Orfaela Center, University of California, Santa Barbara. Her books include *Peaceful Uses of International Rivers: the Case of Euphrates and Tigris* (2002), and *Headscarf Controversy: Human Rights and Freedom of Religion* (2012).

Richard Falk is Albert G. Milbank Professor of International Law and Practice Emeritus, Princeton University and currently Research Fellow, Orfalea Center of Global Studies, UCSB. He was UN Special Rapporteur for Occupied Palestine, 2008–2014. For the last several years he has been Director of the project on Climate Change, Human Rights, and the Future of Democracy. In 1972 he published *This Endangered Planet: Prospects and Proposals for Human Survival*. His most recent books are *Humanitarian Intervention and Legitimacy Wars* (2014), *Palestine: The Legitimacy of Hope* (2015), and *Chaos and Counterrevolution: After the Arab Spring* (2015). Since 2008 he has been annually nominated for the Nobel Peace Prize.

John Foran is Professor of Sociology and Environmental Studies at the University of California, Santa Barbara, where he has taught since 1989. He is the author of *Fragile Resistance: Social Transformation in Iran from 1500 to the Revolution* (1993) and *Taking Power: On the Origins of Revolutions in the Third World* (2005). His books, articles, and public sociology on the global climate justice movement can be found at www.climatejusticeproject.com and at www.iicat.org, where he blogs. Foran is active with 350 Santa Barbara, the Green Party of California, and System Change Not Climate Change, where he co-hosts the Paris Climate Justice project.

Miriam R. Lowi is Professor of Comparative and Middle East Politics at the College of New Jersey. She has written extensively on the natural resource dimension of political behavior in the Middle East and North Africa. She is the author of *Water and Power: the Politics of a Scarce Resource in the Jordan River Basin* (1993) and *Oil Wealth and the Poverty of Politics: Algeria Compared* (2009), and co-editor of *Environment and Security: Discourses and Practices* (2000). She was named "Carnegie Scholar" (2008–10) for her current work on oil and the politics of identity in Gulf monarchies.

Manjana Milkoreit is a Postdoctoral Research Fellow with the Walton Sustainability Solutions Initiative and a Senior Sustainability Fellow at the Julie Ann Wrigley Global Institute of Sustainability, Arizona State University. Her research explores the role of cognition in global climate change governance with a focus on beliefs and emotions among decision-makers and diplomats. She leads the multidisciplinary Imagination and Climate Futures Initiative, and is involved in projects exploring the conceptual development of the Anthropocene, the science-policy and science-diplomacy interface, pop-culture and climate-related mobilization, and the nature of ideologies. She holds a Masters degree in Public Policy from the Harvard Kennedy School and a Ph.D. in Global Governance from the University of Waterloo (Canada).

Simon Nicholson is Assistant Professor and Director of the Global Environmental Politics program in the School of International Service at American University. He also co-directs the Forum for Climate Engineering Assessment, a scholarly initiative that considers the political and social implications of climate engineering proposals. Nicholson is editor (with Paul Wapner) of *Global Environmental Politics: From Person to Planet* (2015) and (with Sikina Jinnah) of *New Earth Politics: Essays from the Anthropocene* (2016).

Matthew Paterson is Professor of Political Science at the University of Ottawa. His research is currently focused on the political economy and cultural politics of climate change. His most recent book is *Transnational Climate Change Governance* (with Harriet Bulkeley and eight other authors; 2014) and he has recently acted as a Lead Author by the Intergovernmental Panel on Climate Change, working on the chapter on international cooperation for the Fifth Assessment Report. His current research project, funded by the SSHRC, is entitled "Cultural Politics of Climate Change," and explores the contested politics of how shifts to a low carbon society produce novel forms of subjectivity and challenge established ones.

Paul Wapner is Professor of Global Environmental Politics in the School of International Service at American University, Washington, DC. His work focuses on environmental ethics, climate change politics, and global activism. He is the author of *Living through the End of Nature: The Future of American Environmentalism*, and *Environmental Activism and World Civic Politics*, and co-editor of *Global Environmental Politics: From Person to Planet* (with Simon Nicholson), and *Principled World Politics: The Challenge of Normative International Relations* (with Lester Ruiz). His most recent work focuses on the relationship between climate change and the inner life.

Acknowledgements

Reimagining Climate Change is the first major book publication resulting from the establishment in 2009 of the project "Climate Change, Human Security, and Democracy," funded and partially conceived by Moulay Hicham ben Abdullah of Morocco, and enjoying the formal auspices of the Moulay Hicham Foundation. The book is the outcome of a process that commenced with a 2010 workshop in Santa Barbara, California, followed by further meetings in Morocco, Turkey, and at several annual meetings of the International Studies Association. Over this time period, chapter authors worked to process the huge outpouring of writings about climate change and collectively identify how scholarship can best assist in creating a more livable and just world.

The editors and contributors want to express their special thanks to Mark Juergensmeyer, director of the Orfalea Center of International and Global Studies at the University of California in Santa Barbara, for hosting the project from its inception and providing logistical support, particularly at the founding workshop that launched the project as a whole. We also wish to thank Victor Faessel, the Executive Director of the Center, for his help in arranging the original workshop and assisting the project over the past few years. We are similarly grateful to Catherine Cornet for her efficient facilitation of the Morocco workshop held in conjunction with the annual meeting of the Moulay Hicham Foundation.

Simon Dalby wishes to express gratitude to the Social Sciences and Humanities Research Council of Canada for supporting his research with a grant focused on "Borders in Globalization." Paul Wapner wishes to thank American University for its support through a Vice Provost Faculty Research Award.

This project would not have been possible without the help of Anne Kantel and Alyssa Brierly. Anne assisted with initial editing of a number of chapters and helped plan the intellectual trajectory of the volume. We are grateful for her conscientiousness and scholarly capabilities. Alyssa prepared the manuscript for publication with extraordinary skill and enthusiasm. We deeply appreciate the care she devoted to the book, her keen editorial abilities, and her generous willingness to volunteer her services to the undertaking.

Finally, we wish to express our deep gratitude to Moulay Hicham for his support, inspirational presence, and hospitality in Morocco during the intellectual development of the project.

1 Introduction

Reimagining climate change

Paul Wapner

Humanity has been trying to respond to climate change for over three decades. During this time, many well-meaning people, organizations, and governments have put their noses to the grindstone and worked to reduce greenhouse gas emissions, enhance sinks, and otherwise attempt to address the intensifying reality of global warming. What have we to show for it?

When the international community signed the Kyoto Protocol in 1997, the world annually emitted roughly 24 billion tons of CO_2 into the atmosphere. Carbon concentrations stood at 364 ppm, and temperatures had risen about a half of a degree Celsius over preindustrial levels. Today, the world annually emits 36 billion tons of CO_2 – with the expectation that this will continue to rise 3 percent each year – and CO_2 concentrations stand above 400 ppm. Global average temperatures have risen 0.8 degrees Celsius since the industrial revolution and, despite international agreement to keep temperatures from rising over 2 degrees Celsius, the going consensus is that the world will push through that threshold over the next few decades. Things are not good. Indeed, we seem to be at an impasse.

The impasse, it should be clear, is not one of inactivity. Plenty of people and organizations are dedicating their careers and indeed lives to addressing the climate challenge. The problem is that such efforts lack traction. There are at least two reasons for this. First is simply the sheer magnitude and complexity of transitioning from a carbon-based economy. Carbon pervades almost all of our lives. It literally fuels our existence. Almost everything we eat, drink, purchase, or otherwise consume has a carbon footprint. Given current energy systems, one cannot write these words without drawing on fossilized life in one form or another, and indeed few cannot get through their days without tapping into the rigs, mines, or pumps lodged into the earth's belly. Our carbon-fueled lives are so ubiquitous that it is inaccurate to say simply that we have a carbon-based economy; rather, we live inside a carbon *world*. Everywhere we turn, carbon.

Many have acknowledged the immensity and complexity of the climate challenge, and analyzed the power relationships that animate humanity's addiction to fossil fuels and carbon's ubiquity. The authors of this volume focus on a second but related explanation for the current impasse. We concentrate on the efforts being taken to address climate change themselves. There is an assumption these days that all the right pieces are in place to tackle climate change, we simply lack the ability to scale them up. That is, while the challenge is immense, we actually have the knowledge and capability to delink ourselves from carbon. We have, for instance, the technological competence, market mechanisms, cultural understandings, and governing tools to transform our fossil fueled civilization; we simply cannot generate enough will, momentum, or collective thrust to enable them to do their work. We live, in other words in an "if only" moment. *If only* markets could capture full climate costs; *if only* states could find common ground and agree to appropriate international measures; *if only* technological innovation was given fuller reign and renewables could compete on a level playing field; *if only* rationality and scientific evidence could root out ignorance or superstition; *if only* we could stop consuming so much; *if only* ... on and on. Framed in this manner, it appears that our climate woes involve the pace, intensity, and scale of our efforts, not their quality, direction, or ultimate destiny. It is as if the main task is merely to accelerate current mitigation and adaptation efforts. Time is running out; we better get on with it.

The authors of this volume question what "getting on with it" means. Rather than sounding yet another alarm and warning that we have to move our feet that much faster to implement the solutions at hand or at least those in the works, we focus on the encrusted character of the so-called "solutions" themselves and their attendant mechanisms of execution and employment. We question the entire climate regime – what we refer to as "Climate Inc." – the routinized system of response that has evolved to address climate change. We do this because getting out of the carbon world is not simply a matter of severing ties to certain industries or particular forms of collective behavior, but envisaging and reformulating first principles.

All of us suffer from what could be called, "hardening of the categories" – the reification of understandings and practices. This is also the case with responding to climate change. Over the years, we have established certain approaches that constitute the landscape of climate response. These are so well known or obvious that they have retreated into the background and now structure climate affairs by streaming through our institutions and practices largely unseen and certainly untheorized. Nonetheless, they have fixed certain horizons and committed us along particular trajectories. Such hardening has thus narrowed the range of possibility for thought and action, and has concentrated attention on the instrumentality rather than the ends of climate measures. This has caused the current climate regime to see the challenge of responding to climate change mainly as a lack of time, commitment, or momentum.

The authors of this volume focus not on scarcity of will, weakness of motivation, or lack of dedication, but on failures of *imagination*. The scarcest resource these days, in other words, is the ability to unleash the mind, heart, and spirit to envision, entertain, and develop hitherto neglected possibilities. Climate Inc. works against this. Most efforts and even proposals for addressing climate change subscribe to conventional political, economic, and cultural understandings and practices. They mimic the larger society of which they are a part and rarely question underlying suppositions. One reason for this has to do with the seeming necessity to appear practical and realistic. No one wants to be accused of being naïve or irrelevant. Starry-eyed utopians rarely find a "seat at the table." Being practical wins one credibility and, even more, widens the degree of resonance within public discourse. One can be understood when talking about, for instance, cap and trade, international negotiated emissions ceilings, technological innovation and technology transfers, and low carbon lifestyles. These fit into existing forms of governance, economic practices, scientific understandings, engineering possibilities, and everyday activities. They can be adopted without major systemic adjustments. The world becomes more tone-deaf when the language switches to, for instance, questions of social justice, the distortions of capitalism, moving beyond mitigation and adaptation, and critically assessing modernity. These latter objects of attention occupy, at best, the periphery of current political consideration. More often than not, they exist completely outside climate conversations and thus beyond the realm of worthy consideration. They involve wholesale change that is either not in the political cards or representative of what the established order deems irresponsible thinking. If one wants to be relevant these days, one needs to adhere to prevailing assumptions of what is possible. Climate Inc. serves as a gatekeeper to relevance. It implicitly polices the content of climate responses by disciplining ideas and deliberations. To be sure, it does so not through authoritative individuals or institutions conducting litmus tests – although this sometimes happens – but through a socializing process that everyone who wants to address climate change goes through in trying to be taken seriously.

The same socializing process takes place at a higher level of abstraction. Beyond determining who gets a seat at the table, Climate Inc. sets the paradigmatic boundaries for thinking itself. Today, many of us assume that our cognitive, emotional, and spiritual lives enjoy infinite extension. That is, we can think, feel, and experience anything we want. The Internet fuels this permissive sentiment as we witness ideas soaring around the planet in micro-seconds and thus believe we inhabit an endless cultural terrain. Proof of this is the seemingly profound multiculturalism that has marked global life for the past decade or so. The world has never enjoyed such a globalized moment wherein cultural containers no longer protect people from external influence. But, as should be obvious, such cultural sharing is not a love fest of democratic expression with limitless possibilities. Rather, it represents a certain form of exchange that is itself bounded by structures of power. Material and ideational systems – encapsulated in, what some call, epistemes, discourses, or simply modes of life – establish the contours of thought and practice. Contemporary multiculturalism, for instance, contains hierarchical structures that privilege certain cultural expressions over others. Racism, sexism, First World-ism, and anthropocentrism, for example, mark global cultural life despite a thick veneer of progressive cosmopolitanism. Furthermore, even the most enlightened cosmopolitanism has limits insofar as we all live in socio-historical contexts that, by definition, circumscribe thought and behavior. Similarly, Climate Inc. lays down certain parameters and authoritative protocols for addressing climate change. These correspond with broader socio-political structures that dominate and establish the originality of the current age. Largely unnoticed, most people internalize such structural constraint and are thus bounded as they wrestle with the challenge of climate change.

Given the constraints of Climate Inc., this volume offers an exercise in what James Rosenau (1990) calls "jailbreaking" – the attempt to unshackle political life from established categories. Jailbreaking, in the context of Climate Inc., involves liberating thought and action from conventional approaches to climate change. It seeks to set to one side the discourses that presently structure standard responses to climate change, explain inherent limitations, and offer alternative orientations. It does this in the service of moving beyond the current political impasse. If the world were on track to reduce carbon emissions anywhere near what scientists say is required to ensure climate safety, Climate Inc. would be something to celebrate. After all, Climate Inc. involves the participation of innumerable institutions, billions of dollars of investment and practice, and the creation and alteration of countless programs in and across various sectors. No one can persuasively argue that the effort is unimpressive. The problem is that, for all its steam and momentum, its achievements are disappointing, to put it mildly and, more consequentially, grossly insufficient. They have taken us into a troubling cul-de-sac in which the efforts may be multiplying and gaining greater public acceptance, but are also circling around, what is essentially, a political dead-end. No one genuinely believes that current measures, even if dramatically scaled up, will provide an effective response to climate change. It is time to move on – to stand back from Climate Inc., understand the ultimate direction towards which it is leading, and chart a new course. As will become clear, doing so requires not simply cosmetic adjustment to current practices, but wholesale reformatting and a transformative outlook. This is what successful jailbreaking ultimately means.

An immediate question arises in this kind of exercise, one that has plagued thinkers throughout time: how can one gain conceptual distance from established categories to criticize them and seek alternative arrangements? How can one practice reflexivity deep enough to disrupt the constant chatter and reproductive mechanisms that set the terrain for social thought in the first place? How can one think outside the proverbial box? There is, of course, no single answer to such questions but at the heart of *any* explanation lies the potentials of the imagination. Imagination represents the ability to dream, envision, conjure, and otherwise subvert existing, conceptual classifications. It involves flights of awareness in which the mind and heart take license to leave the seeming "realities" and "feasibilities" that are supposed to frame experience. Untied to existing mores and self-consciously devoted to poking through conceptual walls, one can go, to use Rilke's words, "a little further, beyond the last of the billboards" (Mitchell 1984, 205), and there recognize not only that one has been imprisoned but also envision and explore empowering alternatives. The imagination, put differently, enhances reflexivity by liberating one from habitual thinking and practice, and opening up the conceptual space to notice the means by which one is structurally incarcerated. To be sure, there are limits to imagination given the inescapable difficulty of completely transcending one's historical age. One can push the very edges, however, and that is the intention of the present volume.

Getting outside of Climate Inc. is somewhat distinctive in that it involves not simply the imagination *per se* but what C. W. Mills calls the *sociological* imagination. For Mills, the sociological imagination is not merely a flight of fancy but the ability to grasp the larger arc of collective experience and interpret it's meaning for the choices we face. It involves stepping away from everyday occurrences, contextualizing them historically, and seeking patterns that render them social in nature and political in possibility rather than personal and individualistic. In other words, the sociological imagination requires a level of abstraction that enables one to see the collective, structural roots of particular encounters, feelings, and thoughts. It allows one to see one's experience and the experiences of others not as natural conditions written into the nature of the universe but as the consequence of broader socio-historical forces. One gains an appreciation for, as Mills puts it, "the larger historical scene" (Mills 1959, 5) that shapes not simply material conditions but also the inner life. With regard to Climate Inc., this involves disciplined inspiration, creativity, and ingenuity that can help contextualize and render strange and questionable existing responses, and cognitively and emotionally allow for criticism and the proposing of alternative futures with radical implications. In this sense, unleashing the sociological imagination in the service of climate protection is an exercise in teleological reflection. It involves scrutinizing the circumscribed trajectories along which the current regime is unfolding and asking fundamental questions that reveal alternative first principles about how to respond to climate change.

The chapters that follow offer radical ideas. As Marx famously wrote, "To be radical is to grasp the root of the matter." Politically, this involves identifying the origins rather than symptoms of particular social or political challenges. Climate Inc. peddles in symptoms. To mix metaphors, it attends to the capillaries of climate change, leaving the heart of the matter unexamined. Such an enterprise *can* take us far. At a minimum, current adaptation plans and measures can certainly prevent much hardship by responding to rising sea levels, droughts, and intensifying storms even though these are the expression, rather than the cause, of climate change. Moreover, conventional mitigation schemes can certainly reduce, to a degree, carbon emissions and thus may make a dent in the severity of future climate suffering. Yet, it is important to keep in mind that these represent merely nibbles at the tip of carbon civilization and leave the structural causes of climate change untouched. As the authors of this book make clear, the politics of symptomatic engineering has limits. It will never do the heavy lifting required to shift the tectonic plates – fundamental levels of injustice, technological hubris, economistic faith, and modernist narratives – that drive climate change. To get at this level of engagement, one must critically assess the industry and ideational support structure that have grown up around climate change. One must step outside the complex of commercial, governmental, and activist enterprises aimed at climate protection. One must interrogate Climate Inc., noticing the ways in which it itself traps us within deeper dynamics that cause climate intensification.

By adopting a radical orientation, *Reimagining Climate Change* destabilizes a number of core elements of the current climate regime to create space for unorthodox thinking and action. Its authors step back from the solution-sets societies are pursuing and show that such "answers" are themselves strictures limiting rather than advancing promising climate alternatives. The chapters go even further, however. In form and content, they exhibit the experimental quality of the sociological imagination. As should be clear, imaginative thinking can deeply move minds and hearts, but it cannot provide a tried and true road to collective salvation. That's simply not its role. Rather, it works to unhinge and subvert conventional orientations, and this is always a form of experimentation. As the reader will no doubt see, the chapters that follow are investigational forays. They provoke, test, question, and may even irritate. This doesn't always make for comfortable reading. In *A Sand County Almanac*, Aldo Leopold writes that the "modern dogma is comfort at all costs" (1949, 71). The pages that follow provide little comfort in the usual sense. They offer not sweet stories that edge one softly toward alternative arrangements but defiant ideas that pose a challenge to appreciate. To assist in this, the reader is encouraged to relax her own standards of "realistic," "practical," and "policy-relevant." The political impasse referred to above stands not as a blip on the screen but a fundamental and predictable result of the causal dynamics of climate change. A shared conviction of this volume is that the world will make little headway addressing climate change until it comes to terms with these dynamics.

Reimagining Climate Change uncovers such dynamics. It unfolds in the following manner. In Chapter 2, Matthew Paterson reminds us that imagination is not reserved solely for social criticism but is part of the reproduction of contemporary thought and practice. He shows, for instance, how the effort to take carbon out of the economy and adopt low carbon lifestyles – conventional approaches to climate change – are themselves forms of imagination insofar as they represent inventive social discourses. There is nothing innate or necessary about decarbonization or lifestyle adjustment; rather, certain social forces came together to constitute these as proper, appropriate responses to climate change. Paterson's contribution rests on reimagining decarbonization and low carbon lifestyles. Enlisting the sociological imagination, he contextualizes the two efforts within a broader historical arc and explores what it would take to enable them to hasten the kind of radical shifts that appear necessary to address effectively climate change. Paterson shows how decarbonization and carbon dieting, although relatively tame in their approaches and certainly compatible with existing structures of power, can tap into and ignite critical reflection on broader political arrangements. For example, he explains how decarbonization can, if conceptually enlarged, call into question the privileged status of fossil fuel companies within the economy and be used as a tool for battling corporate power. Likewise, he shows how the interrogation of low carbon lifestyles can reveal the pervasive individualism that drives consumerism and the kind of self-regarding attitude at the heart of high carbon societies. In short, Paterson demonstrates how reimagining climate change must necessarily arise out of existing practices, subjectivities, and political life, and explains what it would take to turn such an exercise into an instrument of radical change in the service of climate protection.

Chapter 3 reimagines the historical setting of climate change and therewith provides an alternative way to understand security in a climate age. Simon Dalby begins his contribution by contextualizing climate change within the broad historical setting of the Anthropocene. He demonstrates that climate change did not usher in the geological era of the Anthropocene, but that humans have long been altering the planetary conditions of life – including atmospheric carbon concentrations – ever since the Agricultural Revolution and significant urbanization of the human species. In this sense, climate change is not the cause but another effect of longstanding human practices that render *Homo sapiens* participants in shaping planetary ecological conditions. This is significant because it allows us to see climate change not as a catastrophic "end time" but as another wrinkle in a protracted historical trajectory, although one of unprecedented disruptive scope. Climate change, as such, represents simply a "next time," a new historical moment in which humanity must continue shaping and adapting to altered socio-ecological circumstances. Dalby uses this reframing to argue that security, then, cannot be a matter of safeguarding territorial integrity through boundary protecting armaments or restricting mobility across borders, since these represent resistances to the planetary-wide dynamics of which humans play a key part. Rather, climate change as an instance of the Anthropocene calls for dropping humanity's longstanding attraction to national boundaries and resonance with national identity in favor of a more porous, integrated, globalist world order. By reimagining the historical foundations of climate change, Dalby brings traditional notions of security into high relief and therewith ideas about how to secure human wellbeing in the face of climate change. He dispenses with all those efforts that seek security in a climate age by erecting higher territorial barriers, pursuing strictly domestic forms of adaptation, and dividing the haves and have-nots in the quest for climate protection. Put differently, Dalby takes us beyond Climate Inc. strategies as the world wrestles with the challenge of protecting humans from harm in an era of climate intensification.

Chapter 4 continues the logic of questioning Climate Inc. within the framework of separate nation states. Richard Falk points out how conventional approaches peer through a narrow lens when trying to address climate change. This lens privileges spatiality over temporality and thus looks to states, as territorial bodies, as the main agents of response and the best promise for responding to climate change. Falk shows that such privileging limits responses to climate change by discounting the importance of time and the justification to care for the future in climate policies. He explains how the world continues to believe that climate change is a distant threat that need not be addressed with urgency in the present but can be infinitely postponed. Postponement rests on the hope that, when the "real" time to address climate change arrives, some innovation in behavior, technological invention, or nonhuman force will miraculously appear to save the day. According to Falk, this represents the height of irresponsibility but one embedded into the current world order of sovereign states. The international system privileges spatiality – with its emphasis on separate states, balance of power, deterrence, anarchy, and borders – and this occludes a sensitivity to time. Time becomes an abstraction that never fully impinges upon policy makers. They address seemingly present problems without recognizing the degree to which the future is implicated in the present. That is, policy makers fail to realize that problems arrive not as discrete packages but are of a continuum that stretches into the past and future. Climate change, thus, is not some future event that policy makers can wait for and address "when the time comes," but a phenomenon that is happening now and will continue to happen in the future. Policy makers must jump into the temporally flowing river of climate to make a meaningful difference, which contradicts their operational logic based on very short cycles of accountability. Recognizing the dominance of spatiality in Climate Inc., however, Falk is not sanguine about this possibility and thus suggests that the most consequential efforts may be those taken by nonstate actors since they reside outside the rubric of territorially bounded states.

Chapter 5 widens the scope of radical thought by moving beyond a critical view of the Westphalian state system to one of modernity itself. Miriam Lowi does this in a unique way. Lowi focuses on efforts by Gulf States, like Saudi Arabia and United Arab Emirates (UAE), to mimic the Western love affair with technology, economistic thinking, mastery over nature, and capital-intensive development. She shows how Gulf States embrace these tenets of modernity both to impress the West with their level of development and to placate and rule over their citizens in the context of governing rentier regimes. She examines two mega-projects that exemplify such an embrace – an effort to grow wheat in the deserts of Saudi Arabia and one to build a zero carbon city in the UAE. Both projects involved significant investments of capital, the use of high technologies, and the belief that nature can be beaten into shape as humans see fit. As Lowi explains, Saudi Arabia and UAE had to cancel or significantly scale back these projects. In both cases, human artifice rubbed up against the stubborn parameters of nature. Furthermore, and this is Lowi's main point, both projects represented a doubling down on modernity to address challenges presented by modernity itself. In the case of Saudi Arabia, the impetus to farm the desert arose as a response to population growth spawned by medical innovations, high consumptive lifestyles, a rentier state dependent on oil and a global economy run on fossil fuels, and notions of development premised on demonstrating humanity's rule over nature. To address these challenges, Saudi Arabia pulled out all the modernist stops to impose its vision. Likewise, in its effort to build a zero carbon city, the UAE employed all the modernist trappings. Aiming to demonstrate how a "developed" country could address climate change, the UAE enlisted architects, engineers, and various technicians to build, what turned out to be, a mirage of a zero carbon city. Its failure underlines the risks of doubling down on modernity to address modernity's problems. At a broader level of generalization, Lowi offers a cautionary tale about modernity itself and its relationship to climate change. Almost every Climate Inc. scheme relies on modernist instruments. Lowi reimagines this effort by showing modernity's limitations and invoking at least some wisdom from indigenous people who have yet to fall fully under the spell of modernity. She questions relying on a modernist orientation to address climate change.

Chapter 6 takes the climate change challenge into one of the ancient, fundamental, and vital preoccupations of humanity, viz., agriculture and food systems. Hilal Elver starts with the complex relationship between climate change and agriculture. She explains how, on the one hand, climate change is crippling husbandry and, on the other, how large-scale, carbon intensive, industrial farming is exacerbating climate change. To unravel this knot, Elver encourages us to think beyond a productivist model of food and agriculture. Many analysts ask the haunting question of how to feed 9.7 billion in the hot and crowded world anticipated to exist in 2080. In doing so, they implicitly frame the challenge in supply-side terms and encourage deepening humanity's commitment to agro-industrial practices that promise production through endlessly extracting resources from the earth and from, often powerless, agricultural workers. Elver reimagines agriculture and food systems in a climate age by linking issues of production with matters of justice and sustainability. This involves looking beyond large-scale industrial agriculture and adopting a different vision of husbandry by supporting small-holder farmers, local food initiatives, and the promotion of agro-ecology on a global scale. In order to develop her argument she offers examples of emergent alternative models around the world, including organic, biodynamic, bee-friendly, and community-supported food systems. She insists that such models can not only provide food security for a growing population but also offer new patterns of community and human relations that could have broader social impacts on issues such as employment, support networks, internal migration from rural to urban areas, and communal resilience to climate change. Furthermore, she explains how such examples represent a less extractivist mentality and thus encourage a more harmonious relationship between humans and nature. Finally, following an analysis of alternative food production systems, Elver introduces a human rights-based approach to global climate change governance, an important and necessary paradigm shift in dealing with climate justice because the current climate change regime exacerbates social and economic injustices, pushing those who are already vulnerable in society further to the edge rather than acknowledging and offsetting their vulnerability. Elver reiterates the necessity of a profound culture shift to respond to the problems of climate change beyond simple mitigation and adaptation strategies if we are to respect the basic human rights of the peoples of the world and safeguard the sustainability of the earth's resources. She ends the chapter with this strong message: "A truly climate resilient society should embrace such approaches not as an alternative but, in fact, as the only way to ensure the future of the planet and its human population."

In Chapter 7, Simon Nicholson reimagines climate engineering. A growing number of people are starting to realize that conventional mitigation and adaptation strategies are failing to reduce carbon emissions or otherwise protect us from global warming. They have thus started to conjure up technological feats that will enable the world to keep living high carbon lifestyles and pumping greenhouse gases into the atmosphere. These involve altering the very geo-chemical foundations of the planet itself. For instance, some schemes propose shooting sulfates or space mirrors or other substances into the atmosphere to filter out sunlight (and thus heat); others suggest fertilizing the oceans with iron to absorb CO_2 or literally extracting carbon out of the atmosphere and storing it in deep chasms. Nicholson explains that the framework for such endeavors feeds into Climate Inc. insofar as advocates see geoengineering as a "Plan B" for the world. They offer it as an alternative, sitting in the wings, to jump in when all other measures are tried and fail. As Nicholson points out, this overestimates the viability of geoengineering schemes, underestimates the risks and harmful side effects, and completely avoids the broader existential questions that must be asked about humanity's role in shaping the planet itself. To assess geoengineering with accuracy and enable deeper questions to be asked, Nicholson calls for abandoning a Plan B orientation and explores what it might look like to include geoengineering considerations within a broader, more integral menu of responses to climate change. He points out that the kinds of challenges posed by geoengineering – for example, the need for international cooperation or a practical appreciation for ecological interdependence – can contribute to responding to climate change in promising ways. They can only do so, however, if we can reimagine technology in the context of climate protection.

In Chapter 8, Paul Wapner claims that we have entered a new phase of climate change that requires a fresh response. To date, the world has tried to mitigate and adapt to climate change, but a third response is growing increasingly relevant, namely, widespread suffering. Today, untold numbers of people and other creatures are confronting desperate situations and all indicators suggest that this will continue in one form or another, and likely intensify. Wapner explains what it means to take seriously climate suffering. He notes how the poor and marginalized stand at the frontlines of climate hardship and therefore argues for climate strategies that seek to improve their lot. This involves, what he calls, "radical resilience." Conventional ideas of climate resilience involve building flexible systems that can withstand climate assaults and return to pre-existing conditions. In contrast, *radical* resilience responds to climate assaults in ways that transform existing conditions. It entails using climate change as an opportunity to create more just societal arrangements. Put differently, Wapner highlights the anachronistic quality of mitigation and adaptation strategies and reimagines resilience as a relevant response to climate change that contains social dividends through a strong commitment to equity.

In Chapter 9, John Foran reimagines the climate justice movement. Foran looks at the environmental movement in evolutionary terms and notes how it has grown from a nature-centric campaign concerned with protecting pristine landscapes, endangered species, and valuable ecosystems, to one that embraces the concerns for people as well. The epitome of this growth is the recent creation of a climate justice movement – the widespread effort to address inequalities and exploitations involved in a carbon economy and the prejudices that often inform Climate Inc. strategies. As Foran sees it, the climate justice movement represents the greatest hope for genuinely addressing climate change but that the movement can only realize its potential if it radicalizes itself. This means politically engaging realms outside the narrow sphere of carbon and fashioning climate activism into a broader effort entailing social transformation. Foran thus calls on the movement to deliberatively, for instance, resist all forms of patriarchy and militarism, critique capitalism, and work to undermine hierarchical forms of power in general. To Foran, climate change is the atmospheric expression of widespread injustice and thus can only be combatted by addressing the wider causal dynamics that drive societal unfairnesses at large.

In the final chapter, Manjana Milkoreit focuses on the imagination itself and its relationship to climate politics. She suggests that policy-makers, activists, and even ordinary citizens often lack the facility to exercise the imagination as it relates to climate change and offers ways of enhancing that ability. Specifically, Milkoreit calls for studying the emerging genre of writing known as climate fiction (or, as she calls it, "cli-fi") to liberate the boundaries of our current, habitual responses. Cli-fi offers readers mental representations and emotional depictions of what is not yet present. These can include, at a minimum, future climatic conditions – wherein writers portray imagined biophysics of climate intensification – as well as future societal arrangements – wherein writers describe various dystopian or utopian visions of collective life in an age of climate escalation. Such descriptions expand conceptual and affective boundaries, and therewith help people resist the kind of hardening of the categories described above. Milkoreit illustrates the liberating potential of cli-fi by analyzing stories by three fiction writers – Margaret Atwood, Barbara Kingsolver, and George Turner. She highlights how each of these writers joggles the mind and heart by wrestling creatively with climate change. She delineates the added perceptual space generated by each of these authors and explains the degrees of freedom this offers in moving beyond Climate Inc. Rather than reimagine a specific element of Climate Inc., as most other contributors do, Milkoreit directly explains the necessity and promise of the imagination itself to addressing climate change. In short, she reimagines imagination as it relates to climate change.

The authors of the chapters in this book exercise the imagination in the service of climate protection. They recognize that a whole industry of response, premised on routinized practices of mitigation and adaptation, has emerged and that this industry, euphemistically called Climate Inc., has achieved little to derail the world from moving down a path of escalating temperatures, intensified storms, biodiversity loss, and so forth. In fact, they see Climate Inc. not simply as ineffective but also harmful to the degree that it correlates with existing political, economic, and social arrangements that, themselves, dig us deeper into a carbonized world system. Unwilling to accept that the world must go down the rabbit hole of climate change, authors have worked to distance themselves from accepted categories of thought and action, and to reflect wildly about other possibilities. Taken as a whole, the book offers various fruitful ways of stepping back from existing practices, to discern alternative directions and develop the courage to pursue more promising pathways for remaking society in a climate age.

There is much important, innovative, and socially responsible insight in the following pages. However, it would be naïve to think that such acumen can itself generate dramatic action on climate change. After all, the chapters that follow offer "only" ideas. They provide thoughts, notions, concepts, and impressions that entertain the mind and possibly heart, but, in themselves, lack political agency and do not translate easily into political practice. Furthermore, striving to go beyond Climate Inc., they proffer relatively radical ideas that might make them seem marginal to most discussions as they push the conceptual boundaries of climate change politics. The ideational and sweeping character of the chapters, however, should not render them somehow apolitical or irrelevant to climate action. To be sure, they provide no simple answers to climate change but the world will be greatly hampered in its climate protection efforts without their insights. Indeed, in contrast to Climate Inc., which peddles in practicality but ensures climate catastrophe, the chapters that follow may represent the most realistic path to a safer climate. They are what could be called *necessary* ideas. They may be insufficient to herald a new, more promising policy phase in responding to climate change, but their contributions must nevertheless be required in any genuinely strategy toward a hopeful future.

Climate change is not a discrete problem with a given solution set. Rather, as the chapters show, it is a multi-pronged challenge produced by and drawing strength from existing political, economic, and social arrangements. It thus has a long history and is deeply embedded into current structures. Confronting it requires more than snapping into place a specific answer but unearthing its causal momentum strewn across the ligaments that constitute contemporary collective life. The ideas in this volume begin that process of conceptual excavation. Their contribution rests on their ability to detect large-scale, often abstract determinants of climate intensification and render them more receptive to critique and ultimately transformation. Our collective hope in publishing this work is to inspire readers to push themselves to notice the determinative dynamics that give shape and thrust to climate change, and to begin the difficult task of unmasking, critiquing, and transmuting these in the service of a livable, just future.

References

Mills C W 1959 *The Sociological Imagination* Oxford University Press, New York
Leopold A 1949 *A Sand County Almanac* Oxford University Press, New York
Mitchell S ed 1984 *The Selected Poetry of Rainer Maria Rilke* Vintage, New York
Rosenau J 1990 *Turbulence in World Politics* Princeton University Press, Princeton NJ

2 The sociological imagination of climate futures

Matthew Paterson

Introduction

The framing of this volume invokes C. Wright Mills. On rereading the opening passage of his *Sociological Imagination* (Mills 1959), I am tempted simply to cut and paste the entire passage. Mills opens with:

> Nowadays men [*sic*] often feel that their private lives are a series of traps. They sense that within their everyday worlds, they cannot overcome their troubles, and in this feeling, they are often quite correct ... Underlying this sense of being trapped are seemingly impersonal changes in the very structure of continent-wide societies.
>
> (Mills 1959, 3)

This is Mills's purpose in elaborating what he calls a sociological imagination – as a set of intellectual resources that enable people to "understand the larger historical scene in terms of its meaning for the inner life and external career of a variety of individuals" (Mills 1959, 5). He does so with an explicit political and transformative aim: "By such means the personal uneasiness of individuals is focused upon explicit troubles and the indifference of publics is transformed into involvement with public issues" (Mills 1959, 5).

Many of the motifs in these (and other) passages are apposite to understanding the impasse(s) we face in climate politics. Trap, troubles, inner life, uneasiness, indifference, involvement ... all could be used to understand the way that many people around the world experience climate change – as something simultaneously of momentous importance and deep abstraction from daily life, and as the product of activities in daily life that are supposed to be acts of freedom and prosperity but are at the same time often experienced as a trap. Climate change thus provokes trouble and unease. But, following Mills, this trouble and unease can at the same time generate indifference precisely because the traps of daily life prevent us from seeing the "larger historical scene" that might enable our "involvement with public issues." In climate change debates to date, perhaps the best expressions of these are in Kari Norgaard's account of *Living in Denial,* her meticulous study of the complicated avoidance of dealing with climate change in a small Norwegian town, and in Mike Hulme's *Why We Disagree About Climate Change* (Norgaard 2011; Hulme 2010).

This chapter uses the notion of imagination in Mills's most immediate sense to analyze the challenge of climate politics. Its premise is that climate politics is itself a product of a number of imaginations but that, to date, these have been insufficiently expansive enough to reveal a meaningful context from which to mobilize effective public involvement. The chapter illustrates this by focusing on two specific initiatives that have held promise for addressing climate change. The first is decarbonization: the effort to get carbon out of the economy. Emerging at the turn of the twenty-first century, decarbonization has been a conceptual touchstone for political-economic reimagining and thus a guide for policy. In its most narrow technical sense, decarbonization involves feats of engineering that excise carbon sources of energy and replace them with non-carbon substitutes. In its more imaginative and critical forms, it calls for reconstituting the socio-economic fabric of societies so as to generate post-carbon practices (i.e. ways of living together that involve transforming our carbon-dependent economies). The second initiative involves the reimagination of daily life in terms of low-carbon practices: the effort to reduce daily carbon consumption. In its narrow sense, this involves reducing individual emissions. In its more expansive sense, it entails redirecting urban design so as to minimize energy use in buildings, transportation, and food acquisition. In contrast to decarbonization, which aims to alter policy and politics, low carbon reimaginations of daily life seek to shift the cultural parameters of contemporary life.

This chapter analyses both sets of initiatives to understand the place of imagination in contemporary climate politics. It shows, on the one hand, the conceptual quality of decarbonization and low carbon practices – how and why they emerged as imaginative responses to climate change – and, on the other hand, the inherent limitations of each in the absence of further employment of the sociological imagination. At a higher level of abstraction, this chapter treats decarbonization and low carbon daily life as contradictions of current collective realities: they reveal the promise and constraints of building a climate-safe future. From a normative perspective, the chapter views them as thus ripe for further imaginative enhancement. By revealing the larger historical scene of which they are a part, the sociological imagination can conceptually reenergize decarbonization and low carbon daily life as strategies for moving beyond Climate Inc. and generating more promising responses to climate change. In this sense, I use Mills's account of the logic of the sociological imagination to argue that that existing reimaginations of climate change are rather too techno-economic in character, and that actors (and academic analysts) need to build into their political activities the effort to enable people to understand their situation in a "larger historical scene" in order to open up space for further social change in response to climate change.

Conceptual orientation

Before proceeding, some conceptual and theoretical discussion is in order. First, why should we think of climate change politics as an exercise in imagination? To my mind, it is useful in this context to understand climate change in the terms set out by complex systems theory (see notably Hoffmann 2010; Levin *et al.* 2012). Following this logic, climate change is not a problem that is amenable to simple application of existing discourses, economic models, institutional fixes, or governance arrangements, by clearly identifiable sovereign actors. Rather, it engenders an orientation, by a broad range of actors, that is experimental (Hoffmann 2010; Bulkeley and Castán Broto 2013; Bulkeley *et al.* 2015), even playful – in other words, imaginative. Since we have no real idea what will "work" in terms of addressing climate change (and perhaps indeed no real idea what "work" means in this context), and at the same time severe institutional, political, and cultural obstacles in developing any sort of serious strategy at all, imagination can be thought of the cognitive underpinning of experimental governance, in that it provides an account of a "larger historical scene" within which experimental efforts to address climate change may be understood as a means of generating public engagement.

Theoretically, I understand this process in terms of "cultural political economy" (Paterson 2007; Best and Paterson 2009; Sum and Jessop 2013). I use that term to mean that the principal forces we need to understand the politics of "actually existing unsustainability" (Barry 2013) are, on the one hand, the social organization of a political economy dedicated to endless accumulation (capitalism), and the political forces that dominate in such a world, and, on the other hand, the sorts of meanings attached to the practices of daily life that are intimately and constitutively associated with the reproduction of that world. Concretely, I have explored this most extensively in relation to the automobile, or more precisely to automobility (Paterson 2007; Rajan 1996; Böhm *et al.* 2006; Urry 2004). It is perhaps relatively straightforward to establish that the socio-technical regime of automobility was central to twentieth-century capitalist development, and at the same time central to the legitimation of contemporary societies via the deep embedding of its commodities (cars and their associated paraphernalia) in the normative and practical visions of people in their daily lives. But one could extend it to other central aspects of capitalist economies and daily life, from the food system, to money and finance, to electricity, and so on. Indeed, the notion of "Climate Inc.," as used throughout this volume, can be understood precisely to be all of those aspects of daily life and economic imperatives that work to shape and constrain responses to climate change in specific ways.

But the consequences of this for thinking about imagination and climate politics are also important. Notably, it enables us to focus on the precise sorts of obstacles that we face as we seek, for example, to transform or even transcend a vast, globally organized socio-technical machine that is auto-mobility – which are in effect precisely challenges of imagination: what would an economy look like that didn't have the automobile sector, and its myriad associated beneficiaries (road construction and maintenance, insurance, oil extraction and distribution, various other raw materials, mechanics, property developers, golf ... and so on) at its heart? And what would daily life look like (at least for first world majorities and increasingly large developing world middle classes) that wasn't centered on commuting, taxiing children, looking for parking spots, driving to the supermarket, the occasional trip to the countryside or to visit family and friends, as well as routinely complaining about traffic, gas prices, insurance rates, cyclists, etc.? This is an inevitably imaginative task, since both go well beyond the direct experience of large parts of humanity.

But both Mills's invocation of imagination and the cultural political economy perspective sketched above call attention to two aspects of this process that deserve further thought. First is that these imaginations always arise in particular political, economic and cultural contexts. So the possibility of novel imaginations is always to a certain extent constrained by existing contexts. To take one example from automobility – as we imagine post-car futures, the imaginary of a world centered on public transport is constrained perhaps by the legacy of hyper-individualist cultures associated with and nourished by automobility. This might favor imagined future mobilities centered on the bicycle, whose user shares many aspects of their subjectivity with the car driver (indeed some bike ideologists precisely talk of the cyclist as *more authentically automobile* than a car driver). But pursuing a strategy centered on bikes may nevertheless be constrained by political economy questions - the difficulty in imagining an *accumulation* or *growth* strategy centered on bikes (Paterson 2007, ch. 7). This is a clear instance of how Climate Inc., as articulated in the introduction to this volume, constrains the possibilities of enacting more fruitful responses to climate change.

Second is that Mills calls our attention to the imagination as a *sociological* one, meaning that it requires us to think specifically about the historically constituted subjects that exist, and enable them to historicize their own experience in order to open up possibilities for public engagement and social change. In practice, as illustrated below, many imaginative acts in response to climate change already exist. However, most of these fail to develop persuasive accounts for themselves and their promise to address climate change. They are usually couched either in an apocalyptic frame or a blithely optimistic one. Some thus prefer to engage our fears about climate impacts – a trope that one can see from scenario planning to science fiction (Swyngedouw 2010; Clarke 2013; Chapter 10, this volume) – and which, as de Goede and Randalls show very effectively, operate as discourses that "depoliticize and de-legitimate debate and that potentially bring the unimaginable into being" (de Goede and Randalls 2009, 861). Others focus on the "win–win" dimensions of low carbon transitions, the advantages in terms of development of new technologies, rebuilt urban infrastructure, restructured food systems, enhanced quality of life, and so on. As a well-known cartoon that first appeared in *USA Today* in December 2009 puts it, showing a speaker at a conference outlining all the positive spin-off benefits of eliminating fossil fuels: "what if it's a big hoax and we create a better world for nothing?" (Pett 2012).

The latter of these is certainly the better starting point for the pursuit of low carbon futures, as fear usually produces either stasis or reactionary politics, but the success of positive imaginaries of low carbon futures depends on addressing Mills's important point as well. By success I mean that such an imaginary needs to create novel ways of thinking and acting across a broad range of social and political actors, in particular perhaps mobilizing them via the positive effects – hopes, desires, enthusiasm – for a low-carbon future that can transform how people see their "interests." In this way an imaginary is a powerful part of the process of creating a set of self-sustaining processes of social transformation, where the visceral desires for specific low carbon futures is an important component in overcoming the visceral resistance generated by affective attachments to existing high carbon objects (cars) and socio-technical assemblages (automobility as a whole), and generates new socio-technical assemblages that enroll others across society into low carbon practices via the logics of the systems themselves.

But to get to this transformative potential, following Mills, to transform inaction into public engagement, imaginaries need to be able to enable people to situate their current lives in their historical contexts in order to facilitate them imagining how those lives may be transformed. Indeed, as illustrated below, some of the more successful efforts to open up political space for transformative action are precisely those that foster broad, open, deliberative spaces for thinking about contemporary life and its potential transformation, yet which don't pursue an illusory "consensus" and keep the possibility of continued conflict alive (Machin 2013).

Imagining decarbonization

Sometime around 2000, although I have been unable to identify exactly when, policymakers, business people, and NGOs started to use the term "decarbonization." The concept took off fairly quickly in northwest Europe (most notably, Germany, Holland, the UK, and Sweden). Its use in public discourse started a good deal later, with Google News Archive suggesting it took off in news media only in early 2010. Its use reimagines climate change very clearly as a problem of transformation.

Dominant accounts within policy circles had previously been (and in many contexts continue to be) focused on relatively short-term aims – stabilizing emissions (as in the United Nations Framework Convention on Climate Change in 1992), reducing them by modest amounts (in Kyoto, and in various national targets associated with that treaty). While the United Nations Framework Convention on Climate Change did announce a long-term objective of the "stabilization of greenhouse gas concentrations in the atmosphere at a level that would prevent dangerous anthropogenic interference with the climate system" (United Nations 1992, article 2), and the first Intergovernmental Panel on Climate Change (IPCC) report had suggested that greenhouse gas (GHG) emissions needed to be reduced globally by around 60 percent over 1990 levels to achieve such stabilization, these nevertheless framed climate change as an emissions problem – focused on the outputs of industrial economies, not their internal dynamics.

Decarbonization produced a significant shift in the conception of the relationship between GHG emissions and the economy that produced them. The term reimagined climate change in terms of the economic metabolism and invites us literally to "take the carbon out" of the economy. In other words, climate change is no longer conceived as strictly speaking an "emissions problem," but rather a problem of socio-technical transformation. Many of the associated academic literatures that emerged at the same time posed the question in terms of "sustainability transitions" (Kemp *et al.* 2007).

At the same time, even in emissions terms, it affects a quantitative jump-shift. No longer are we thinking about 10 percent cuts, then another 10 percent, and so on, but rather we are jumping to the end game and thinking, in the most radical (i.e. it gets to the root) version, about 100 percent cuts, and then working backwards from that end. As soon as attention is focused on that end, it becomes obvious that we are aiming at a radical transformation of the socio-technical fabric of contemporary societies. To take one example as a heuristic – when you aim at 10 percent cuts, you're looking for more efficient air-conditioners (or cars, industrial processes, power stations, etc.). When you aim for over 90 percent cuts, you are building houses to not need air-conditioning (and transport systems not centered on cars, electricity systems without coal, etc.).

While it would of course be absurd to say decarbonization magically "solves" the problem, it has been nevertheless instructive. Those places that have so far managed to get more ambitious policy initiatives in place are those places where this reimagining of climate change has taken off most fully (see for example Lachapelle and Paterson 2013). At national levels, countries like the UK, Germany, and Sweden, have been able to imagine a process of economic development that entails radical reductions in GHG emissions, and my argument is that in part this is due to the space opened up by the decarbonization frame. Decarbonization has been a productive reimagining of climate change. More recently, countries like South Korea,

Ethiopia and others have joined these European countries, deploying the less radical but nevertheless transformative "low carbon economy" discourse. Central to many of these efforts has been the way that decarbonization/low carbon economy imaginings have generated a focus on planning "transitions" to low or zero carbon societies (Shove and Walker 2010). In the UK for example, there is now an institutionalized process of "carbon budgeting," where governments are required to regularly set 5-year carbon budgets, and be guided by a long-term target of at least 80 percent reductions by 2050. Within government, this is accompanied by an enormously elaborate set of governing arrangements to follow these macro-level carbon budgets within every aspect of government activity and the parts of the economy or society they govern.

The central question that arises for the imagineers (Weber 2000) of a decarbonized future involves political economy, classically understood. If the future is to be imagined as a world without fossil fuels, then it comes up against the immediate trap posed by existing understandings of the "larger historical scene" – that historical capitalism has been organized, and continues to be so, around fossil fuels themselves. It remains the case today that economic growth (as measured in the problematic and increasingly contested unit of gross domestic product) has more or less a linear relationship with fossil fuel consumption, if measured at a global level. Individual countries may experience a "decoupling" of fossil fuel use from economic growth, but the global economy has not. The question then becomes how to imagine a growth process (since capitalism cannot survive without such growth, the propositions of ecological economics notwithstanding) that no longer has fossil fuels at its heart – the pursuit of what Peter Newell and I have elsewhere called *Climate Capitalism* (Newell and Paterson 2010).

But this is not only a technical question – how much energy can renewables deliver? What technology can replace oil in transport? – but a political one concerning the power of fossil fuel interests to resist change. The countries that have gone furthest have been the ones that have identified constituencies that benefit directly from emissions reductions and that might therefore help overcome short-term opposition from coal or oil interests. These are various (and often politically controversial) – financial interests in the United Kingdom (mostly) that benefit from carbon markets, solar cooperatives (in Germany) that benefit from feed-in-tariffs, for example. From a political economy point of view, building on a powerful reimagining entails identifying those who will materially benefit from it and encouraging patterns of investment, production and consumption that can sustain growth processes to compensate from the de-accumulation of capital in fossil fuels. A key challenge in political economy terms is precisely that many of the beneficiaries are decentralized and relatively small economic actors (those with small-scale solar installations, bicycle manufacturers) and thus both more difficult to mobilize politically than the small numbers of large companies (E.On, Shell, Western Fuels) with vested interests in the status quo, and less capable of accumulating sufficient capital to scale up their efforts.

Again, none of these magically "solves" the problem, or avoids the messy day-to-day politics provoked by particular crises involved with energy (Fukushima), vested interests seeking to undermine low carbon transitions (Keystone XL), co-optation of technological transition (carbon capture and storage), or unanticipated and complicated developments (fracking, biofuels). But it is instructive to compare countries where decarbonization has become part of the institutionalized discourse with, say Canada, where it has not, and where indeed the *recarbonization* of the economy is both a material reality as well as a normative and strategic discourse within governing elites.

These low carbon or decarbonization imaginings are also central to many of Hoffmann's experimental initiatives or the worlds of transnational climate change governance (Hoffmann 2010; Bulkeley *et al.* 2012, 2014). Some put it in their name – Transition Towns for example. But more broadly, imagining a decarbonized future is often central to the ability of these initiatives to enroll actors in these novel governance arrangements among cities, regions, corporations, NGOs, and others, attempting to reshape urban environments, shift investment patterns, generate and govern carbon markets, or diffuse low carbon technologies.

But this imagination of climate change as a problem of decarbonization, while useful, remains for the most part abstracted from the processes that Mills emphasizes as crucial for the generation of processes leading to social change. For the most part, the imaginations collapse into techno-economic scenarios, working out where the radical emissions reductions will come from, which technologies will enable the appropriate breakthroughs. Individual lives in most of this imagination become precisely objectified, entrapped, through the technocratic language of "behavior change," and the reduction of individuals to the abstract conceptualizations of psychology and/or economics, rather than active agents continually remaking their lives in complex social settings (Shove 2010). Such a framing radically limits the potential of an otherwise highly imaginative reframing of climate change. I return to what it might involve to go beyond this in the conclusion to this chapter.

Imagining low carbon daily lives

If the development of decarbonization as a techno-economic discourse has become institutionalized in various contexts, the imagining of what a low carbon life might look like is more speculative and difficult, although not impossible, to think through. We can see two sorts of these imaginations readily in a wide range of discourse.

The first is entailed in those series of individualized carbon governmentalities that seek to get people to reduce their own emissions (Paterson and

Stripple 2010) Examples include carbon dieting, carbon footprinting, carbon offsetting, joining a Carbon Reduction Action Group, and so on (Paterson and Stripple 2010; Stripple and Paterson 2012).

Take carbon dieting as an example. Carbon dieting proceeds from the logic of measuring individual carbon emissions and renders them especially visible in two different ways. It makes carbon emissions visible on an individual, emotional level, through the analogy with the management of one's body through dieting. Such a connection is at once visceral (literally) and (allegedly) universal – speaking to the purportedly universal concern of westerners with nutrition, body image, and weight. But it also engages with us in a moral register, suggesting that like the management of our body, the management of our emissions is something that we have obligations to address. The dieting metaphor of course invokes a morality that is simultaneously narcissistic – our obligation to reduce our emissions connects immediately to competitive desires to impress those around us. Carbon dieting thus entails a form of subjectivity centered on the relationship between guilt and emotional reward, peer-pressure and mutual judgement. It also makes climate action a specifically *bodily* practice, entailing *work*. This is a significant contrast to carbon offsetting – while in the latter, emissions can be eliminated through the artifice of the offset project investment, in carbon dieting, one is stuck with one's own bodily practice: the only way to act is through self-discipline and restraint.

Technically, a dieting metaphor draws attention to the minutiae of practice in a way that goes beyond simple carbon footprinting. With footprinting, we could stay at the macro-level of overall consumption; with dieting, we count calories for every single tiny practice. Typically, books on carbon dieting have appendices for carbon emissions from a huge range of practices. Harrington, for example, distinguishes even between different cuts of meat; beef tenderloin apparently produces 68kg of CO_2 per kg of meat, beef top-round only 42 kg (Harrington 2008, 174). Within the rationality of dieting, consumers must know this in order to manage their emitting behavior. But the relationship of denial to luxury is also established; this knowledge enables them to plan their self-denial in order to allow themselves specific treats. To earn a couple of bottles of wine from New Zealand, you must save 3.6 kg of CO_2; to fly from London to Paris, you need to find 88 kg (Siegle 2007, 29).

As an imagination, to follow Mills's logic, this is a sort of discourse that attempts to imagine low carbon futures via radically individualized activity. It thus reproduces precisely the traps, troubles and uneasiness he identifies as central to individuals' experience of modernity, and fails to contextualize individual life within broader social structures and practices. The imagined climate future thus becomes one of progressively more obsessive individuals working on their own daily lives but unable to see the contexts that determine large parts of their carbon-generating practices and the limits to such individualistic action (see also Maniates 2002; Luke 1994).

But there is a second sort of low carbon imagining that is much less individualistic. Assuming the majority (and an increasing proportion) of humanity continues to live in urban areas, the challenge is to make it so that at least:

- all buildings have radically reduced energy consumption and many generate their own electricity from renewable sources;
- they are much closer together than the current norm, especially in North America and Australia but also even in some "emerging economies," so that transport systems can be based on walking, cycling and public transport as the dominant practice;
- food systems and energy generation systems are organized to be much closer to urban areas.

Many people have generated imaginings of what urban life looks like in that sort of a scenario (Sheppard 2012), and visionary examples such as the BedZed ("Beddington Zero Energy Development") community in south London exist as sorts of prefiguring of what such urban life might entail (Chance 2009; Greenwood 2012; Lovell 2007).

What is more difficult is thinking about this process in political terms. Such envisioning can itself generate precisely the sense of entrapment, unease and trouble that Mills writes about. Context is going to be radically important in the capacity for this imagination to take hold easily and how activists might pursue it. A citizen of Amsterdam (or perhaps Busan) is going to be much more readily able to imagine such a vision than one of Atlanta (or perhaps Lagos). For the latter, it is likely to provoke a sense of despair, as the reader recognizes the attractiveness of the vision of urban life where everything they need on a daily basis is within easy walking distance, where they no longer ferry their children constantly around, where their houses are comfortable and self-sufficient in energy, but finds the contrast between that and their present existence too much to be able to imagine the transition. It thus increases the sense of entrapment.

Or alternatively, it might provoke in them resistance, even anger, as the vision provokes a radical threat to established ways of life that they strongly value. This is the response famously mobilized by the fossil fuel lobby in the 1997 campaign that helped undermine support for the Kyoto Protocol in the US, contributing to the Byrd–Hagel resolution in July of that year, with the campaign having a stereotypical "soccer mom" state that "the government wants to take away my SUV" (Schneider 2002). This affective response, and its mobilization by corporate interests, arises because of the way the established practices threaten deeply established norms and routines of daily life. The soccer mom is not just a dupe of corporate interests in this discursive formation; she has become someone whose obligations as a *mother* are at stake when a low carbon future is imagined. Climate change thus contributes to the uneasiness surrounding the entrapment that Mills identifies, since it calls into question these established values, identities and the practices associated with them.

Mills's account of the sociological imagination is important to reinvoke here, since it insists that we not only imagine a climate future itself, but that we deploy our capacity for imagination to show the importance of the "larger historical scene" for these "inner lives." The sociological imagination of climate change thus might be important for the first sort of reaction to the imagination of a low carbon urban future mentioned above. This would entail providing resources that do two specific things. First, they would have to contextualize historically and socially the specificity of the experience of the low-density city dweller – the patterns of urban development driven by planners, road construction companies, property developers, low agricultural land prices, as well as historical discourses of racism and class discrimination – that have historically produced such forms of urban development. And second, they would have to show the myriad paradoxes of such development – the reduced access to services for many, the gender inequalities, the reduced freedom and mobility for children and anyone unable to drive, the health costs from reduced physical activity and air pollution (the "obesogenic environments" of contemporary cities; see Lake and Townshend 2006), or the daily death toll from car crashes. Devising means of visualizing and imagining these social aspects of both high and low carbon futures would be integral to developing climate change narratives that work effectively so that the "indifference of publics is transformed into involvement" (Mills 1959, 5).

The Transition Towns network (www.transitionnetwork.org) is relevant to decarbonization, and is also instructive for appreciating how low carbon daily life transitions can be scaled-up or repoliticized at the hand of the sociological imagination. Transition Towns is a network of initiatives organized at the municipal level. It originated in the UK but has spread across a number of parts of the world, both North and South (Transition Network 2013a). The notion of Transition Initiatives, in the network's own words, are "actively and cooperatively creating happier, fairer and stronger communities, places that work for the people living in them and are far better suited to dealing with the shocks that'll accompany our economic and energy challenges and a climate in chaos" (Transition Network 2013b). There is an underlying set of premises of the need to transition away from fossil-fuel based economies, but the frame, the reimagining, is about the creation of new forms of community (Aiken 2012; Smith 2010). They thus seek precisely what Paul Wapner calls (this volume) "radical resilience." The activities of Transitions Initiatives are frequently focused on workshops of community members brainstorming on how to shift their larger community in a low carbon direction, and on generating direct action within communities to enable further social change. Transitions is thus an example of a climate change reimagining that seems focused on enabling space for the sorts of reflection on how existing entrapments and troubles of daily life can be explicitly confronted and transcended, rather than ignored.

Conclusions

This chapter attempts to sketch (nothing more) a way we might think about the role of imagination in reflecting on climate futures. It elaborates the importance of Mills's insistence to think about this imagination (both by researchers and the participants in political processes around climate change themselves) in sociological terms. This involves recognizing the historical context of the socio-economic and political regime constitutive of climate change and the traps that prevent people from seeing and practicing meaningful decarbonization and low carbon practices.

Returning to the volume's core concerns, the implications of this chapter's analysis are two-fold. First, it suggests the limits of treating "Climate Inc." as a totalizing regime that needs to be escaped. The reimaginations of climate change explored here are rather more immanent than transcendent, arising out of the internal logic of climate change that rather forces us to be extravagantly imaginative. To be sure, pre-existing structures, discourses, and power relations constrain the types of imaginations that emerge and the possibility of pursuing particular ones, but given that climate change engenders an experimental mode of operating in all agents, there is a good deal of fluidity in where such reimaginings might lead us.

Second, there is a danger in seeing reimagining as occurring at the heroic level of social transformation as a whole – a new worldview, ideology, and associated practices. Such things certainly exist, but they draw our attention away from the many small-scale reimaginings and the practices they enable, on which concrete social change can be based. If we are to see imagination as a social process, we need to be attentive to context and place.

We can combine elements of these two points. One example of the effects of the technocratic reimagining of climate change as decarbonization, for all of its problems, has been to trigger radical uptake of solar and wind energy in those countries that have started top-down, policy-driven efforts to shift economies to low carbon energy. Such things are highly visible – a visit to countries like the UK or Germany now reveals a rapidly changing visual landscape where solar panels are ubiquitous on roofs and wind turbines dot the land- and seascape. For example, the average street in the UK now has two houses on it with solar on the roof, a 120-fold increase from 2008 (Evans 2014). While this is yet to look particularly significant in the overall figures regarding the proportion of electricity coming from those sources, it does constitute a change in the "larger historical scene" that structures people's daily experience and thus their sense of entrapment, as people cannot now navigate their daily lives without encountering this shift in urban life. Arguments against solar energy that may reinforce such entrapment are immediately refuted by the daily experience of their reality, thus opening up space for further sorts of reimaginings of daily life in a low carbon direction. No-one can now say that a solar future is "impossible" without confronting major cognitive dissonance. Such space must be grabbed and mobilized, but it nevertheless will be able to explore further possibilities by thinking through these complex, context-specific interactions between imaginaries, their instantiation in new technologies, social practices and economic life, and the space for further reimaginings that can shift the whole process yet further.

References

Aiken G 2010 Community transitions to low carbon futures in the Transition Towns Network (TTN) *Geography Compass* 6(2) 89–99

Barry J 2013 *The Politics of Actually Existing Unsustainability: Human Flourishing in a Climate-Changed, Carbon Constrained World* Oxford University Press, Oxford

Best J and Paterson M eds 2009 *Cultural Political Economy* Routledge, London

Böhm S, Jones C L, Land C and Paterson M eds 2006 *Against Automobility* Blackwell, Oxford

Bulkeley H and Castán Broto V 2013 Government by experiment? Global cities and the governing of climate change *Transactions of the Institute of British Geographers* 38(3) 361–75

Bulkeley H, Andonova L, Bäckstrand K, Betsill M, Compagnon D, Hoffmann M, Levy D, Newell P, Paterson M, Kolk A, Pattberg P, VanDeveer S and Duffy R 2012 Governing climate change transnationally: assessing the evidence from a database of sixty initiatives *Environment and Planning C: Government and Policy* 30(4) 591–612

Bulkeley H, Andonova L, Betsill M, Compagnon D, Hale T, Hoffmann M, Newell P, Paterson M, Roger C and VanDeveer S 2014 *Transnational Climate Change Governance* Cambridge University Press, Cambridge

Bulkeley H, Castán Broto V and Edwards G 2015 *An Urban Politics of Climate Change: Experimentation and the Governing of Socio-Technical Transitions* Routledge, London

Chance T 2009 Towards sustainable residential communities: the Beddington Zero Energy Development (BedZED) and beyond *Environment and Urbanization* 21(2) 527–44

Clarke J 2013 Reading climate change in J. G. Ballard *Critical Survey* 25(2) 7–21

de Goede M and Randalls S 2009 Precaution, preemption: arts and technologies of the actionable future *Environment and Planning D: Society and Space* 27(5) 859–78

Evans S 2014 Five things we learned from DECC's annual energy statement 7 November (www.carbonbrief.org/blog/2014/11/five-things-we-learned-from-deccs-annual-energy-statement) accessed 11 February 2015

Greenwood D 2012 The challenge of policy coordination for sustainable sociotechnical transitions: the case of the zero-carbon homes agenda in England *Environment and Planning C: Government and Policy* 30(1) 162–79

Harrington H 2008 *The Climate Diet: How You Can Cut Carbon, Cut Costs, and Save the Planet* Earthscan, London

Hoffmann M J 2010 *Climate Governance at the Crossroads: Experimenting with a Global Response After Kyoto* Oxford University Press, Oxford

Hulme M 2010 *Why We Disagree About Climate Change* Cambridge University Press, Cambridge

Kemp R, Loorbach D and Rotmans J 2007 Transition management as a model for managing processes of co-evolution towards sustainable development *International Journal of Sustainable Development and World Ecology* 14 78–91

Lachapelle E and Paterson M 2013 Drivers of national climate policy *Climate Policy* 13(5) 547–71

Lake A and Townshend T 2006 Obesogenic environments: exploring the built and food environments *The Journal Of The Royal Society For The Promotion Of Health* 126(6) 262–7

Levin K, Cashore B, Bernstein S and Auld G 2012 Overcoming the tragedy of super wicked problems: constraining our future selves to ameliorate global climate change *Policy Sciences* 45(2) 123–52

Lovell H 2007 The governance of innovation in socio-technical systems: the difficulties of strategic niche management in practice *Science and Public Policy* 34(1) 35–44

Luke T W 1994 Green consumerism: ecology and the ruse of recycling in Bennett J and Chaloupka W eds *In the nature of things* University of Minneapolis Press, Minneapolis 154–72

Machin A 2013 *Negotiating Climate Change: Radical Democracy and the Illusion of Consensus* Zed Books, London

Maniates M 2002 Individualization: plant a tree, buy a bike, save the world? in Princen T, Maniates M and Conca K eds *Confronting Consumption*, MIT Press, Cambridge MA 43–66

Mills C W 1959 *The Sociological Imagination* Oxford University Press, Oxford

Newell P and Paterson M 2010 *Climate Capitalism: Global Warming and the Transformation of the Global Economy* Cambridge University Press, Cambridge

Norgaard K M 2011 *Living in Denial: Climate Change, Emotions, and Everyday Life* MIT Press, Cambridge MA

Paterson M 2007 *Automobile Politics: Ecology and Cultural Political Economy* Cambridge University Press, Cambridge

Paterson M and Stripple J 2010 My space: governing individuals' carbon emissions *Environment and Planning D: Society and Space* 28(2) 341–62

Pett J 2012 The cartoon seen "round the world" *Lexington Herald-Leader* 18 March (www.kentucky.com/2012/03/18/2115988/joel-pett-the-cartoon-seen-round.html) accessed 1 June 2015

Rajan S C 1996 *The Enigma of Automobility: Democratic Politics and Pollution Control* University of Pittsburgh Press, Pittsburgh PA

Schneider W 2002 America keeps on trucking *National Journal* 23 March 894

Sheppard S 2012 *Visualizing Climate Change: A Guide to Visual Communication of Climate Change and Developing Local Solutions* Routledge, London

Shove E 2010 Beyond the ABC: climate change policy and theories of social change *Environment and Planning A* 42(6) 1273–85

Shove E and Walker G 2010 Governing transitions in the sustainability of everyday life *Research Policy* 39(4) 471–6

Siegle L 2007 The low-carbon diet or how to lose half a tonne in just one month *Observer Magazine* 21 January 24–9

Smith A 2010 Community-led urban transitions and resilience: performing Transition Towns in a city in Bulkeley H, Castán Broto H, Hodson M and Marvin S eds *Cities and Low Carbon Transitions* Routledge, London 159–77

Stripple J and Paterson M 2012 Carbon's body politic, paper presented to the conference on Culture, Politics, and Climate Change, Boulder CO

Sum N-L and Jessop B 2013 *Towards a Cultural Political Economy* Edward Elgar, Cheltenham

Swyngedouw E 2010 Apocalypse Forever? Post-political populism and the spectre of climate change *Theory, Culture and Society* 27(2–3) 213–32

Transition Network 2013a Transition Initiatives map (www.transitionnetwork.org/initiatives/map) accessed 20 August 2014

Transition Network 2013b What is a Transition Initiative? (www.transitionnetwork.org/support/what-transition-initiative) accessed 20 August 2014.

United Nations 1992 *Framework Convention on Climate Change* United Nations, New York

Urry J 2004 The "system" of automobility *Theory, Culture and Society* 21(4) 25–39

Weber C 2000 Imagineering value: good neighbourliness in an era of Disney in Youngs G ed *Political Economy, Power and the Body* Palgrave, London 94–111

3 Climate security in the Anthropocene

"Scaling up" the human niche

Simon Dalby

Anthropocene musings

Since Paul Crutzen made his now famous statement in 2000 that we are no longer living in the Holocene, but rather in a geological period better termed the Anthropocene, the debate about the term has grown and spread into many genres (Crutzen 2002). Concerned that the scale of human activities was such that a new designation for present times was necessary, Crutzen's contention has been worked over thoroughly in the pages of academic journals, in the conference halls and seminar rooms of earth system sciences, and increasingly in popular culture and the media. Climate change is a substantial part of the discussion, but far from the only factor that is being considered. Numerous other aspects of human activity, and the extraordinarily rapid expansion of our capabilities, are also part of the Anthropocene formulation. All of which suggests that while climate change is a pressing issue for humanity, care must be taken to understand it as a subset, as it were, of the Anthropocene if political innovations and cultural changes are to be clearly formulated and appropriately implemented in coming decades.

Climate change is part of a larger quite fundamental transformation of the biosphere and of the human condition, one on a scale large enough that earth system scientists are now seriously discussing the addition of this new geological epoch of the Anthropocene to their long established scheme of the stages of earth history. If humanity is causing transformations on a scale similar to those that ended the age of dinosaurs, then clearly climate is an important matter, but part of a number of simultaneous transformations set in motion by the rapid expansion of the human population since the last ice age, and crucially by its appropriation of ecological and geological entities to remake its habitat on a scale that is now truly global. The expansion of humanity to become the dominant species in the biosphere has led to its reorganization to suit the most powerful parts of the species, a process reordering human affairs in the often-inadvertent process of reordering many other things. Welcome to the Anthropocene!

Much of the discussion of these matters is told in tropes of fear, alarm and various registers of human immorality. The world as we know it is being destroyed. Catastrophe looms! Violence and warfare caused by environmental scarcities will doom civilization. In more explicitly religious tropes, we have sinned and will be punished by floods and droughts; plagues and famine will once more spread across the earth to punish us for our hubris. We are killing off many of the species that matter globally; humanity is the terminator species. There is no such thing as a wild world anymore; defaunation is triumphant (Kolbert 2014). Dark ages are ahead. The Anthropocene is the end times, degradation and destruction is the future and even if intelligent planning does emerge soon it is probably too late to save the world. These pessimistic renditions all rely on at least some clear understanding of particular trajectories. Indeed, declensionist narratives are a popular part of modernity, often driven by the assumptions of imperial decline that pervaded European political narratives in the twentieth century. The cultural politics of end times, in Slavoj Žižek's (2011) terms, are a matter of hopelessness and defeat for progressive forces loosely understood.

However, some other readings of the Anthropocene put climate change arguments into a rather different context, one of "next times," rather than "end times." One sees this kind of thinking in, for instance, James Lovelock's (1979, 2014) recent reworking of the Gaia hypothesis coupled to the common futurist argument that humanity is merely a means to the end of an electronic intelligence that will emerge to regulate the planet (albeit one that may not have need of humanity once its tasks are accomplished). More generally the "optimistic" or "eco-modernist" version of the Anthropocene, epitomized by the work of the Breakthrough Institute (www.thebreakthrough.org; Nordhaus and Shellenberger 2007) is that while the earth is being remade by humanity, it isn't just a tale of destruction, but one of new human opportunities and remade ecological processes, in which industrial artifacts are an increasingly large and productive part of the new assemblages we are making. Yes, pristine nature no longer exists, as humanity has imprinted its signature everywhere and has become a geological force in its own right. But new, attractive, horizons exist in a post-natural world. The Anthropocene represents a potential bright promising future, especially as humans embrace their role as governors of the earth (Ackerman 2014).

This chapter reimagines climate change as an instance of the Anthropocene. In doing so, it underlines that humanity's role in changing the biosphere dates back long before contemporary climate industries. The chapter suggests that ever since humanity started living in cities and practicing agriculture in extensive ways, it has assumed a geological role. Thus, making sense of climate change, at an intensified moment of human geo-dominance, requires coming to terms with urbanization and the agricultural revolution, and all that these have involved. Put differently, climate change is simply another, albeit large, wrinkle in the Anthropocene's protracted unfolding and it is best understood in this context.

While this chapter fundamentally aims to delineate the connection between the Anthropocene and climate change, it has additional aspirations, some of which aim directly toward policy. Climate change poses many dangers to both the human and more-than-human worlds. For many, it presents its most threatening challenge to security, specifically the protection of humans from harm. Policy makers, activists, and ordinary citizens have tried to understand this challenge and propose responses that minimize climate suffering and enhance widespread safety. As I will show, such efforts have been inadequate because they have failed to see climate change in the broader context of the Anthropocene. They have thus proposed at best stopgap measures that offer merely the veneer of security. Contextualizing the challenge of security in a climate age within prolonged historical patterns of urbanization and agricultural expansion, enlarges the conceptual boundaries within which to conceive appropriate measures for enhancing security. A sensitivity to climate change's Anthropocene roots enhances humanity's ability to pursue security in a warming world.

In this sense, the chapter reimagines climate change in the service of boosting human security. To use the language of the volume as a whole, the chapter argues that Climate Inc. has amnesia when it comes to contextualizing historically climate change. It sees climate change as the engine rather than a consequence of the Anthropocene and thus precludes itself from devising appropriate responses, especially when it comes to security. In fact, as I will suggest, Climate Inc.'s misperception commits itself to exacerbating security challenges rather than meeting them. It operates according to a narrow optic and thus offers only limited insight and guidance. By reimagining climate change as an instance of the Anthropocene, this chapter opens up new and broader possibilities of securing human safety as we move into greater climate intensification.

Rethinking security in light of humanity's geological role

Security involves protection. It entails safeguarding wellbeing and enhancing stability. Often such stability gets equated with existing social orders and thus security becomes a matter of ensuring current political, social, and economic conditions. At this historical moment, those conditions revolve generally around the nation-system and the world order of which states are apart. A key element of this is our carbon-based civilization. This has been the order that has been secured for the last few centuries and yet it is precisely this order that presents humanity with the problem of climate change. And indeed it is this contradiction that lies at the heart of current impasses when it comes to responding to climate change. As climate change deepens, one increasingly must ask not only how to provide security but, more fundamentally, what ought to be secured, by whom, and toward what end (Stiglitz and Kaldor 2013). Humanity can no longer be simply defined as a species that seeks to protect the status quo. There is thus a deep contradiction in our traditional conceptualization of security as an attempt to secure a status quo that is no longer present.

What future matters enough to invoke the use of extreme measures and the often-violent logics of security? The "intellectual jailbreak" needed to reimagine climate change in innovative ways is in part a matter of abandoning modern state focused versions of security and thinking again about what it is to be insecure. We need to reimagine rapid change as something other than a threat to various modern social practices. It also requires recognizing that the Westphalia state system and the related geopolitical rivalries among state elites may be part of the political problem rather than an arrangement that facilitates dealing with climate change (Harris 2013).

Doing so requires among other things abandoning the crucial modern distinction of humanity and environment, of culture and nature as either separate or opposite. Reimagining climate in these terms requires us to think of ourselves not only as animals in many ways but as part of earth, not visitors. We are not apart from earth, but a part of earth. Understood in these terms we are geological actors, involved in earth system processes, not merely living within a given environment. Ecology has a history in the composition of rocks, oceans and atmosphere and if we understand ourselves in these terms it challenges many of the myths that perpetuate modernity, and its economic rationalizations for our current situation. The emergence of humanity as a geological force poses inevitable questions as to the beginning of our role in the earth system. Looking closely at the emerging science of these matters suggests that the focus on carbon fuels isn't the whole picture.

Such a change in perspective emphasizes that humanity has both been an agent of change for a long time, and, albeit inadvertently, effectively taken its fate into its own hands. We no longer face a situation understood in terms of protecting a given set of environmental circumstances, effectively trying to secure the status quo, but rather face political questions concerning what kind of earth we will bequeath to future generations. We are, in Paul Wapner's (2010) terms, "living through the end of nature" in a world where the future is increasingly artificial, and as this chapter emphasizes, one that is urbanized. What we decide to make is key to what climate the planet will have millennia hence. How we understand who that "we" is, and what environmental contextualization is most appropriate for discussing climate change are also changing in light of further current research into the Anthropocene.

Reimagining climate change, and what who should do about it, now requires engaging this discussion in detail. It does so because what is underway isn't just climate change, it's a larger transformation of the biosphere, one in which humanity is becoming an urban species and remaking the conditions of its existence quite fundamentally. How this transformation is shaped in coming decades is crucial both to the future configuration of the biosphere and of human society. The Anthropocene formulation makes it clear that these are two sides of the same coin. More so than this, the discussion of the Anthropocene suggests that humanity has been a much more active part of the biosphere than has usually been realized; human actions have been shaping climate for much longer than the current discussion of climate change, with its focus on industrial carbon emissions usually recognizes.

We have already remade the biosphere in crucial ways; now we need to do so once again, this time aware of what we are doing and to what end. Getting the fact that humanity has been changing many things for much longer than conventional thinking on climate change usually realizes clear is important because it recontextualizes the climate issue. As the later parts of this chapter suggest this reimagining of the human role in the biosphere requires us to think about adaptation to rapid climate change in terms of what we make, how we construct future cities, and how we power them, not just in terms of governance mechanisms and attempts to update traditional notions of security in particular. The Anthropocene discussion suggests that while protecting parts of "nature" in particular to keep numerous species alive is important, as plans are made for living in a rapidly changing world, we need to focus more explicitly on what we are making and how these artifacts and related social arrangements might secure humanity's future in a rapidly changing biosphere.

Methane and climate change

Discussions of humanity and its "forcing mechanisms" in the earth system inevitably raise questions of the origins of these new geological processes. When, in other words, did the Anthropocene start? James Lovelock (2014) has recently suggested that it can be precisely dated to 1712 when Thomas Newcomen patented his ideas for a steam engine. This eventually allowed miners to pump water from mines and hence to dig deeper and more effectively. Most other commentators locate the start of the Anthropocene closer to the end of the eighteenth century pointing to James Watt's innovations with the steam engine, dated to 1784, which made it much more practical as a power plant for manufacturing. It subsequently underpinned locomotion with the advent of railways and steam engine ships both of which fueled the expansion of global trade.

The extraordinarily rapid expansion of the global economy, powered largely by coal and petroleum, the period now widely known among earth system scientists as "the great acceleration," began after the Second World War, and perhaps the Anthropocene could be more usefully dated from then (Steffen *et al.* 2011). In geological terms, the introduction of artificial radioisotopes into sediments worldwide, the consequence of the manufacture and use of nuclear weapons, coincides with this dating too. This is a matter of some practical utility to stratigraphers trying to locate a "golden spike" geological marker at the beginning of the new geological epoch.

All these discussions focus on carbon from first coal and then petroleum as key to the Anthropocene. There is good reason to do so, not least because the technologies that set the extraordinary expansion of humanity in motion relate first of all to steam engines, and subsequently petroleum powered propulsion units of various sorts. In so far as most of the discussion of contemporary climate change is about the consequences of carbon combustion, all this makes sense. But another debate in the earth sciences is also worthy of attention on the questions of the origins of the Anthropocene, because it suggests that focusing only on carbon fuels is missing the larger story of the emergence of humanity as a geological force. Methane is getting much more attention recently with growing alarm about its emergence as natural gas replaces much coal as a source of energy and as methane is liberated from the seabed in northern waters and from thawing permafrost (Reay *et al.* 2010).

Methane may have had historical effects on climate many climate analysts have been slow to appreciate. William Ruddiman's (2005) research into historical dimensions of climate change suggests that methane was critical in shifting climate after the last ice age ended. In previous "inter-glacials," geological intervals of warmer global average temperature, the world had slid back into a further period of glaciation fairly quickly. Looking through the geological record Ruddiman noted that the level of methane in the atmosphere is apparently higher early in the current "inter-glacial" than in previous ones, and that this coincided roughly with the emergence of agriculture. Methane from agricultural activities, forest clearing, paddy fields and domestic livestock might have had a significant impact. In atmospheric terms these are trace amounts, but in terms of the thermal balance of the planet, that is enough to make the difference between a trend to cooler times or not. If this thesis continues to hold up to further scientific scrutiny then the question of the origin of the Anthropocene can be formulated in terms of the emergence of agriculture, not of industrialization. Indeed the argument that the Anthropocene is a redundant geological category, because such things are already implicit in the designation of the present period as the Holocene, gains traction by such considerations. After all, as Smith and Zeder (2013) emphasize, changes to the human niche, dating from the domestication of animals and plants in its early millennia, stretch through most of the Holocene.

However, this discussion suggests a couple of further points that are key to thinking about the origins of the Anthropocene, and how such a formulation at least nuances the climate change discussion. Agriculture has usually required both the selection of particular species for cultivation and once selected efforts at breeding versions of those species to emphasize attributes that produce food for humans. It has also required clearing "natural" vegetation and artificially moving plants and animal species around, and in the process changing the species mix in particular ecosystems in ways that have dramatic ecological effects. Effectively this has involved "scaling up" the human niche in the biosphere. This suggests much more than just climate change is resulting from human activities even if climate change is the most obvious large-scale consequence. This "scaling up" is, if Ruddiman is right, a global-scale phenomenon, given that it has already had the effect of at least postponing the next ice age, something that it did long before the current concerns with fossil fuel generated global heating.

Recent estimates suggest that this earlier intervention in the global climate system may be cumulatively as significant as the emissions in the last 150 years, effectively doubling the impact of human climate activities (Ruddiman *et al.* 2014). Therefore it makes sense to argue that humanity had already changed the climate of the planet drastically. If, the logic of this argument goes, humanity had not started doing agriculture seven thousand years ago, now the planet would probably be in the midst of a further period of glaciation. Sea levels might be hundreds of feet lower than at present, perhaps the North Sea would be dry land, and the boundaries of most coastal states as we know them would be unrecognizable to cartographers! No doubt much of central North America would be under thousands of feet of ice and the University where this author is based in what is now called Southern Ontario, would have to be … well, it wouldn't exist at all!

Early farmers were unaware that their animal husbandry or their rice cultivation practices were preventing the planet from undergoing another "ice age," but if the Ruddiman thesis about the early effects of humanity is correct, this is indeed the consequence of their actions. Such ruminations run directly contrary to most human assumptions in modern culture that humanity has been a relatively small factor in ecological considerations until recently. Environmental determinist arguments, ones that suggest that climate patterns and environments have shaped, and even caused the course of human history, turn out to be misconstrued even more than earlier critiques have suggested (Dalby 2015a). Above all this argument suggests that the focus just on carbon fuels and the present climate change crisis, while very serious and extremely urgent, requires a further recontextualization to emphasize that humanity is an actor in shaping the planet in geological terms. It requires a clear understanding that the biosphere is a much more dynamic entity than most environmentalist arguments usually assume.

The consequences of this argument suggest that part of the problem with climate change discussions is that environmentalist premises, and the assumption of a fairly stable ecological system that recent human activities are destabilizing, isn't contextualized accurately enough to be helpful in formulating appropriate political and policy responses. Protecting a stable system, assuming change as a problem, and human interference with a naturally functioning system as necessarily something to be avoided, is predicated on a modern assumption of humanity as separate from a given nature (Wapner 2014). The argument about methane and "early" human causes of climate change, in the sense of preventing an ice age, suggest that this premise needs to be reimagined in how we address climate. None of this in any way reduces the need to tackle climate and curtail the growth of greenhouse gases in the immediate future to slow the pace of change so humanity can better cope with what is coming. But it does firmly suggest that while climate is a matter of human actions, humanity's impact on the planet is not as novel as many of the discussions of contemporary climate emergencies suggest. What is novel is the scale, and crucially the speed, of contemporary changes (Barnosky *et al.* 2012).

Habitat change: the urban question

As noted in the introduction to this chapter, humanity has become an urban species. At least numerous commentators in recent years have suggested that in the first years of the new millennium more than half of us now reside in towns and cities. The significance of this is profound for all sorts of reasons, not least that it suggests a fundamental shift in the human condition that has happened simultaneously with the rise in carbon dioxide levels in the atmosphere. In so far as climate plays out in terms of more extreme weather, floods, heat waves, and the like, the new habitats that humanity has constructed, the towns, cities and related infrastructure, are the context in which people experience, and often suffer, the direct consequences of change (Dalby 2009).

It is also of course precisely that infrastructure, the long commodity chains that bring food, fuel and consumer goods to the cities, and the pipes and electricity lines that power urban life, and take away its wastes, that, when disrupted, makes us vulnerable to extreme weather. The increasingly artifactual nature of our urban existence, and the necessity for the networks to function if our lives, jobs and the contemporary economy are to continue, make our world an increasingly artificial one. This is the context in which the current concern with climate change is playing out. Imagining climate in these terms then raises a number of further questions about cities, their origins and the significance of urbanization for how we think about climate.

Many of the discussions of our contemporary predicament are posed in terms of the survival of our civilization, and whether prior human experiments with civilization that ended in apparent decline or disaster, have lessons to teach us in terms of the failure to consider resource exhaustion, agricultural limits, or vulnerabilities to climate change (Diamond 2005). Most of the understandings of civilization are ones that presuppose urban existence; indeed the roots of the term refer to ways of life made possible by city life; modes of existence distinguished from rural and agricultural life ways. Many of the discussions of city life and of the rise of civilizations also rely on unquestioned assumptions about an evolutionary path for humanity from hunter-gatherers through subsistence agriculture, where surpluses gradually accumulated allowing for the emergence of villages and later towns, to the growth of cities and then the emergence of civilizations. But recent discussions of the beginnings of urbanization suggest an alternative sequence, one that tells a different story that may have further useful insights into how we reimagine climate change and the politics of security in contemporary times.

In his work on cities and the rise of the global economy as networks of cities Peter Taylor (2013) suggests that the conventional assumption of cities emerging only after the gradual rise of villages and towns may be misconstruing the historical record in at least one crucial dimension. Following Jane Jacobs's (1992) work in thinking about innovation and economic growth, he suggests that the stimulus for agriculture came from early urbanization. Demand for food and other commodities was, so he argues, a key part of the emergence of agriculture. The nascent division of labor in early societies drove the beginnings of commerce, and this is key to the rise of cities and the gradual transformation of ecosystems to producers of agricultural products. Urban innovation, the division of labor at the heart of specialization of economic function, the rise of commerce and the emergence of agriculture are, in this view, integral parts of one story, not a sequence of happenstances that gave rise to civilization. The focus on single cities, and on the rise of states as the political drama of our species, is also reformulated here suggesting that trading along networks of cities is integral to innovation. That innovation was frequently interrupted by the power struggles of emergent political elites struggling for control in military rivalries between various cities.

If this argument is then linked to the Ruddiman thesis about the emergence of agricultural activities and the slight elevation of the global levels of methane a few thousand years into the Holocene, it follows that economic innovations, based in cities that generate demand for commodities from both immediate hinterlands and indirectly through trading networks, are a key part of the story of the Anthropocene. Economic activities can then be directly linked to the construction of new urban habitats and thus to changed atmospheric circumstances. Viewed in this way climate change is an accidental side effect of economic activity, but with a history much longer than the conventional story of recent carbon combustion as the culprit in a new set of urban and globalized circumstances. The upshot is that we are involved in terraforming the earth, but have yet to act in a way that makes this explicit rather than an afterthought. That mode of thinking needs to change quickly.

Rethinking security and climate

Cities are new habitats that effectively extract resources from surrounding landscapes, and transform them in the process. They do this by changing the species mix in terms of agriculture, reworking hydrology for water supplies and irrigation, mining minerals and fuels, or somewhat less directly, altering marine environments through fishing and waste disposal. Urbanization is simultaneously a process of colonization (Cronon 1991). Extending the frontier from which resources are extracted, and changing the surrounding landscapes to facilitate the production of commodities for the urban economy, are two sides of the same historical process. This urban driven change is a key part of the human story that has been relatively neglected in modern narratives that have emphasized the superiority of European civilization and ignored the material transformations involved, often at a distance, as empires exploited colonies for commodities to enrich their metropoles. These commercial patterns of demand in cities driving rural transformation long predate the rise of European imperialism and its more voracious offshoots in contemporary globalization.

In so far as artificial climate change is something novel in the earth system, then understanding it as part, albeit mostly an inadvertent part, of the rise of economic activity, and that economic activity as primarily driven by innovations in cities, suggests a narrative that relegates states, and largely empires too, to relatively minor players in the story. Understanding cities and hinterlands, that may or may not be within the same territorial and state jurisdiction as the city, as the key forces behind economic activity, suggests that the implicit geographies in the discussion of global environmental change need more explicit attention than they usually get in either discussions of political or technical matters of ecological transformation. Crucially it suggests that territorial states, and discourses that link environmental change to matters of climate change and specifically to national security, may be a misfit with the processes that matter most in understanding contemporary transformations. At least they are with the notable exception that now these states are the entities that write the rules for the international economy and hence partly shape how innovations play out geographically (Lewis 2014).

This argument links to the larger discussion from Jane Jacobs and Peter Taylor which suggests that the two main modes of social interaction, perhaps unfortunately named "moral syndromes" of human cultures, those of commerce and of "guardian" activities, have very different attributes that will inevitably lead to different modes of conduct. Where guardian functions require assumptions of distrust, potential violence and competitive social relations, commerce requires degrees of trust, an ability to trade and have a reasonable expectation that contracts will be honored. Guardian cultures, with the threats of violence, the ever-present focus on potential threats, and the importance of honor in social interactions, are not useful settings for thinking about climate specifically or the Anthropocene generally. Confusing the rise of states, civilizations and cities, obscures the key function of city commercial networks in changing the human condition. Trade and commerce, not the activities of the "guardians," matter the most in changing the ecological condition of humanity. Competitive state relations, the taken for granted premise of much geopolitical thinking, isn't helpful in climate matters, as a generation of climate negotiations focused on relative gains, free riders and the dangers of defection from collective endeavors has shown repeatedly (on the limitations of statist logic for addressing climate change, see Chapter 4 of this volume).

While in many ways cities also compete in economic matters and attempt to work their way up the hierarchies of the global economy, their competition isn't as zero sum as that of states in terms of power competition. Innovation is key to attracting new industries and new activities in the global system. In terms of municipal politics most cities are energy consumers, not producers and that matters in terms of the possibilities for cities to improve their relative performance in economic terms. And adding climate change, cities can usefully learn from each other in terms of practical innovations in greening their infrastructure as well as the related question of new governance mechanisms; they do so in part precisely because they aren't states (Magnusson 2011). As such cities may be much more useful sources of climate change innovation than many states; their institutional context gives them possibilities for innovations, such as supporting power purchases from green electricity suppliers, which makes a difference in energy matters. Reducing coal consumption simultaneously helps with urban air pollution, a lesson that Chinese urban managers are currently relearning the hard way. Networks of environmental activists and innovative organizations in cities offer ways of collectively learning that frequently bypass state structures too (Bouteligier 2012).

All this suggests that in terms of climate change and what the future of the Anthropocene will look like, it is production decisions that in many ways matter more than traditional environmental notions of limiting and regulating pollution, resource extraction and preserving traditional land uses. All these matter, and will continue to matter, but the more important point is that how decisions about what is demanded by urban markets, and hence what gets produced, are taken, are now the key to the future of the Anthropocene. Reimagining climate change, in this context, means elevating the role of cities and urban living to a central place in our accounts of the Anthropocene. It requires thinking about security in particular in terms of what is needed to enhance urban life rather than maintain the territorial integrity of competing national states. It is a matter of focusing more on city and commercial activities rather than the traditional preoccupation of state "guardian" functions.

In the short term this is a matter of making urban infrastructure much more robust to deal with storms, droughts and other weather disruptions (Graham 2010). In the longer term this requires rebuilding cities as places to live that are much less dependent on fossil fuel systems, a matter of regenerating neighborhoods while also rethinking urban economies and key things such as the ownership of municipal energy systems (see Chapter 2 of this volume; see also Klein 2014). Now we need to rapidly think about political systems that can produce low throughput affluence, rather than administrative arrangements that further colonize peripheral peoples and places while extending property rights to facilitate further rural extractions. Communal land ownership and leasing arrangements for wind and solar energy generation now provide much more sustainable ways of reconstituting rural ecologies than do distant commercial property markets (Mackenzie 2013).

For city residents concerned to slow down the pace of climate change, whether because of the dangers of severe weather or, in the case of port cities, their vulnerabilities to rising sea levels, practical innovations in terms of energy supply and more robust infrastructure should allow them simultaneously to mitigate climate change and facilitate adaptation. However this is not a call for simple market logics; as Peter Taylor (2013) ruefully notes, the provision of relatively cheap air- conditioned housing in the American South has produced energy inefficient sprawl. Cities, if thoughtfully designed, rather than driven only by the dictates of property market logics, ought to be able to buffer their inhabitants from the worst consequences of climate change. Indeed James Lovelock has suggested greater urbanization as the appropriate mode of human adaptation to deal with the coming transformation of the climate.

Urban futures/territorial securities

In the face of climate change, or to be much more precise, rapid climate change, and its potential disruptions to present human arrangements, suggestions for deliberately engineered solutions to climate difficulties, whether by injecting sulfate aerosols into the stratosphere or by other means, are now common (Keith 2013). Viewed in Ruddiman's terms humanity has actually been doing a version of this for a long time by adding agricultural methane to the atmosphere. Critics are aghast at the apparent hubris in deliberately attempting to try to adjust planetary temperatures, suggesting that the solution may be much worse than the problem to which it is a putative response (Hamilton 2013). But the very fact that there is now a serious discussion of the issue emphasizes both the severity of climate disturbances, and more importantly, the failure at least so far, of efforts to negotiate an international climate regime to constrain greenhouse gas production effectively (see Chapter 7 of this volume).

James Lovelock (2014) is among those horrified that humanity should try to geoengineer its way out of climate change by attempting to adjust the whole system through solar radiation management. He suggests that over the long-run the earth is a self-regulating system within which life operates to maintain optimum conditions. As such letting the planet self-regulate while humanity air conditions only greater concentrations of cities or "hives" in Lovelock's terms, rather than the whole planet, is a better option. What he largely neglects to deal with directly in this account is how the self-regulating system – Gaia, in his famous theory – will provide food and other ecological necessities for humanity's hives as it deals with the rapid rise in global temperature that is now inevitable.

Adapt the planet will! How humans will fare is in part a matter of what they decide to try to secure in coming decades. Humanity has already remade many key terrestrial ecosystems. Plants and animals will have to move in order to deal with new climate conditions, many of the decisions about what will move where and when will be artificial decisions as farmers, agricultural corporations, foresters and land-use planners decide what to plant and build where and when. How the ocean ecosystems will respond to heating, beyond more Arctic and Antarctic ice melting, is far from clear. Increased acidification, unsustainable fish extraction and pollution from industrial and urban activities will all combine in ways that have yet to be worked out by oceanographers. Lovelock's (2014) argument doesn't provide any guarantees that in the long term the planet will remain conducive to human life. But in the foreseeable future at least it is clear that humanity will be adapting to circumstances that its actions are continuing to change.

In these circumstances twentieth century modes of security provision premised on territorial sovereignty and mobility restrictions are likely to be unhelpful. Crucially adaptation requires the ability of species to move, to colonize more conducive ecological conditions, both higher up mountains and in some cases further towards the poles. In these circumstances traditional assumptions of preservation of nature in particular places will have to be relaxed to facilitate adaptation and the migration of species. Understanding environmental security as a matter of stability, of new species as a threat because they are "invasive," is not helpful, especially given the wholesale movement of species by gardeners, farmers and pet owners around the world (Fall 2014). The territorial states that are the major spatial arrangements for administering human affairs may here too be an obstacle to securing the flexibilities that adaptive systems require. Thinking of security as a matter of facilitating change rather than preventing people and species crossing national boundaries is a key innovation that suggests flows rather than stasis, and connections and networks rather than demarcations, are most important. In Jacobs's and Taylor's terms commercial rather than guardian functions would seem to be much more appropriate in terms of security provision in the next phase of the Anthropocene.

Here the irony of modern modes of administration, the use of stable borders and demarcated geographical spaces as the basis for sovereign authority, when rapid transformation is the essence of modernity, is palpable (Brown 2010). Security understood in terms of stability, rather than adaptability is more likely to be an obstacle than a help to rapid adaption. If however security is reformulated in global and human terms, rather than national terms, it might be a useful political concept in helping facilitate the innovative focus on what humans need in specific places in the face of global changes (Dalby 2013). The Anthropocene discussion of global politics isn't about states or the themes that usually relate to either peace or war; putting climate security into the traditional terms of national security is misguided.

The fearful prognostications of Malthusian pessimism in the form of fears of nomadic hordes that threaten imperial centers – tropes that animate some of the more rhetorically compelling sections of Malthus's text of two centuries ago – no longer apply in a global system where such nomads are a tiny fraction of the human population, and where high-tech industrial militaries are what matter in terms of combat (Malthus [1798] 1970). However, such imputed environmental causations related to pre-modern territorial arrangements, and in Malthus's case the fall of the Roman Empire, are remarkably persistent in contemporary security narratives, especially those linking environment and conflict in Africa (Hartmann 2014). Now we don't set off in search of greener pastures; nomadic war bands are a thing of the past, or at least they were if most of the currently popular post-apocalyptic fictional genres are ignored!

While global corporations do seek out new frontiers for production schemes and new lands to incorporate into their global operations, it is important to emphasize that imperial centers disrupt peripheral ecologies, while peripheral peoples do not seriously threaten urban civilization. Portraying peripheral areas as threats to metropolitan security is a pattern powerfully reinforced by the geopolitical formulations of the war on terror, but not an accurate representation of the dramatic disruptions of rural areas that contemporary processes of resource extraction involve (Sassen 2014). Neither is it the appropriate geography for understanding how sustainable practices require simultaneously reducing the urban footprint on rural areas in the global south while regenerating their ecologies. If innovations driven by cities are to be an important part of the future, they cannot be about ever-larger extractions of energy and resources from rural ecologies (Sachs and Santarius 2007).

Ironically one of the key themes in the language of security is protecting particular social orders, and most obviously the social order of global capitalism. This is precisely the order that has produced extraordinary innovations including the global trading system that has changed the ecological conditions of the planet. That interconnectedness has also made it clear that the global economy provides what urban humanity needs to sustain its mode of life, and in so far as global security means anything, making a functional economy work is now key (Stiglitz and Kaldor 2013). The ambiguities and contradictions in such formulations are noteworthy, but now, and this is the key point, unavoidable in any serious effort to engage politics with ecological transformations. It is so because the global economy is what is producing the future configuration of the planet and the conditions of human existence in that future. Decisions about what gets produced and built are key to the future of the increasingly artificial biosphere; this is where crucial decisions are being taken. Investors and property speculators rarely understand their actions in quite these terms even if they have to file environmental impact statements as part of their "development" plans.

No longer is this about economy versus environment. As the authors of the 2012 *Global Environmental Outlook* put it in the subtitle of their report, it is now about "environment for the future we want" (UNEP 2012). It is about what kind of environment the economy will produce in future. That key insight is what makes the Anthropocene such a useful concept, one that renders the assumptions of separate environments and economies redundant, and in the process makes geopolitics a matter of considering such things as the rules and regulations for how the global economy will be remade. The key point here in terms of how security is rethought in the Anthropocene is that current geopolitical calculations in trade negotiations are shaping the future climate of the planet, not that climate change may have impacts on the future of geopolitics (Dalby 2014). Arcane points of international trade negotiations are now the terms of geopolitical competition that matter most in terms of building economies less dependent on carbon fuels (Wang *et al.* 2012). If global corporations can invoke local content rules in international trade agreements to effectively prevent some attempts to revive local economies, then clearly geopolitical power, and with it decisions about the future configuration of production systems on the planet, are not located "in" sovereign states, even if they write the rules that corporations use.

Gaia and geostory

Lovelock's arguments about earth's planetary life as a self-regulating system have been enormously productive in terms of rethinking how geology and life interact. The obvious point is that coal and oil, the substances that we are now using as fuels with such profligacy, are in fact the remnants of past life. Geology is about many processes, volcanic, sedimentary, metamorphic and geomorphological. But a key part is the impact living systems have had in changing the composition of the atmosphere. The history of the planet has, until very recently mostly been understood as separate from human history, a matter for science, not a matter in which the humanities or social sciences have much to say. Indeed the conventional division of academic labor in universities has until very recently kept them apart. Now, driven by the new insights of earth system science and the discussion of the Anthropocene, such divisions are increasingly seen as anachronistic; science and politics are interconnected, so too are, as this chapter argues, matters of security and production (Dalby 2015b).

Related to this is the additional point, highlighted in Bruno Latour's (2013) reflections on natural theology, that the traditional notions of nature that have structured modern thinking are also no longer tenable as useful concepts. Nature has frequently acted as a theological concept, a matter of the divine, as a given, beyond human actions. In light of the Anthropocene discussion such distinctions are no longer useful. While preserving species diversity is a key theme in any discussion of the future, it is important to recognize that maintaining habitat *in situ* and anchoring species to particular locales is no longer necessarily appropriate given changing climatic conditions. Neither is resilience, for all its implicit flexibilities, necessarily useful if it presupposes a return to a prior state after a disturbance (see Chapter 8 of this volume). The point about the Anthropocene is that rapid change is now the norm, and what it is that has to be preserved may now be the ability to adapt!

In these terms, where Nature is no longer a given, and change is the norm while the distinction between science and humanities is collapsing, Latour suggests that we need some new vocabulary. He suggests "geostory" as a synthesis of geology and history; a dynamic unfolding drama rather than matters written in stone. With that goes the need to think without nature too, and here Gaia may work better as a category given both its self-regulating adaptive attributes and its ability to accommodate humanity as but the latest of many innovations within its changing configuration. The point about Gaia isn't that any species matters, but that the combinations have in the past worked as a regulatory system regardless of any particular species and in the absence of any design or intention. Indeed it is that insight that encourages Lovelock (2014) to warn against attempts to geoengineer the planet and to focus instead on protecting the new urban "hives" that are now humanity's most important habitats.

Viewed in these terms, the debate about whether there is such a thing as a "good" Anthropocene or not seems misplaced (Dalby 2015c). If the Anthropocene is merely used as a synonym for a period marked by the human destruction of the natural world then its conceptual richness in rethinking the human condition is not being invoked. The point about the Anthropocene is that it isn't the end times; it's the next time. It's a time in which humanity is beginning to live, and in which, while there is both a dramatic decline in biodiversity and the destruction of many places that have been shaped by the post ice age conditions of the last dozen millennia, nonetheless new assemblages are being constructed rapidly. The legacy of the carboniferous period in geological history in particular is being reworked very rapidly in geological terms, for that is what is now being done given the current human proclivity for turning rocks back into air. This is now the key to anthropogenic climate change.

The rich and powerful parts of humanity are now at least implicitly deciding how many polar ice caps the planet will have in future millennia, and where the most convivial climates for particular kinds of agriculture are likely to be. How cities are built in coming generations, with an eye to reducing their ecological throughputs for lives marked more by sufficiency rather than excess, or as extensions of North American style suburban sprawl, matters greatly in terms of how the Anthropocene plays out. In the very long run humanity will leave some kind of fossil record, some strata in the geological record, but while that may be an interesting topic for academic speculation (Clark 2012), what matters more immediately is the speed at which geological transformations are undertaken.

The crucial point in Latour's (2013) invocation of geostory is that neither humans nor ecosystems are in control; and that their mutual constitution in coming decades is something that at least some parts of humanity can actively shape. To be sure, powerful corporate and state actors will certainly be co-authors of the geostory. However, so might social activists. As Naomi Klein (2014) makes clear, social movements, both those resisting the worst excesses of extractive activities and those actively seeking more just and sustainable ways of life, can shape key political choices. Such actions can simultaneously deal with the most outrageous injustices of the present global economy while reducing the ecological footprints of urban life, and in the process start addressing climate as a matter of human security.

Scaling up the human niche

Understanding ourselves as geological actors allows a more careful linkage of geophysical matters of atmospheric composition with such practical matters of crop choice and architectural design. Understanding geopolitics as relating more to the necessity of arranging international trade matters as key to the future of the human habitat that we are all reshaping, rather than to traditional games of prestige, status and influence among heads of state, will be key to security in any meaningful sense in coming decades. Humanity has scaled up its niche, and in the process changed both its immediate practical contextual arrangements, effectively becoming "hive" dwellers, and indirectly set in motion a much larger transformation of the biosphere. Getting these contextualizations clearly in focus is necessary if climate change is to be appropriately understood as part of the human condition. Then we can think about security in terms of innovative ways of building low energy consumption cities and facilitating biological adaptations and migrations. This is not how security has been understood in recent decades but climate change demands that we understand the security context in these new ways, and act accordingly.

The geopolitical categories of the Westphalia system, and its guardian functions in terms of states, national security and violence, are clearly in need of a very substantial overhaul. Cities provide both the possibilities of innovation, and a more prominent place for commercial rather than guardian modes of behavior for the next phase of the Anthropocene. None of this gives license for the unconstrained market logics of neoliberalism. What it does suggest is that rethinking the human niche, as part of a rapidly changing world that urban humanity is remaking, is a key part of what needs to be reimagined in the climate change discussion. This requires thinking well beyond the conventional views of "Climate Inc." that at least so far fail to question fundamental assumptions of contemporary collective life. Instead we need to work to reimagine security in ways that both slow down climate change and adapt our modes of urban life to deal with changes that are now unavoidable. Thinking of humanity as a geological scale actor is a key part of this rethinking.

Without such reimagining apocalyptic fears of imminent catastrophe might come to pass. Given the abilities of cities in particular to innovate quickly, however, the global economy might yet be reshaped to slow greenhouse gas emissions and hence make adaptations easier in coming decades. The longer such innovations are postponed the more difficult adaptation is likely to be. But adapt humanity certainly will. Whether it will do so relatively easily and embrace forces that lead to a more just, humane, and ecologically sound future, or do it the hard way, with much human suffering, in part depends on how the appropriate contextualization of what needs to be secured is now imagined. Hence the importance of understanding climate change as part of the production of new urban habitats that have been key to scaling up the human niche. The necessary focus has to be on what should be secured for urban humanity in the next stage of the Anthropocene, one in which our role in Gaia is now dramatically enhanced.

Acknowledgement

The research in this chapter was supported by a Social Sciences and Humanities Research Council of Canada grant on "Borders in Globalization."

References

Ackerman D 2014 *The Human Age: The World Shaped by Us* Harper Collins, Toronto

Barnosky A D, Hadly E A, Bascompte J, Berlow E L, Brown J H, Fortelius M, Getz W M, Harte J, Hastings A, Marquet P A, Martinez N D, Mooers A, Roopnarine P, Vermeij G, Williams J W, Gillespie R, Kitzes J, Marshall C, Matzke N, Mindell D P, Revilla E and Smith A B 2012 Approaching a state shift in Earth's biosphere *Nature* 486 52–8

Bouteligier S 2012 *Cities, Networks and Global Environmental Governance: Spaces of Innovation, Places of Leadership* Routledge, New York

Brown W 2010 *Walled States, Waning Sovereignty* Zone, New York

Clark N 2012 Rock, life, fire: speculative geophysics and the Anthropocene *Oxford Literary Review* 34 259–76

Cronon W 1991 *Nature's Metropolis: Chicago and the Great West* Norton, New York

Crutzen P J 2002 Geology of mankind *Nature* 415 23

Dalby S 2009 *Security and Environmental Change* Polity, Cambridge

Dalby S 2013 Climate change: new dimensions of environmental security *RUSI Journal* 158(3) 34–43

Dalby S 2014 Rethinking geopolitics: climate security in the Anthropocene *Global Policy* 5(1) 1–9

Dalby S 2015a Environment: determinism to the Anthropocene in Agnew J, Mamadouh V, Secor A and Sharp J eds *Wiley Blackwell Companion to Political Geography* 2nd edition Wiley Blackwell, Chichester 451–61

Dalby S 2015b Climate geopolitics: securing the global economy *International Politics* 52(4) 426–44

Dalby S 2015c Reframing the Anthropocene: the good, the bad and the ugly *The Anthropocene Review* (forthcoming)

Diamond J 2005 *Collapse: How Societies Choose to Fail or Succeed* Viking, New York

Fall J 2014 Governing mobile species in a climate changed world in Stripple J and Bulkeley H eds *Governing the Climate: New Approaches to Rationality, Power and Politics* Cambridge University Press, New York 160–74

Graham S ed 2010 *Disrupted Cities: When Infrastructure Fails* Routledge, London

Hamilton C 2013 *Earthmasters: The Dawn of the Age of Climate Engineering* Yale University Press, New Haven CT

Harris P 2013 *What's Wrong with Climate Politics and How to Fix It* Polity, Cambridge

Hartmann B 2014 Converging on disaster: climate security and the Malthusian anticipatory regime for Africa *Geopolitics* 19(4) 757–83

Jacobs J 1992 *Systems of Survival* Vintage, New York

Keith D 2013 *A Case for Climate Engineering* MIT Press, Cambridge MA

Klein N 2014 *This Changes Everything: Capitalism vs the Climate* Knopf, New York

Kolbert E 2014 *The Sixth Extinction: An Unnatural History* Henry Holt, New York

Latour B 2013 Facing Gaia: six lectures on the political theology of nature The Gifford Lectures, Edinburgh (www.bruno-latour.fr/node/486) accessed 2 July 2015

Lewis J I 2014 The rise of renewable energy protectionism: emerging trade conflicts and implications for low carbon development *Global Environmental Politics* 14(4) 10–35

Lovelock J 1979 *Gaia: A New Look at Life on Earth* Oxford University Press, Oxford

Lovelock J 2014 *A Rough Ride to the Future* Allen Lane, London

Mackenzie F 2013 *Places of Possibility: Property, Nature and Community Land Ownership* Wiley Blackwell, Chichester

Magnusson W 2011 *Politics of Urbanism: Seeing Like a City* Routledge, New York

Malthus T [1798] 1970 *An Essay on the Principle of Population* Penguin, Harmondsworth

Nordhaus T and Shellenberger M 2007 *Break Through: From the Death of Environmentalism to the Politics of Possibility* Houghton Mifflin, New York

Reay D, Smith P and van Amstel A eds 2010 *Methane and Climate Change* Earthscan, London

Ruddiman W F 2005 *Plows, Plagues, and Petroleum: How Humans Took Control of Climate* Princeton University Press, Princeton NJ

Ruddiman W, Vavrus S, Kutzbach J and He F 2014 Does pre-industrial warming double the anthropogenic total? *The Anthropocene Review* 1(2) 147–53

Sachs W and Santarius T eds 2007 *Fair Future: Resource Conflicts, Security and Global Justice* Zed, London

Sassen S 2014 *Expulsions: Brutality and Complexity in the Global Economy* Harvard University Press, Cambridge MA

Smith B D and Zeder M A 2013 The onset of the Anthropocene *Anthropocene* 4 8–13

Steffen W, Persson Å, Deutsch L, Zalasiewicz J, Williams M, Richardson K, Crumley C, Crutzen P, Folke C, Gordon L, Molina M, Ramanathan V, Rockström J, Scheffer M, Schellnhuber H J and Svedin U 2011 The Anthropocene: from global change to planetary stewardship *Ambio* 40 739–61

Stiglitz J E and Kaldor M eds 2013 *The Quest for Security: Protection without Protectionism and the Challenge of Global Governance* Columbia University Press, New York

Taylor P 2013 *Extraordinary Cities: Millennia of Moral Syndromes, World Systems and City/State Relations* Edward Elgar, Cheltenham

UNEP 2012 *Global Environmental Outlook GEO5: Environment for the Future we Want* United Nations Environment Programme, Nairobi

Wang L Gu M and Li H 2012 Influence path and effect of climate change on geopolitical pattern *Journal of Geographical Sciences* 22(6) 1117–30

Wapner P 2010 *Living Through the End of Nature* MIT Press, Cambridge MA

Wapner P 2014 The changing nature of nature: environmental politics in the Anthropocene *Global Environmental Politics* 14(4) 36–54

Žižek S 2011 *Living in the End Times* Verso, London

4   Climate change, policy knowledge, and the temporal imagination

Richard Falk

> Time present and time past
> Are both perhaps present in time future,
> And time future contained in time past.
>
> (T. S. Eliot, "Burnt Norton," *Four Quartets*)

Points of departure

A few metaphors ruthlessly govern the political imagination. Globally, by far the most influential modern metaphor reminds us that we inhabit frag-mented spaces.[1] Images of sovereignty, balance, equilibrium, deterrence, anarchy, and borders continue to grip the mind and reify certain actualities despite the recent intrusion of cyberspace. The master metaphoric repre-sentation remains the conventional map organized into territorial domains of separate sovereign states. This conception of political space ignores the increasing role of transnational forces and non-state actors, and tends to level the conceptual playing field, glossing over the unevenness of states in all dimensions of behavior relevant to policy and law. (Maps make clear that there is no transnational or meta-national juridical entity able to shape or impose order on a fragmented, sovereign system.)

Like all metaphors, spatial ones obscure as much as they reveal. The prevailing one ignores temporality – time, motion, flows, and change, as well as any sense of historical agency or causation. This is unfortunate since it limits the horizon of political possibility by discounting changes in world order that require transcending statist logic. Further, to the extent that time *is* taken into account, it is beneath the sway of a spatially configured world order. This reinforces the economic advantages and ecological resilience of the more powerful and developed states while imposing disproportionate harm and risks on the least developed and most ecologically challenged ones as it tends to discourage an affirmative action approach to close inequality gaps or to address the distinctive afflictions of the least developed states.

Nowhere is this more obvious than in confronting climate change. Global warming scrambles the dominant spatial metaphor. It ignores state boundaries and requires that an extra-territorial, non-national orientation be taken into sufficient account. To date, scattered mitigation and adaptation efforts have arisen within global civil society, parts of the world economy, and related realms of transnational life. Yet these have had an insignificant impact on the dark shadows cast by the statist, spatial mindset. Spatiality restrains and, in fact, perverts, the political imagination when it comes to climate change. It must be complemented or, better, replaced by an outlook sensitive to *positive* temporality so as to make meaningful progress toward climate sanity and equity. Positive temporality involves contextualizing climate decisions within long time horizons so as to use past experience and future assessments to prudently assess risk. This contrasts with negative temporality, which downplays risks by relying on nonhuman power (i.e. God) to determine the future or by assuming that technology will find a solution when it is needed. At present, *negative* temporality mainly shapes policy. The most developed countries tend to mitigate, adapt, and defer, while the least developed countries are too preoccupied with their respective urgent territorial challenges and too limited by resources and constrained political imaginations to accord climate change the attention it deserves.

This chapter considers how the dominant spatial metaphor limits the political and moral imagination and makes the case for positive temporality in our conceptualizing and responding to climate change. Conventional orientations to climate change – what this volume calls, collectively, "Climate Inc." – presuppose a spatially constructed view of world order accompanied by a dysfunctional treatment of time. Focused on the category of the state and selectively tone-deaf to the immediacy of climate harm, national governments either assign climate action to the future and ignore or underplay its present relevance, with a belief that, *when the time comes*, humanity will miraculously mobilize the will and the means to respond appropriately. The problem is that, committed to a static, statist analytic, the *right* time will *never come* for meaningful action on a global scale; it will be either too early or too late. Postponement, rather than engagement, is the modus operandi of the state-system as a whole, with various degrees of self-interested responses taking place on a state-by-state basis.[2] Climate Inc. thus guarantees climate intensification and widespread suffering arising from ecological deterioration. Emphasizing the importance of time, motion, historical agency, and social acceleration, this chapter aims to expand horizons of political awareness and provide some resources for a better grasp of the promise of a climate-safer future.

Put differently, this chapter reimagines climate change by strongly encouraging greater attention to the dimension of temporality in our analytical, theoretical, and prescriptive approaches to policy formation and norm creation. From this point of departure, the chapter recommends adhering to a precautionary approach that combines the perspectives of "climate justice" with "climate security." This kind of prescriptive outlook may seem like nothing more than an admonition to heed common sense. But given cultural compulsions toward infinite material growth, various forms of indebtedness, and a deferring of burdens to future generations, such advocacy implies profound adjustments. In effect, positing a healthy and sustainable climate as a human right and a prerequisite to species survival, and therewith employing positive temporality, calls into question the whole modern consumerist, carbon-based mode of life.

The climate change challenge

Part of the argument being set forth is that governments representing states are operating primarily on the basis of *spatial* categories with the dimension of time made relevant mostly as a matter of diplomatic exhortation, but not in ways that exert a constructive influence on problem-solving and governmental policy forming mechanisms. National interests not global interests are given priority, which tends to privilege the preoccupations of territorial states rather than the necessities of the global community. If global interests shaped climate policy then future prospects and current unevenness of impact and capabilities would be given much greater weight. Spatially oriented actors are particularly ill-adapted to address climate change because the states most threatened are generally not the biggest emitters of greenhouse gasses, and besides, the richest states can better afford to pay the higher premiums resulting from deferring a response.

For instance, the countries in the Middle East and Africa are the most seriously harmed by climate change at present with worse to come in the near future. Yet states in these regions contribute only a small fraction to global emissions, face significant domestic challenges like meeting basic needs and addressing internal conflict, and lack diplomatic leverage to exert much influence on global policy formation (Al-Olaimy 2013). By comparison, major emitting states are not as severely harmed in the present period and possess greater adaptive capabilities. This engenders complacency based on expectations of being able to adjust *when the time comes*. Such inequality, based on differential experiences and perceptions of risk and harm, complicates meeting the challenge of climate change in a prudent and equitable manner. Spatiality, in the form of territorial fragmentation and uneven capabilities, undermines possible transnational and globalist approaches to climate change. It promotes negative temporality in climate change contexts.

The current conceptualization and organization of the world into territorial, sovereign units help explain the disappointing and costly inadequacy of current international responses to climate change. The 194 states party to the UNFCCC differ not only in their historical contribution to the problem but also enjoy varying degrees of exposure, perception of harms experienced, and capability to respond. Furthermore, constituting a large group of sovereign units, states must engage in a procedurally unwieldy process that includes both free rider problems and incentives for a few states to forge an agreement that serves their particular interests. For instance, the Copenhagen Accord in 2009 sought a "consensus" based on a text drafted at the eleventh hour by an ad hoc coalition of five political actors led by the United States. By the time the document was presented to the other 189 governments for approval, negotiations had already taken place. Such a hegemonic process was an affront to the majority of states that had worked for many months negotiating a more ambitious agreement that would regulate emissions as a matter of legal obligation. Such an approach proved to be an insult in the post-colonial political atmosphere that prevailed at Copenhagen, and besides was viewed as falling far short in safeguarding the planet from global warming.

In one respect the American initiative was an understandable reaction to the mood of domestic and Congressional politics in the United States that embraced a narrowly focused nationalism coupled with a pro-business outlook and a relatively relaxed perception of climate change threat. This made it politically untenable for the United States to engage in a global lawmaking process that had meager support in the US Congress. Undoubtedly, the United States wanted to avoid a repeat of the disappointment arising from the pronounced unwillingness of the Senate to even consider ratifying the 1997 Kyoto Protocol, which had been negotiated in the form of a binding set of legal commitments (Pielke Jr 2010).[3]

From a positive temporal perspective, the more voluntaristic and minimal Copenhagen approach is not sensitive to the immediacy of more serious impacts of climate change in some parts of the world, which cannot afford to wait if they are to avoid even more serious hazards in the future. Such vulnerability is particularly acute for islands and coastal areas subject to flooding if ocean water levels rise due to polar melting or if, as in the Middle East, water scarcities are aggravated by rising temperatures. In effect, positive temporality both needs to calibrate policy with national circumstances and to conceive of global policy by taking account of universal human interests as well as national concerns.

Acting in time

The temporal dimension is relevant to an understanding of the resistance encountered in all efforts so far to implement the scientific consensus in a responsible fashion. An aspect of the climate change debate is whether to conceive of the risks and harm to be matters primarily of *future* concern, implying that "we have time." Particular attention has been given to that part of the scientific assessment that posits a safe ceiling for global warming to be an increase of 2° Celsius, which situates the main danger in the domain of "not yet," subtly signaling that present governmental officeholders will not be held accountable. This creates temptations for politicians to avoid taking action unpopular with voters and powerful private sector interests or to portray what must be done in ineffectual ways to avoid imposing burdens on existing businesses or current day consumers.

This evasive course of action is also encouraged by the invisible nature of climate change, as compared to many forms of environmental pollution, accentuating the impression that the dire warnings are more "speculative" than "scientific," misunderstanding the policy relevance of climate models.[4] Locating the threats posed by global warming in the future is also encouraged by the technophilic confidence that the marketplace will, whenever it becomes truly necessary, generate innovative solutions. This kind of corporate mysticism strengthens the push back argument that climate alarmists are exaggerating the dangers posed by climate change in ways that will needlessly impede development by reducing the efficiencies of markets.

Relying on technological fixes by way of geoengineering also creates promising opportunities for major profitmaking ventures, and tends to minimize the uncertainties posed by such novel and large-scale manipulations of nature. Again this kind of outlook, working generally well in earlier phases of industrialization, seems insensitive to the peculiar nature of the climate change challenge. It is untenable to wait until the harmful effects are punishingly severe (for instance, by the rise of ocean levels, release of large quantities of methane from tundra regions, and unsustainable rises in average temperatures). Such attitudes risk negative temporarily in its most extreme form, the crossing of thresholds of irreversibility.

This temporal dimension of the *present* is misleadingly reinforced due to an excessive stress on *future* thresholds as posited by climate scientists who exhibit their professional reluctance to put forward tentative and probabilistic assessments about present harms attributable to global warming. For example, a growing body of research suggests that recent severe droughts in Syria and Darfur, partially responsible for the extensive civil strife in both countries, may be tied to anthropogenic climate change. Yet policymakers have completely ignored such evidence (Fountain 2015).[5] Likewise, the media and most politicians in the US have treated severe storms like Katrina and Sandy merely as "normal" extreme weather events best understood as periodic gyrations within natural weather cycles. No influential policymaker has called for any regulation of human activities as a result.

Such silence is pervasive. Instead of acknowledging the obligation to address climate change in the present, economic elites, the media, and politicians search for, and draw attention to, more tangible factors such as mismanagement of water resources, negligent storm protection, and/or societal pressures. In the cases of Syria and Darfur, for instance, reports discussed, at best, heightened ethnic tensions caused by the severe water shortages. They failed to address the background relevance of climate change as a triggering mechanism in fragile societal and environmental circumstances.

In other words, there are multiple reasons for this pattern of reluctance to read the future into the present, including the absence of sufficient proof and the inability to conduct acceptable scientific tests. Hence, since even the scientific community holds back in its ability to link present harms with climate change, political leaders feel little public pressure to act prudently in response to immediate climate realities. Such assessments are made even more disturbing when particularized in terms of uneven present and future vulnerability – confirming that those most in need seem least aware and are not being helped by better endowed governments. With respect to temporality, this unevenness of states makes the perceptions and responses even more dysfunctional than if all territorial communities were more or less equally vulnerable to climate change or if climate policy was shaped by regional and global perspectives.

One aspect of this failure of prudent response is the epistemological style of scientific discourse that withholds a definite pronouncement until there is near certainty of evidence validated by empirical tests, as well as formal simulation models. In the case of climate change, complexities and probabilities are hedged with surrounding uncertainties that could make projected harms more or less serious (Oreskes and Conway 2014). As a result, the level of validation that would be required for the scientific community to take a firm, public stance on climate change has not been reached. This conservative approach to new knowledge is arguably sensible and appropriate within epistemic communities composed of scientists. However, as policy should be premised on assessments of behavior from the perspective of societal wellbeing and prudent risk-taking, a different calculus of reliable knowledge is essential. For instance, the issue was not confronted in relation to pollution and the environmental agenda of the 1970s where there was some dependence on scientific assessments of actual and potential harm, but the views of scientists were far less centrally related to the formation of policy than in relation to climate change. The Stockholm Declaration on the Human Environment, for instance, formulates a "precautionary principle" that views the assumption of risk through an optic of common sense prudence rather than insisting upon the optic of scientific pronouncement prior to validating the threat.[6]

This cautious approach lends a certain credibility to climate skepticism. Scientific reluctance makes it difficult to attribute devastating droughts, wild fires and extreme weather to global warming despite the strong likelihood that these present harms are being *caused* by rising average earth temperatures. Such withholdings of judgment, allow climate skeptics to argue more effectively that harms from global warming are merely speculative, can be in all likelihood be explained by variations in natural weather cycles, and should not form the basis for adding to costs of production that diminish economic growth and discourage consumption. In other words, treating the zone of danger as something that is not sufficiently established in the present shifts the issue of adaptation into the future. This shift makes it reasonable to go slowly with fashioning costly and burdensome present responses until there is much greater assurance as to future realities so that scientists would become willing to affirm this expectation.

Such epistemological patience is particularly troublesome in the context of achieving a desirable climate change policy. There is an immediate consequence exhibited by this refusal to link present harm to global warming, as has been the case with respect to the frequency and severity of storms or droughts. Instead of mobilizing wider responses when such events do occur, the failure of most scientists to affirm the causal connection (as distinct from urging present adjustment to heed the implications of an anticipated future), weakens the motivation to accept local, national, regional, and global initiatives to prevent future such events that are likely to occur with greater frequency and result in even more serious forms of human suffering, and make responsive action more difficult and expensive.

By the time that the scientific community becomes willing to connect the dots between events on the ground and their links to the carbon and other greenhouse gas density in the atmosphere immediate dangers exacerbate and thresholds of irreversibility grow closer and require exponentially more expensive costs. And surely, given expectations about population increase and persisting economic growth, there is every reason to suppose that the longer the wait for measures of genuine adaptation and mitigation to be taken, the more difficult it will be to adjust, not only economically, but also with respect to fundamental societal life style patterns bearing on health, diet, shelter, and consumption.[7]

In effect, the prudential wisdom with respect to time embodied in the lines from T.S. Eliot's poem quoted above is trumped by the scientific caution that makes it more difficult to act prudently in the present. Putting this point differently, pre-modern views of coping with future threats posed by nature seemed more in line with sustainable living than do those of our modern scientific civilization (Latour 1993; Diamond 2006). This bias toward "science" leads to the formation of a scientific consensus that is adopted at *a rhetorical* level by society and its political leaders, but given the obstacles along the path of implementation is not acted upon effectively even in its minimal formulations.[8]

Because the dangers associated with global warming are not visible in the same way as conventional pollution and not correctible without big burdens or complex tradeoffs as was the case for ozone depletion, the epistemological conservatism of climate scientists is significant, and their reluctance to reach closure at sufficiently high levels of concerns creates a space within which the skeptics and special interests gain traction to slow things down further.[9] This situation underlines the importance of the formation of an epistemological community with respect to public risk that operates more in accord with the precautionary principle – without awaiting scientific closure, which of course may never come or come when it has become too late (Beck 1992). Moving in such a direction with respect to risk analysis bearing on climate change would in effect heighten respect for and enhance the influence of positive temporality.

There is a final observation relevant to taking account of possibly grave risks relating to future catastrophe. The response to the advent of nuclear weaponry is a prime example of the hegemony of negative temporality, and should serve as a kind of instructive experience for the climate change debate and movement. With respect to nuclear weaponry, scientists are essentially irrelevant except to create a dire picture of what a post-nuclear world might be like, which may induce a certain degree of caution in policymaking circles, but does not give guidance as to making the central choice between "deterrence" and "disarmament" (Lifton and Falk 1986; Falk and Krieger 2012; Nye 1986). In my view a comparable failure to that of climate change exists on the part of the policy community to address properly future risks posed by the threat posed by nuclear weaponry, but its essential character is different than that bearing on climate change due to the greater relevance of the interaction between temporal categories of present and future.

Instead of "scientific certainty" those that make security policy are guided by an epistemology that is best known as "political realism" drawing on views of the past, premised on history and a skeptical view of human nature. It bases its policy logic on interpretations of human nature and historical experience that correlate security primarily with physical strength, military capabilities, political distrust, and the susceptibility of human reason to expectations of gain and loss. The major premise of political realism lifts a line out of context from the ancient Greek historian, Thucydides: "The strong do what they will, the weak do what they must" (Thucydides 1954).[10] In this regard nuclear weaponry can be rationally accommodated, and even prudently sought after, as a means to increase security against some of the threats that arise within a framework of sovereign states. Thinkers such as John Mearsheimer (1984–5) and Kenneth Waltz (1981) believe that we should be thankful for the presence of nuclear weapons as probably responsible for the avoidance of World War III. In this regard, there is no way to resolve the argument between those who favor deterrence and those who seek disarmament by an appeal to prudence in relation to addressing future risks as what is at stake are contradictory conceptions of prudence. As with climate change, I believe we are addressing a fundamental question of the appropriate epistemology in relation to somewhat indeterminate future risks.[11]

Unlike climate change where a precautionary approach to knowledge would provide an appropriate guide to policy, for nuclear weapons I would argue for the adoption of a moral epistemology that unconditionally prohibits certain forms of behavior including genocide, torture, and weaponry of mass destruction whatever the instrumental justifications that can be advanced (Thompson 1982). It is true that the adoption of such a moral epistemology does not entirely eliminate the policy problem as it can still be argued from the perspective of use that the contrasting risks of possession and abolition are incalculable. In response, I agree with E.P. Thompson that the threat to use such weaponry is itself genocidal if not omnicidal, and therefore any kind of benefits from deterrence are tainted by the nature of the threat being made. In this regard it should be recognized that from the perspective of international law and morality threats can be as unacceptable as actual uses of force (Falk 2013).[12] Admittedly, this somewhat begs the question as it is not clear that mere possession of the weaponry entails a threat to use (International Court of Justice 1996). Despite this degree of ambiguity, the case for reliance on a moral epistemology in a globalizing world seems indispensable if there is to be created the kind of global political community that will become capable of upholding the *human* interest as well as processing the interplay of *national* interest calculations (Johansen 1980).

Discussion of the analogous concerns with respect to the status of nuclear weapons is intended to convey the differing ways that temporality in these two instances of ultimate concern is relevant. In relation to climate change, since the underlying causes of harm and risk are associated with intrinsically benign behavior, restrictions need to rely on a precautionary or prudential epistemology that is sensitive to present harms, unevenness of perception and experience, and the prospects of increasing costs and uncertain thresholds of irreversibility. In contrast, the role of nuclear weapons rests on threats and acts that are intrinsically criminal, and the elimination of this weaponry by prudent arrangements for phased disarmament relies on the authority of a moral epistemology. To assess the disarmament arrangement advocated and implemented does depend on a more prudential calculus as distinct from the categorical rejection of nuclear weaponry as instruments of protection or security. Positive temporality for nuclear weaponry concentrates on the means to attain the desired end, whereas for climate change the focus is how to adjust the means in light of competing values and risks.

Modern modes of coping with the future

The temporal imagination is not absent from the modern sensibility, but its ways of coping with the future have not been helpful to date in responding to climate change. Science fiction is one influential way to offer critiques of present societal arrangements, including the destructive nature of consumerism or the failure to arrange for sustainable energy (Lessing 1971; Chapter 10, this volume). The depiction of alternative worlds can highlight what is going wrong with the way human society has evolved, but it offers literary and deliberately unattainable models of alternative worlds and life styles, and makes no claim to know how to alter current practices and policies sufficiently to make sustainable living and security patterns politically achievable. Science fiction provides opportunities to gain insight into the destructive patterns associated with current life styles as well as depicting more sustainable and satisfying ways of living together on the planet. In these ways, it can soften resistance to adopting less growth oriented economic policies, which would also be more compatible with reducing greenhouse gas emissions.

In many respects, the utopian tradition is apolitical as it projects idealized futures without bothering to work out transition scenarios. Such a utopian tradition was condemned by Karl Marx and Friedrich Engels in *The Communist Manifesto* because they believed it distracted energy from achieving a transformative politics needed to liberate workers from oppressive societal conditions. There are many types of "utopias," that is, political futures that are radically different in conception and embodiment than present realities. Utopias tend to be idealized alternatives to the present that seek to overcome alienation and inequities encountered in past and present social and political structures. There is a recent sub-genre of "green utopias" that seek to glorify sustainable living patterns as related to species survival and ecological stability, profiling how we might live well, yet in greater ecological harmony (Callenbach 1975). In a more conventional political mode, proposals for world government are ways of responding to present challenges by establishing strong central institutions of government that are expected to promote the human interest on a global scale. This utopian tradition either disavows any expectation that the vision is realizable or leaves this task to others. It is merely introduced as a desirable alternative as was the case with Plato's *Republic*, the classic example of this genre. There is a definite role for both science fiction and utopian literature in seeking to explore how a future society might live well yet not disturb the cosmic equilibrium in the manner that has been occurring since the Industrial Revolution. This is especially the case with charting climate futures.

The World Order Models Project (WOMP), a transnational, multi-decade scholarly enterprise, represents an ambitious foray into such conceptual terrain. Reacting to the criticism that proposals for the centralization of political control on a global scale were tainted by Westcentric advocacy, WOMP invited scholars from non-Western civilizations to develop their own vision of a desirable future within a framework of universally agreed values (Mendlovitz 1975). It turned out that none of the supposedly realistic utopias prepared by the non-Western participants looked toward political centralization as a solution to the issues then confronting humanity (Mazrui 1975; Kothari 1975; Sakamoto 1975). When in a second phase WOMP attempted to produce a collective model of a realistic or achievable utopia it failed to achieve a consensus and abandoned the effort. Two relevant points emerged from this exercise: when radical reform is contemplated without the inhibition of practical politics, there are deep cleavages as to policy priorities and attainable goals; when attention is given to the transition from "here" to "there" with respect to realizing a vision, the unevenness of values and material circumstances undermines the capacity required to construct a viable political project. WOMP did seek to turn loose the power of an imagined future to address the dangers and wrongs of the present, but without any success in allowing desired futures to reshape a deformed present. In other words, neither rationality nor ideas have political traction without transformative agency, which is so far lacking in relation to fundamental ecological challenges even if seeming to threaten species survival (Falk 2014).

WOMP was carried on for a 25-year period in the last part of the twentieth century before climate change had impacted in any serious way on the public imagination. Its work finished before the threats associated with global warming were appreciated, which can be associated with the aftermath of the 1992 Earth Summit held in Brazil. It may be that the mobilization of public awareness together with the presence of a consensus among climate scientists would give a WOMP approach to these issues more chance of devising a globally acceptable format for integrating future expectations into policymaking venues. In this sense, what WOMP contributes is a normative sensitivity to the future that is different from the rigorous strictures of scientists on reaching closure. A WOMP-type normativity could provide a conceptual template for framing climate debate and policy formation. It would certainly induce political leaders to wed near-term national interests and private sector predispositions with long-term global needs and concerns. Furthermore, it would challenge technophilic confidence in purely mechanical fixes to climate change. A WOMP-like normativity would also offer a sensitivity to the relevance of positive and negative temporality as providing policy guidance.

What is meant by "normative sensitivity" to temporality is far from obvious or free from controversy. As used here it implies a postmodern worldview grounded in the interactive realities of the ethical/spiritual with natural surroundings and with human endeavor.[13] It implies human and animal rights, as well as maximal reliance on sustainable energy sources, and a lifestyle that respects the carrying capacity of the earth.

Translating normative sensitivity into the dynamics of a political project is also part of the challenge that was never met by WOMP, nor by various aspirational texts relating to climate change, including the foundational Framework Convention on Climate Change. The increasing tendency within global arenas under UN auspices has been to settle for pledges and voluntary contributions to the control of carbon emissions. This way of registering future concerns is both an acknowledgement of the weakness of the present political will relevant to implementing the scientific consensus and of resistance to translating normative sensitivity into political action, especially on the part of leading governments, none more so than the United States. The advantages of an obligatory framework is both an acknowledgement of the greater likelihood that an obligation will be upheld as compared to a pledge that is vulnerable to a host of reasons for failing to follow through. Imagine basing tax obligations on a framework based on voluntary contributions even if formalized by public pledges made in advance.[14] Given the conflicting attitudes toward whether past contributions to the atmospheric densities of carbon and other greenhouse gasses should be taken account, as well as the extremely uneven behavior of states regarding the regulation of emissions and with respect to meeting material needs, it is especially important to have agreed obligatory arrangements that override subjective interpretations of relative responsibilities, priorities, and capabilities and lessen the temptation to give in to immediate pressures for jobs and growth.

What is to be done when the positive temporal imagination is not strong enough to impress itself upon the political agenda of important actors? What happens when the privileging of spatiality prevents embracing the precautionary principle? One sees the answer to these questions in the way the world has moved from obligatory to voluntary climate commitments. The main perpetrator of this shift has been the US. The failure of the US to adhere to the Kyoto Protocol or even submit this treaty to the US Senate for ratification, has underscored the inability of the United States Government to offer credible leadership in shaping global policy on climate change, and yet there has not stepped forward any alternative leadership. There is present a broader realization that if the United States is unwilling to accept obligatory controls, then enough others will follow suit and thereby undermine the contributions that could otherwise have been made by an agreement engaging most governments in the world. In this regard, the post-Kyoto consensus accepts limiting lawmaking goals to a largely voluntary framework, at least rendered credible by being made explicit and reinforced by monitoring and reporting mechanisms to achieve verification as to compliance.[15]

It should, of course, also be acknowledged that the acceptance of obligations in binding international agreements never guarantees compliance, and that there are generally no mechanisms to address non-compliance beyond some loose verification procedures designed to establish whether treaty violations have occurred. In a situation of the sort posed by climate change where strong economic and security incentives for non-compliance might emerge, it can be argued that the effectiveness of a treaty is dependent on essentially *voluntary* patterns of adherence.[16] There is influential writing, including by ecologically minded authors who accept the scientific consensus: that it is politically futile to enact any regulations that will be seen to impinge upon the operation of "the iron law" of economic growth or deny access to energy on the part of those that are energy deprived (Pielke Jr 2010). It can be expected that circumstances of immediate economic stress would lead governments to suspend compliance with emissions restraints if perceived as reducing productivity, profits, growth, and jobs. These considerations do not undermine the need for obligatory commitments but rather emphasize the importance of a strong cultural commitment to positive temporality in relation to climate change to ensure the prudent balancing of conflicting present pressures by political leaders.

One reason to welcome ambitious voluntary arrangements as clearly preferable to the frustration associated with failed obligatory frameworks is the relevance of public opinion and civil society activism.[17] If a civil society mobilization occurs that draws its substantive thresholds from the scientific consensus as interpreted through the optic of the precautionary principle rather than by adherence to the strict epistemic requirements of science a more sensible set of policy relevant recommendations are likely to emerge. One test will be whether civil society pressures can be usefully mounted to induce compliance with the sort of voluntary framework that emerged in 2015 at Paris UN Conference of the Parties, which was seen as the last chance for the governments of the world acting under UN auspices to meet the underlying challenges posed by climate change. That is, the norms that are agreed upon even if denominated as "voluntary" give civil society thresholds of reasonableness upon which to base demands from below and mobilize people for action (Brecher 2015). There are also strong incentives to uphold undertakings between powerful political actors even if framed as "voluntary." For example, respecting the bilateral agreement of 2014 between the United States and China on modestly restricting their emission levels also functions as a test of overall trustworthiness of cooperative relations between these two dominant states, and the related possibility of providing responsible joint leadership with respect to the climate change agenda. There is some fragility embedded in such arrangements to uphold policies that follow from implementing the precautionary principle with respect to climate change, exhibiting a greater readiness to integrate a calculus of positive temporality into present behavior.[18] Political leaders change, risk assessments vary, pressure to meet present needs arise.

Confronting the future in the present

From ancient times, many thinkers have tended to conceive of time in a chronological or linear manner. This has been the principal way in which the relevance of the future has been understood – as a progressive forthcoming unfolding of experience. For reasons argued above relating mainly to the formation of political will, the statist structure of world order, and the epistemological enclaves generating tensions between science and policy, the efforts to address climate change in conformity to the imperatives of the precautionary principle have been disappointing. Prospects for the near future are more hopeful, but still far below the level of sufficiency. In the context of conventional images of time, the precautionary principle appears relatively impotent as a source of policy guidance at governmental and inter-governmental levels.

Time can also, however, be conceived from the perspective of ruptures or, transformative events. The concept of *kairos*, in Christian thought, in which the crucifixion is seen as a breach of historical continuity, represents this alternative understanding (Carey 1978). In relation to climate change, some sort of awakening occurrence that seemed undeniably linked to global warming might function in a comparable mobilizing manner (e.g. abrupt and unprecedented rises in temperature; Griffin 2015, 391–404). It would seem that some kind of rupture in the flow of time is needed to overcome resistance to the emergence of an appropriate globally oriented approach to upholding the human interest with respect to policies bearing on energy use and other human activities responsible for the release of large quantities of greenhouse gasses. It is not at all necessary that the rupture be linked to catastrophe. In unpredictable ways a transformative movement could emerge that challenges the established order in a variety of ways, including its failure to protect society against global warming. The shape of a *kairos* moment is its unanticipated intrusion on historical expectations.[19]

There is an element of wishful thinking in describing certain develop-ments as if *kairos* moments. For instance, the noted environment author and climate change activist, Bill McKibben, points to two such events in 2014. The first involves reports that the West Antarctic Ice Sheet is "desta-bilized" in such a way as to make its melting "irreversible." McKibben quotes Thomas Wagner, a NASA research scientist, as contending that this could result in a disastrous four-foot rise in ocean levels. McKibben claims that these reports might be remembered in the future as a decisive turning point in relation to managing the planetary ecosystem.

A second *kairos* candidate mentioned by McKibben, and closer to his own engagements, was the Peoples' Climate March of September 21, 2014, when demonstrators in 2,800 cities around the world took to the streets to protest a carbon-based, unjust economy. McKibben calls the event "a turn-ing point in the scale and impact of the grassroots fight against climate change" (McKibben 2014). It seems doubtful that either of these happen-ings, significant in their own right, should be viewed as *kairos* moments, as nothing seems to have changed fundamentally with respect either to the political will of leaders or the durability and intensity of popular mobiliza-tion. As such, then, these developments seem more appropriately in the domain of *chronis* (i.e. as steps in a process rather than a clean historical rupture). In this sense, they may be part of a cumulative set of events that could conceivably lead to a *kairos* moment in the future. It is certainly possible that if the rise in oceans levels does in the years ahead generate the political will required to put the precautionary principle into practice, either or both of these events will be viewed in retrospect as transformative.

Waiting for a *kairos* moment has a Beckettian feel of delusion about it. Seen "realistically" it seems to depend upon something that is dreaded, a catastrophic shock to the complacent refusal to act in accordance with the precautionary ethos.[20] In effect, if the *kairos* moment occurs before future thresholds of irreversibility are crossed then there could take place a refash-ioning of behavior with a heightened sense of urgency that also informed the political will of public and elites. We need to realize that for some particularly vulnerable communities, such as low-lying islands such thresholds have already been crossed, and a tragic future is expected. For most of the world although the hour is late there is still seems time to insinuate the future into the present in a precautionary spirit. We may not yet appreciate that we have experienced a *kairos* moment, and will not be able to identify its occurrence until years and possibly decades have elapsed. There may have occurred already a shift in public consciousness that has yet to penetrate the political realm in an effective form. To be sure, all evidence suggests that this is indeed the epitome of wishful thinking, but such optimism should not be completely dismissed. In the same way that few observers foresaw the consequential magnitude of the fall of the Berlin Wall or the beginnings of the Arab Spring, most of us are simply intellectually incapable of recognizing abrupt moments of historical change. They often happen under the surface of phenomenal observation, only to reveal their significance in hindsight. It may be that the release in June 2015 of the papal encyclical on climate change crafted by Pope Francis will be viewed as either a confirmation of a *kairos* understanding of climate change or as a major effort to induce such an understanding.

Despite such hopefulness, this essay, as an exercise in climate imagination, is less interested in fantasizing unlikely occurrences than in posting warnings about the constraints of Climate Inc. Current efforts to address climate change are animated by, and further lock us into, the straightjacket of negative temporality. Negative temporality proposes that climate change is a distant threat, substantiated by weak science, and thus not urgent or significant enough to require immediate, dramatic policy responses. It encourages a politics of postponement so as not to rock the boat of a world order constituted by sovereign states concerned fundamentally with their territorial, short-term, national interests rather than global or even regional imperatives. Saturated by such a narrow and skewed view, often the most one can do is engage in wishful thinking. However, as this chapter has tried to suggest, one can also work to dismantle the conceptual perversions that privilege spatiality and thus negative temporality. Such criticism demands imagination to recognize limitations and identify opportunities.

In concluding, I would observe that time is a crucial aspect of (re)imagining climate change, especially in relation to seeking agreement among territorially oriented state actors. Embodying the precautionary ethos in political consciousness may come more naturally to civil society actors, individuals whose *primary* loyalty is to the species and its natural and cosmic surroundings rather than to a particular nation, ethnicity, religion, and so forth.[21] There is also reason to celebrate the kinds of localism that embody the future in the present because of their understanding of the meaning of life as exemplified by the lifestyle and worldview of many indigenous peoples and by notions of "voluntary simplicity". One might also celebrate the benefits of autonomous small communities as experiments in adaptive lifestyles.

Notes

1   Ancient societies lacking maps and a sense of the world as a whole lived to a far greater extent by reference to cycles of time, whether astronomical, seasonal, or generational. Among indigenous peoples practical wisdom derived from thinking about action from the perspective of seven generations earlier and later than the present.

2   Also relevant is an unevenness of space/time adjustments within states, reflecting differing perceptions and priorities even without taking into account civilizational differences (e.g. the outlook of native Americans). For instance, in the United States, some states impose carbon emission regulations, others do not; similarly, some particular cities and local communities are more ecologically conscious and sensitive to arguments about global warming and climate justice than others.

3   The internal conservatism of the US in the law of the seas context has led to a standoff of decades as between the Executive Branch adhering as a matter of policy to the treaty while the Senate refuses to this day to ratify, but with climate change the situation is different because the treaty is useless if not funded and implemented by Congressional action. Also with regard to the public order of the oceans delay may be inconvenient and costly, but with respect to climate change delay raises risks to high levels difficult to even ascertain and raises adjustment and mitigation costs to levels that strain capabilities. Beyond this, there are well-financed pressure groups that challenge the scientific consensus that posits the need for constraints on emissions, oppose regulatory burdens on market freedoms, and are indifferent or hostile to considerations of climate equity. Such a situation of gridlock is further reinforced by "the iron law of growth" that sees encroachments on market-driven behavior as inhibiting growth and development, and as such, not politically viable. This has been well argued by Pielke Jr (2010).

4   In this respect, it was easier in the West to mobilize public support for environmental protection because of the visibility of pollution during the last decades of the twentieth century. In this regard, the current pollution of Chinese cities makes the public and leadership more responsive to overall ecological threats than in those Western states that acted earlier to avoid environmental harm, and are now reluctant to grapple with the unseen hazards of climate change.

5   There is beginning to emerge a willingness of scientists to posit causal connections on the basis of a prudential assessment that falls short of the near certainty that had led most scientists and their professional associations to refrain from connecting the dots. It also had the effect of making those scientists who stood apart and expressed their deep concerns appear to be "alarmists" or "headline grabbers."

6   Cf. Stockholm Declaration on the Human Environment and subsequent formulations in declaratory documents of the UN. In climate change contexts the issue is accentuated due to two additional factors: a vigorous well-funded cohort of scientists who are climate skeptics, diluting the policy impact of the scientific consensus that does exist as a result of IPCC reports and numerous other confirmations; the perception that accepting even the understated consensus among climate experts would burden development, economic growth, and the profitability of business operations. These concerns partly explain the prevalence of negative forms of temporality in relation to climate policy debates as for instance in the efforts by the Heartland Institute to influence policy debate on the basis of negative temporality.

7   Stern (2009) rather authoritatively established that the costs of regulating emissions rises geometrically as time passes.

8   Some actions taken on basis of avoiding future heightened risks and costs: Kyoto Protocol, but only involving 12% of global emissions; development subsidies for clean energy (Friedman 2015).

9   Compare the dire warnings of respected climate scientists that depart from their epistemological community such as James Hansen, James Lovelock, Clive Hamilton with the more restrained warnings of the IPCC and other scientific bodies. The more disturbing assessments of threats are often dismissed as "alarmism" by mainstream scientists and ignored by policymakers. There are two levels of problems here with temporal implications: warnings about the future outside the scientific paradigm are not treated as "scientific" even if put forward by renowned scientists; more moderate warnings from scientists exhibiting more restrained concerns that accord with the scientific paradigm are opposed by those that contend that God will take of any future hazards according to divine plan, that the market will prompt technological innovations capable of satisfying human needs, or that global warming is either not occurring or attributable to natural variations in weather over time.

10 From the Melian Dialogue, and in my view a misreading of Thucydides; I interpret Thucydides as arguing that reliance on this power ethos that puts morality to one side is indicative of Athenian decline and imminent collapse, and not of the world as it is; Kissinger, Herman Kahn, and others invoke this passage as disclosing the nature of historical experience in line with realist thinking in international relations.

11 How would we estimate a risk of nuclear accident or recourse? Positing any finite level of risk projected over time suggests how "crazy" it is to retain nuclear weapons until one appreciates that the alternatives of renunciation or disarmament are also "crazy" as finite risks are present, and we lack a metric to compare the level of risk. Negative temporality is also at work in relation to nuclear weaponry, leading to an unwarranted sense of safety and security because no weapon has been used since 1945. I believe higher standards of prudence are called for due to human fallibility, and thus that the disarmament option should have been chosen. In effect, a world with nuclear weapons seems more dangerous than a world without them. A probabilistic pessimism underlies Schell (1982). See also Schell (1998).

12 One form of negative temporality is to safeguard the present by making threats to act in the future in unacceptable ways.

13 In contrast, the modern sensibility breaks these connections (Tarnas 2007).

14 There exists a presumed link between compliance and obligation as a means to minimize the so-called free rider problem, and a further link between obligation and enforcement that gives insight into the relative effectiveness of the obligation; compare nonproliferation aspects of the NPT regime with the disarmament aspects due to political will of nuclear weapons states to enforce, at least selectively, the commitment to forego the acquisition of nuclear weapons.

15 As with human rights, naming and shaming are available to civil society actors, governments, and international institutions. Whether such efforts to achieve compliance can make up for the weakness of pledges, as distinct from legal duties, will be disclosed by the future. It may be that if the United States does uphold its pledges it will exert pressure on others to follow suit. If the pledged constraints turn out to be insufficient from the perspective of climate stability, then the whole framework is likely to be quickly dismantled.

16 In effect, the distinction between what is voluntary and what is obligatory is not so clear in the absence of effective enforcement mechanism; for instance, members of the UN withhold their obligatory dues from time to time without

adverse consequences or engage in uses of force that are inconsistent with the UN Charter. See Arend and Beck (1993) on erosion of law with respect to use of force; and the other side of this observation is the realization that under certain circumstances "voluntary" undertakings can have a great impact on behavior, which has been the experience of the Universal Declaration of Human Rights.

17   It would seem that a pro-regulatory leader such as Obama opts for voluntary international arrangements so as to circumvent the need to submit a mandatory agreement to the US Senate for ratification. Of course, this is a risky approach as Congress can fight back in various ways if it believes that its constitutional role is being eroded by such tactics.

18   A weakness of democratic polities, especially if polarized, is their unreliability in the event that there occurs a drastic shift in the orientation of political leadership. Authoritarian governments in this regard can offer great assurances of continuity under most conditions. It would seem likely, for instance, in the event that a climate skeptical leader is in the White House, and controls Congress, that any arrangements based on pledges to cut emissions would be put aside, especially if seen as burdening industrial growth.

19   In this respect, the *kairos* idea is linked to the "black swan" notion of historical change being so closely connected with events and social forces that were not taken into account. Arguably, the Soviet collapse, the release of Nelson Mandela from a South African prison, the Arab Spring were recent examples of *kairos* happenings or black swans (Tepper 2012; Taleb 2007).

20   This is analogous to those science fiction scenarios of the aftermath of nuclear war that exhibit the fears and slim hope of the apocalyptic imagination (Žižek 2010).

21   I have tried to (re)imagine citizenship in this manner under the rubric of the "citizen pilgrim," with the idea that the spiritually and ecologically attuned citizen is seeking a future political community that lives in harmony with nature to the extent possible (Falk 2012).

References

Al-Olaimy T 2013 Climate change impacts in MENA: North Africa (http://adoptannegotiator.org/2013/11/21/climate-change-impacts-in-mena-northafrica) accessed January 2014

Arend A C and Beck R J 1993 *International Law and the Use of Force: Beyond the Charter Paradigm* Routledge, London

Beck U 1992 *The Risk Society: Toward a New Modernity* Sage, London

Brecher J 2015 *Climate Insurgency: A Strategy for Survival* Paradigm, Boulder CO

Callenbach E 1975 *Ecotopia* Banyan Tree Books, Berkeley CA

Carey J J 1978 *Kairos and Logos: Studies in the Roots and Implications of Tillich's Philosophy* North American Paul Tillich Society, Cambridge MA

Diamond J 2006 *Collapse: How Societies Choose to Fail or Succeed* Viking Penguin, New York

Declaration of the United Nations Conference on the Human Environment (1972) Stockholm 16 June (www.unep.org/Documents.multilingual/Default.asp?DocumentID=97&ArticleID=1503) accessed 5 October 2015

Falk R 2012 The citizen pilgrim in *The Writings of Richard Falk: Towards Humane Global Governance* Orient Black Swan, Delhi 480–87

Falk R 2013 Threat diplomacy in world politics: legal, moral, political, and civilizational challenges in Chaterjee D K ed *The Ethics of Preventive War* Cambridge University Press, Cambridge 87–100

Falk R 2014 Does the human species wish to survive *Kosmos* XIV(1) 13–15

Falk R and Krieger D 2012 *The Path to Zero: Dialogues on Nuclear Dangers* Paradigm, Boulder CO

Fountain H 2015 Researchers link Syrian conflict to a drought made worse by climate change *New York Times* 2 March (www.nytimes.com/2015/03/03/science/earth/study-links-syria-conflict-to-drought-caused-by-climate-change.html?_r=0) accessed 5 October 2015

Friedman T 2015 Germany, the green superpower *New York Times* 6 May (www.nytimes.com/2015/05/06/opinion/thomas-friedman-germany-the-green-superpower.html) accessed 5 October 2015

Griffin D R 2015 *Unprecedented: Can Civilization Survive the CO_2 Crisis* Clarity Press, Atlanta GA

International Court of Justice 1996 *Advisory Opinion on The Legality of the Threat or Use of Nuclear Weapons* 15 October A/51/218

Johansen R C 1980 *The National Interest and the Human Interest: An Analysis of American Foreign Policy* Princeton University Press, Princeton NJ

Kothari R 1975 World politics and world order: the issue of autonomy in Mendlovitz S H ed *On the Creation of a Just World Order: Preferred Worlds for the 1990s* Free Press, New York 39–69

Latour B 1993 *We Have Never Been Modern* Harvard University Press, Cambridge MA

Lessing D 1971 *Briefing for a Descent Into Hell* Knopf, New York

Lifton R J and Falk R 1986 *The Political and Psychological Case Against Nuclearism* Basic Books, New York

Mazrui A 1975 World culture and the search for human consciousness in Mendlovitz S H ed *On the Creation of a Just World Order: Preferred Worlds for the 1990s* Free Press, New York 1–37

McKibben B 2014 Extreme heights: just how fast is the world approaching the demise of humanity? *Foreign Policy* November/December 70–71

Mearsheimer J 1984–5 Nuclear weapons and deterrence in Europe *International Security* 9(3) 19–46

Mendlovitz S H ed 1975 *On the Creation of a Just World Order: Preferred Worlds for the 1990s* Free Press, New York

Nye J 1986 *Nuclear Ethics* Free Press, New York

Oreskes N and Conway E M 2014 *The Collapse of Western Civilization: A View from the Future* Columbia University Press, New York

Pielke Jr R 2010 *The Climate Fix: What Scientists and Politicians Won't Tell You About Global Warming* Basic Books, New York

Sakamoto Y 1975 Toward global identity in Mendlovitz S H ed *On the Creation of a Just World Order: Preferred Worlds for the 1990s* Free Press, New York 189–210

Schell J 1982 *The Fate of the Earth* Knopf, New York: Knopf

Schell J 1998 *The Gift of Time: The Case for Abolishing Nuclear Weapons Now* Metropolitan Books, New York

Stern N 2009 *The Global Deal: Climate Change and the Creation of a New Era of Progress and Prosperity* Public Affairs, New York

Taleb N N 2007 *The Black Swan: The Impact of the Highly Improbable* Random House, New York

Tarnas R 2007 *Cosmos and the Psyche: Intimations of a New World View* Penguin, New York

Tepper R G 2012 Kairos: a political post-history of the concept of time Sample chapter from forthcoming dissertation (www.academia.edu/1468890/Kairos_-_A_Political_Post-History_of_the_Concept_of_Time) accessed 5 October 2015

Thompson E P 1982 *Exterminism and Cold War* Verso, London

Thucydides 1954 *A History of the Poloponnesian War* Finley M I ed Penguin, New York

Waltz K 1981 The spread of nuclear weapons: more may [be] better *Adelphi Papers* 171 (www.mtholyoke.edu/acad/intrel/waltz1.htm) accessed 5 October 2015

Žižek S 2010 *Living in the End Times* Verso, London

5 Modernity on steroids

The promise and perils of climate protection in the Arabian Peninsula

Miriam R. Lowi

Introduction

In the Arabian Peninsula, the discovery and exploitation by foreign companies of vast oil reserves, beginning some 70 years ago, initiated a complicated process of economic development and social change. Modern states were created as dynastic monarchies in what had been largely nomadic, tribal societies engaged in pastoralism, subsistence agriculture and some trade, alongside small, settled communities engaged in trade and maritime activities. The blueprint for development was that provided by the West – directly by design and via transplanted technicians who followed the oil companies, and indirectly by imitation on the part of diffident rulers who depended, to varying degrees, on support from foreign patrons.

As exposure to the European and his technology persisted, the need and desire to be like him, and to be acknowledged by him, gained in importance.[1] Furthermore, as the financial means to acquire the Europeans' techniques grew with the growth in oil exports, the promise of modernity loomed large in Gulf practices, and in ways that extend well beyond the myopia identified as characteristic of rentier states (Mahdavy 1970; Ross 1999). Some decontextualized notion of what it means to be "modern" – that is, like the European – and attendant fantasies, have distinguished numerous development projects in Gulf states, beholden as rulers have remained to foreign governments and advisors, and seduced by their accomplishments in the realms of state power, capitalist progress and profits, technological innovation, and the entire cultural ensemble that often defines progress.[2] Hungry for recognition, anxious about image, and uncertain about their place in an increasingly globalized world, Gulf rulers have spent oil rents lavishly to create, or even outdo Europe in the desert,[3] at times – and not surprisingly – in defiance of nature.

Spending practices have also had a crucial, domestically focused political objective, and this has functioned in tandem with modernist aspirations. Unsure of their subjects' allegiance, anxious about national cohesion, and coveting vast resources, Gulf monarchs have remained preoccupied with dynastic "staying power" and regime stability. Hence, they channel oil revenues to themselves, their families, and their subjects in ways that shore up their power, enhance their control over society, and purchase acquiescence.[4]

The combined effort to both mimic the West (and its materialism) and maintain rule in a rentier environment has prompted Gulf states not only to engage in extravagant spending while adopting – indeed, going beyond – a Western-dominated development model (pursuing a type of hyper-modernity), but also to systematically encourage (and finance) hyper-materialism and unbridled consumption among their subjects. This has led, almost necessarily, to increasingly carbon-intensive lifestyles. Indeed, the relatively small petro-states – members of the Gulf Cooperation Council (GCC)[5] – currently lead the world in their carbon footprint. According to the World Bank, per capita carbon emissions in Gulf monarchies range from two to ten times the world average.[6] To be sure, the degradation of the natural environment happens to be a principal product of the modernity project which Gulf rulers have bought into so eagerly.

While modernity has welcomed GCC states into the carbon club of energy intensive, highly consumptive societies, it has also invited them to join the effort to confront environmental challenges, especially climate change. Environmentalism has become a defining characteristic of late modern life. To be fully modern these days, one needs to at least pay lip-service to environmental protection, if not genuinely pursue it. Gulf states appear to have adopted the aspiration of environmental wellbeing, and have sought to take their place among nations willing to advance environmental protection. This is especially the case with climate change. Insofar as action on climate change provides a ticket for further acceptance by the West, GCC states have tried to demonstrate their climate response credentials.

Like their efforts to out-do the West in their development programs, GCC states have tried to out-perform the West in their response to climate change. Here too, they have pursued large-scale, extravagant projects that incorporate the latest, state-of-the-art technologies in an attempt to appear pioneering. Their main strategy in doing so has been to turn modernity into a tool for confronting one of modernity's most entrenched problems: they rely on economistic and technological techniques to battle climate change. In this sense, they subscribe to and adopt what this volume refers to as "Climate Inc." – the business of addressing climate change through conventional mitigation and adaptation measures that are compatible with high modern societies.

Climate Inc. does not aim to transform contemporary structures of power or to otherwise destabilize the globalizing, neoliberal, capitalist regime. Rather, it offers measures that grow out of and deepen the commitment to energy-rich, consumptive, and technologically based collective life. The problem is that these tools and related practices have been integral to propelling the dynamics of climate change in the first place, and thus, aggressively employing them offers neither innovation nor progress toward addressing climate change. In fact, it further deepens the world's inability to respond in clearly effective ways. In other words, Gulf states' efforts to confront the negative effects of technological advancements with more technology perpetuates, rather than challenges, the status quo of Climate Inc.

In this chapter, I describe two state-driven initiatives in the Gulf that epitomize Gulf states' aspirations to gain recognition and consolidate their rule. The first concerns the program to grow wheat and produce dairy in Saudi Arabia. At great expense and with the use of high technology, the Saudi regime sought to show that it could farm like the western United States and Canada, even though its desert geography poses huge challenges to doing so. The second concerns the project, pursued by the United Arab Emirates, to build a zero-carbon city, and demonstrate that the UAE could be a pioneering laboratory for a post-carbon world. Although diametric opposites in that the first was pursued in total disregard for the natural environment, while the second was meant to address climate change, both of these initiatives reflect the over-riding commitment of Gulf rulers to highly capitalized, technologized trajectories that mirror Western development models, and to methods of rule aimed at securitizing and stabilizing rentier states and societies.

As they have evolved, both initiatives, as we will see below, highlight the contradiction between priorities and possibilities, but also between fantasy and materiality. Both have had to be shelved or drastically scaled back precisely because of the materiality of place and the limitations of mimicry. After all, water-intensive farming in the desert makes little environmental sense, and the fabrication of zero-carbon living via the importation of technology and expertise in a setting where consumption and gain are paramount is unrealizable.[7] Both initiatives represent the unstable politics of image, profits, and social control. Insofar as the response to climate change is concerned, both demonstrate that highly capitalized, technologized projects exacerbate, rather than minimize or reverse, the engines of environmental degradation. Driven by modernist aspirations and the desire for recognition, as well as the economic and political dynamics that support dynastic rentier rule, they are inappropriate for addressing climate change.

As I suggest at the end of this chapter, GCC states, like all states, must reimagine responses to climate change so that they no longer dig the world deeper into modernist practices that seek to dominate nature and encourage material excess. They can do so by looking inward to and reviving the relevance of local resources – such as an indigenous moral-ethical structure and/or religious-cultural traditions – that can cast a critical eye toward modernity and its excesses, while proposing a more salutary way of conceiving the relationship between humans and the natural environment.

I begin this chapter by describing the linkage between resource distribution and rentier rule in GCC states. I then go on to outline Gulf states' natural resource endowment – specifically, hydrocarbons and water – and some of the environmental effects of natural resource exploitation. With this as context, I discuss the two initiatives, in Saudi Arabia and Abu Dhabi respectively, underscoring their origins, evolution, and outcomes. I contextualize these projects in terms of, on the one hand, how each aims to realize goals and interests of rentier states and, on the other, what they mean for addressing climate change. I conclude by reflecting on the implications of such initiatives and prospects for sustainability. My overall aim is to propose that we reimagine responses to climate change beyond a modernist narrative. By focusing on hyper-modernist states, I hope to bring the category of modernity itself into high relief and exercise the imagination in moving beyond it.

Resources and distribution – the politics of government spending

As classic rentier states, the six countries of the GCC have been, until recently, absolutely dependent on their narrow resource base and the external environment: for most, their petroleum sectors account for the lion's share of government revenues and national exports.[8] Moreover, as rent accrues directly to the state, distribution is a primary task of national governments and a principal source of their legitimacy. Furthermore, the GCC states have among the largest hydrocarbon reserves in the world, but relatively small populations. It is the combination of small size with vast hydrocarbon endowments that accounts for high per capita income.[9]

Given the size and importance of petroleum rents in state budgets, there has been no perceived need to tax individuals. Moreover, nationals enjoy important transfers and an array of free, or heavily subsidized goods and services. For example, they are guaranteed free access to (public) education and health care, are entitled to a plot of land and until very recently, they could secure public sector employment quite easily. In addition, transportation, gasoline, water and electricity are heavily subsidized by the state, as are, in most countries, staple food items (Woertz 2013a, 13–14). In Qatar, for example, water and electricity are absolutely free of charge, while elsewhere in the Gulf, the cost to users is minimal. Subsidies encourage over-consumption and waste; with prices at or close to zero, there is little incentive to exercise moderation and conserve. Hence, governments' channeling of hydrocarbon revenues to society via the subsidization of utilities, for example, discourages environmentally sustainable practices.

While income inequality is considered to be substantial, consumer subsidies are universal (Woertz 2013b); they are allocated to every national equally, rather than targeted to those in need so as to promote equity and distributive justice. In addition to being extremely wasteful, extending universal subsidies is enormously costly – amounting to as much as 20 percent of government budgets in some cases.[10] Nonetheless, universal subsidies of this sort are thought to assure the continued loyalty of all nationals, especially the rich. Ruling families allow their subjects to consume, and consume extravagantly, with the expectation that they will remain complacent; thus, royals are able to consolidate their power and dominate society more effectively.

Access to land offers important insights into states' distributive practices and their goals. As noted above, each GCC national has the right to a plot of land of a certain dimension. However, despite the universal right, it has been reported that some nationals do not receive any land, while others may acquire several plots and of larger dimensions than the norm.[11] In Saudi Arabia today, the matter of access to land is especially contentious since the country suffers from a severe housing shortage that, combined with rising unemployment among young Saudis primarily, has become a major social issue. It is not that there is no land on which to build, but rather that the royal family exercises a monopoly over real estate in the kingdom. Referred to disparagingly as "land whales" (*hawameer al-aradi*), very rich, well-connected Saudis own land on peripheries of cities. They neither exploit these lands for productive purposes, nor do they plan to sell them; rather, they maintain them thus as long-term investments, while real estate values and land pressures increase (Luciani 2005, 152–3). Moreover, it is said that 40 percent of the land in Riyadh is owned by princes who had received plots as gifts, while 70 percent of the Saudi coastline had been gifted by the former king Fahd to five princes.[12]

To be sure, the concentration of land among royals is not unique to Saudi Arabia: across the Gulf, vast tracts were distributed by rulers, in the early years of state formation, to family members and tribal leaders (Crystal 1990, 148; Jones 2010, 8, 233). The practice would continue and evolve into a lucrative trade, embracing over time members of the business and financial elite – many of whom would happen to be royals, but including their "commoner clients," as well (Hertog 2010, 94–111; Yom 2011, 229–30). Indeed, across the Gulf monarchies, "land was preempted by the princes, distributed to their clients, subdivided into plots, exchanged against political acquiescence" (Menoret 2014, 91). Where privately held land was sought by the state, it was routinely, and at times "coercively" purchased, albeit at greatly inflated prices; this was yet another means to distribute oil revenues to citizens and in so doing, buy their loyalty and assert state power (Yom 2011, 229–30; Menoret 2014, 87–94, 105–9).

Landowning elites and their business clients would be the recipients of additional, most generous financial facilities. This is especially so when they engaged with fetishized government obsessions in the form of "pet projects" that enjoy considerable symbolic capital and are underwritten by the state at considerable expense. Among such projects are various urban development schemes in Doha (Qatar), Abu Dhabi and Dubai, the transformation of Mecca, and agricultural development in Saudi Arabia.[13] These efforts have been deeply infused with state-imposed nationalism, image-making, and social control. They carry the implicit message, designed for both external and internal consumption, that modernity is firmly in place and the (dynastic) state is both pervasive and – foreign consultants, companies, technology, and labor notwithstanding – self-sufficient.

Gulf resources and their exploitation

The six GCC states' hydrocarbon endowment comprises 40 percent of global oil reserves and 24 percent of global gas reserves. Their hydrocarbon sectors account for about 75 percent of their combined total export earnings, 70 percent of government revenues, and 40 percent of GDP. Within the region, per capita oil and gas consumption is very high: for the year 2012, Kuwait, Qatar, Saudi Arabia and the UAE figured among the top ten per capita consumers in the world – ahead of Canada and the United States – with Kuwait in third place. All six GCC countries are in the top ten for per capita natural gas consumption – ahead of Russia, Luxembourg, Canada and the US – with Qatar in second place (World Bank 2014a). The high consumption is the result not only of the energy demands of economic growth and industrialization, population increase and urbanization, but also because of the very low, politically motivated domestic prices for liquid fuels. Furthermore, high domestic consumption of oil and gas drives CO_2 emissions. GCC states are among the world's top 15 emitters of per capita CO_2 – with Qatar in first place in 2009–12, and four of the six GCC states surpassing the US and Canada. While their overall contributions to global warming are negligible when compared with Russia, China, the US and the European Union, their per capita contributions are certainly disproportionate.[14]

The effects of global warming, including anticipated rising sea levels, are bound to be severe on the Gulf region, given the already very high temperatures and extensive coastlines. An arid and extremely arid region, with semi-aridity in Yemen and southern Oman, the Arabian Peninsula is more than 90 percent desert. Average temperatures in the central part of the region are roughly 38° Celsius (100°F), while temperatures over 50° Celsius (122°F) for extended periods are not uncommon. There are no rivers or lakes to speak of, and rainfall over much of the peninsula is sparse and irregular. Four of the six GCC states are ranked among the ten most water-scarce countries in the world – with Kuwait ranked first, the UAE third, Qatar fifth, and Saudi Arabia eighth. Historically, the principle sources of water were springs and shallow wells. Today, the principal sources are desalinated seawater – that provides 85–99 percent of drinking water in Kuwait, Qatar, Bahrain and the UAE, 70 percent in Saudi Arabia, and less than 50 percent in Oman – and subterranean aquifers, many of which contain non-renewable fossil water. Despite the fragile hydrology, domestic exploitation of water in the Gulf in 2006, for example, was reported to be about six times above the natural renewal rate (Kumetat 2009). Added to that, rapid population growth in these states – exceeding 2.3 percent per annum – has required the burning of increasing amounts of oil to desalinate water for drinking. Indeed, strains on natural resources are bound to intensify.

Government projects and the natural environment

Highly visible "pet projects" in Gulf monarchies, defined and overseen by the ruler, infused with symbolic capital, financed by burgeoning oil and gas revenues, and producing important (social and) environmental effects display states' modernist credentials while substantiating their rule. In addition to exhibiting states' priorities, many of these projects reveal the complicated, contradictory nature of regimes' commitment to sustainability. As the two cases discussed below demonstrate, highly technologized, capital intensive, economistic efforts to master nature in the service of political objectives fail to advance environmental sustainability. In fact, they often undermine it. This is because they instrumentalize, in a hyper fashion, the very dynamics that created environmental challenges – especially climate change – in the first place. In short, that which had contributed to creating environmental problems cannot be relied upon for providing solutions.

Wheat production in Saudi Arabia

With the exception of the province of Asir in the southwest corner of the country, Saudi Arabia has a desert climate throughout, characterized by extreme heat during the day – often reaching 54 degrees centigrade (129°F) – an abrupt drop in temperature at night, and slight, erratic rainfall. While average rainfall is 100 millimeters per year, entire regions of the country may not experience rainfall for several years, and drought conditions are not uncommon. Precipitation of this sort, reflective of aridity and extreme aridity, supports pastoralism and nomadic pastoralism since native vegetation is either absent or sparse. Farming is possible in the arid, but not in the extremely arid zones and only via irrigation. The kingdom has one of the lowest reserves of freshwater on earth: there are no rivers in the country, and the Red Sea and Arabian Gulf, to the west and the east respectively, are highly saline. According to World Bank Indicators, the renewable internal fresh water resources of Saudi Arabia in 2013 were equivalent to 83 cubic meters per capita, ranked, with Yemen, sixth from the bottom in the world, after the Bahamas, Qatar, Egypt, UAE, and Bahrain (World Bank 2014a).

Despite extreme scarcity of water "in one of the largest bodies of sand in the world" (Pearce 2012), the Saudi monarchy has been farming the desert for the past 30 years, growing wheat and raising dairy cattle, avowedly to pursue a nationalist dream of food self-sufficiency. At enormous expense, equivalent to hundreds of billions of dollars of oil revenues, it has been mining the once vast underground reservoir of water, more than one mile below the surface, to irrigate fields of wheat for domestic consumption and some export, and provide mist for dairy cattle (to keep them cool).

While some have argued that the program, touted by the monarchy as the answer to the quest for food security, had been spearheaded by the threat of boycott of Arab states in the post-1973 geopolitical environment, its antecedents can be found, as Eckart Woertz (2013a, 63–74) argues, in Ibn Saud's kingdom in the 1940s. Fascinated by American machinery and expertise (and the Americans' eagerness to sell them), awed by new sorts of consumption goods, and anxious to secure his power and authority over his subjects, Ibn Saud enlisted the help of American advisors, already engaged in developing the oil sector, to introduce mechanized agriculture into the kingdom (Jones 2010, 40–58). Doing so served several of Ibn Saud's interests: it demonstrated that his kingdom was becoming modern, and assured an on-going connection (and business relationship) with the West; it offered a means to ensure the loyalty of the king's best-placed subjects insofar as royals and businessmen would receive land for farming; and it was a way to supply the king's palaces, family and close associates with an array of consumer goods. With oil rents that grew substantially over time, Ibn Saud imported farm equipment and inputs, technique and expertise, and made them available at attractive rates to relatives and other well-connected individuals to whom he had distributed land. These related practices – copying the American farmer and consumer, distributing land for free, and incentivizing landholders with an array of financial facilities – would be continued by Ibn Saud's successors. Of course, as Woertz (2013a, 77) points out, "alongside import licenses, sponsorship schemes, government contracts, and land grants, subsidized agriculture was an important tool of the state to distribute oil rent and buy political quiescence."

For the sake of agricultural production, neither financial nor hydrologic constraints were deemed worthy of attention. With burgeoning oil rents, that grew "more than 8,500 times between 1938 and 1973" and roughly tenfold over the next twenty years (Vassiliev 1998, 401), nothing was considered beyond the limits; there were simply no limits. As for dwindling groundwater supplies and the threat of salinization, Saudi rulers had internalized that core notion of the modernity project: that humanity both dominates and masters nature. They were confident that western technology would save the day.

While the distribution of land began with Ibn Saud's seizure of power, it was formalized by King Feisal in 1968, when via the Public Lands Distribution Ordinance, cultivable land – in plots ranging in size from 5 to 20 hectares – was distributed *gratis* to private individuals (while institutions could receive up to 400 hectares). Nonetheless, land distribution took off in earnest after 1980, once the wheat producing program was well underway (Woertz 2013a, 74, 81). From the program's inception in the 1970s, an array of enormously generous producer subsidies were introduced to encourage large-scale agricultural expansion.[15] Indeed, from the late-1970s, with the inception of a wheat price support program, the government not only incentivized and enriched farmers – who were, in fact, absentee landlords who happened to be royals and well-connected businessmen, while those who actually ran the farms were Western companies – in a variety of ways, including by guaranteeing them a purchasing price for wheat that was "about six times the world market price at that time" (Woertz 2013a, 76). The government also charged nothing for the water, while providing "virtually free electricity for pumping water to the surface" (Pearce 2012). Despite its great expense, the scheme enriched well-placed individuals, tying them more closely to the regime.[16]

Between 1978 and 1992, wheat production increased 1200 times, and the kingdom became the sixth largest exporter of wheat in the world (Woertz 2013a, 77). Blinded by the enrichment of royals and their clients, and by the program's other intended political effects, the state disregarded the overproduction, over-consumption, and tremendous waste that resulted. Not only was Saudi Arabia producing more wheat than it could consume and export, it was also exploiting natural resources recklessly (Woertz 2013a, 77–8).

Over time, the project had disastrous effects on the fragile ecosystem. It is estimated that about 70 percent of the water used for wheat-growing came from non-rechargeable fossil aquifers. For the wheat fields alone, 22.7 billion cubic meters of water were pumped annually from aquifers through wells. As more wells drew up more water, the water table dropped and salinity invaded the aquifers. To access non-saline reserves, it became necessary to drill deeper and deeper wells, at greater and greater expense, and by burning increasing amounts of oil, causing irreversible ecological damage: (non-renewable) fossil water was rapidly being depleted, and water quality in neighboring zones plummeted.[17] When the farming began some 40 years ago, it was estimated that there were about 500 cubic kilometers of water underground. In recent years, however, with extraction rates of up to 20 cubic kilometers annually and without any replacement to speak of, the kingdom would have exhausted at least four-fifths of the fossil water by 2008 (Pearce 2012). As fossil deposits constitute a strategic reserve for human consumption, Saudi wheat farming had mostly destroyed the only remaining cushion, in the form of a "last ditch" source of water available to consumers.

In 2007, the Saudi state decided to gradually phase out the program. It was forced to acknowledge, belatedly, that there really was not enough water locally for large-scale agriculture and food self-sufficiency and that, in the post-2008–9 global financial environment, there had to be somewhat closer attention to how oil rents were allocated. Hence, the government embarked upon a gradual transition to 100 percent reliance on wheat imports by 2016 (Woertz 2013a, 78–80). However, it has faced significant opposition from those who had benefitted for years from the generously endowed agricultural activities; they have vigorously resisted cutbacks in water consumption. In 2010, in fact, water use in the kingdom remained very high: it was almost double (959 cubic meters) the per capita global average of 500 cubic meters, with 85–90 percent of consumption from the agricultural sector, of which about 80 percent was coming from deep aquifers (Pacific Institute 2013). With the rapid growth of the Saudi population (more than 2.3 percent, per annum) and of industry, combined with the determined opposition of Saudi farmers to ending cultivation of water-thirsty crops, unsustainable water usage is likely to continue to increase at a rapid rate.[18]

Wheat farming in Saudi Arabia represents the dual objectives of emulating the West and consolidating dynastic rule in a rentier state. In an effort that epitomizes hyper-modernity, the kingdom used all its technological, economic, and environmental might to advance the project. In its demise, the project offers a cautionary tale about over-extending modernity's capabilities. One can only inject so much mastery onto nature without ecological consequences or unsustainable financial costs. Saudi Arabia reached that limit, but only after depleting precious water and other resources, and spending significant amounts of money. Be that as it may, the kingdom, like other GCC states, continues to pursue a high modern development trajectory. Its energy consumption and carbon emissions remain among the highest in the world; and Saudi lifestyles remain dedicated to consumption, material comfort and abundance. Like most states, it has not moved beyond the minimalist gestures of Climate Inc.

Masdar City, Abu Dhabi, UAE

In 2006, Abu Dhabi launched the Masdar Initiative – a multifaceted program for the promotion of renewable energies in the Emirate. A centerpiece of the program is Masdar City, a planned carbon-neutral town of 7 square kilometers, 30 kilometers from the capital of the UAE. At completion, it was meant to house 40,000 residents, 40,000 daily commuters, hundreds of businesses, and an MIT-affiliated research university – the Masdar Institute of Science and Technology (MIST) – and serve as "a cleantech city cluster" (Alusi *et al.* 2011, 7; Reiche 2010, 378–82; Luomi 2012, 120–30). The declared aims of the initiative were threefold: first, to diversify the economy, transition from a carbon-based to a sustainable economy, and transform "oil wealth into renewable energy leadership;" second, to respond to the global demand for alternative energy sources and become a "global center of excellence for renewable energy research, development, and innovation;" and third, to contribute to global policy development by providing "a blueprint for future cities striving for sustainability ... a model for how all future cities should be built" (Masdar Abu Dhabi Future Energy Company 2009). As described, therefore, the Masdar Initiative was the Emirate's grandiose response to both the growing trend in international fora to address climate change, and the negative press the UAE had been getting about their own, heavy carbon footprint.[19] The details, and their implementation, however, would uncover other interests and priorities, and reveal the limits of turning technology on technology.

In charge of the Masdar Initiative is the Abu Dhabi Future Energy Company (ADFEC), established in 2006 as a wholly owned subsidiary of the Mubadala Development Company, a public joint stock company that "manages a multi-billion dollar portfolio" focused on economic diversification, with the Government of the Emirate of Abu Dhabi as the sole shareholder (Mubadala Development Company 2007). At the outset, the Abu Dhabi government earmarked $15 billion for the Initiative, of which roughly $4 billion was allocated for Masdar City. The anticipated total price tag, initially evaluated at $19–20 billion and expected to come largely from oil revenues, increased to $22 billion in 2012. Work on the project began in 2007, with a projected completion date of 2016. Because of financial difficulties, the Masdar Initiative was scaled back and the completion date extended to 2021–5, with the first phase of the City to be completed in 2015 (Alusi *et al.* 2011, 9).

According to the publicity, Masdar City was designed as the "world's most sustainable city" – the "first zero carbon, zero waste, zero car city," which, "at the cutting edge of technology and design ... incorporates advanced energy and water saving techniques modeling the sustainability practices of the future" (Stillwell and Lindabury 2008). The city's net energy demand would be 70 percent less than that of the average city, while net water demand and net waste production would be significantly less, as well. How would all this be achieved?

To begin, the city was to be built atop a fabricated base 7 meters (23 feet) high so as to capture desert breezes. For the purpose of achieving zero carbon emissions, renewable energy would supply 100 percent of the city's power needs. Solar energy – via photovoltaic power plants and solar panels, as well as solar thermal power using mirrors – would provide more than one-half of needs, with the other half coming from a combination of wind turbines, geothermal pumps, and a variety of waste-to-energy and hydrogen technologies. Urban design and architectural features would reduce energy demand, as well, by, for example, orienting the city in a way to provide "an optimum balance of sun and shade," and constructing narrow streets, with buildings designed to let air in and keep sun out, and wind towers to encourage a breeze (Stillwell and Lindabury 2008, 3). To achieve zero waste, extensive water reuse and composting programs would be implemented, and state-of-the-art recycling facilities built. All remaining waste would be diverted to a "combustion waste-to-energy power plant" which would contribute to the city's energy needs. To achieve sustainable transport, walking and cycling would be the principal forms of transit, while two electric transportation systems – one, a light rail system connecting Masdar City with Abu Dhabi, and the other, an underground "personal rapid transit system" comprised of fully automated "podcars" [PODs] moving along magnetic, electricity-charged tracks – would provide quick travel over longer stretches. As for sustainable water use, all the water would come from a desalination plant run on solar power outside the city, and 80 percent of the water would be "repurified and recycled back for household and irrigation purposes" (Stillwell and Lindabury 2008, 4). Soil for agriculture, to grow the city's food needs, would come from composting, while irrigation water would come from recycling, as noted above.

But just how eco-friendly is Masdar City? The original design drew inspiration from traditional Arab settlements, which, in order to manage the elements while providing maximum security, tended to be built at an elevation, practiced mud-brick construction, and maintained narrow streets oriented in ways to maximize shade. However, that the high ground for Masdar City had to be constructed from scratch, so that the city could take advantage of greater wind and superior air quality, implies the totally fabricated, almost surreal nature of the project, rather than its adaptation to the natural environment.

Indeed, seven years into the project, the plan to build at an elevation and house the PODs within the concrete-filled dome providing the elevation, so as to separate built space from transportation, was scaled back considerably: in fact, work was terminated on the 7-metre foundation once MIST had been built.[20] Today, only MIST and related buildings are at an elevation and serviced by PODs; besides, the PODs make only one stop and can move in only one direction within the dome. Representing a tiny fraction of the total planned area of the Masdar Initiative, MIST is the microcosm of what the initial plan was meant to be.[21] According to well-informed administrators and technicians at Masdar, it had simply become far too expensive for Mubadala and the Abu Dhabi government, who were, alas, anxious for attractive returns on their investments. While they had been keen to show that "green living" was not only feasible, but also profitable, they found that given both their principal (financial) interests and the limitations of the technology and know-how which they could access, the project, as initially designed, could not be realized.[22]

In 2010, the entire project was reviewed. The budget of the City was cut by more than 25 percent, and the goal to complete it by 2016 was withdrawn. While the new completion date has been revised several times, the latest decision is that further building would respond to market demand; land in the Masdar enclave would be sold to private developers who would be required to build according to some basic, yet-to-be-defined Masdar guidelines (Luomi 2012, 127). Moreover, while Masdar City was first described as a "zero-carbon" project, it is now not even "carbon neutral," but rather, simply "low carbon" (Luomi 2012, 125–6).

To date, the diffusion effect of the Masdar Initiative has been scant. There are few solar panels in use in Abu Dhabi beyond the City, while legislation and other incentives to encourage the installation of solar panels or even reduce wasteful consumption of energy are few.[23] The combination of the radical scaling back and the weak diffusion effect, compared to the initial audacity and lofty ambitions, confirms for its detractors that the "desert eco-city is more glitz than substance" and "the whole project is just a big show" (Rueter 2012).[24]

One should not be surprised by the "glitz" factor. The UAE pursued the Masdar Initiative to display its facility with state-of-the-art technology as a way to gain international recognition, "out-westernize" the West, and make its subjects proud of the regime's leadership in environmental sustainability. (In this latter regard, the project represents the ruler's effort to win public support and affirm his authority.) But the "show" factor should raise critical concerns. Building a zero-carbon city was not simply recreation or amusement. Rather, it aimed, at least in its substantive form, to address a critical challenge facing humanity. It sought to provide a model for confronting climate change. Its radical scaling back – if not demise – is therefore not simply a missed opportunity or momentary distraction, but a deeply disturbing indicator of the limits of conventional approaches, or what this volume calls, Climate Inc. In its attempts to offer mitigation and adaptation measures that are compatible with existing socio-economic structures, Climate Inc. doubles down on the technological and economistic promises to deliver mastery over nature. The Masdar Initiative demonstrates the poverty of Climate Inc.

Implications and conclusions

With their enormous cost and grandiosity, as well as deep ecological footprint, what do these two projects suggest about Gulf monarchies' interests and priorities, and commitment to the environment? To be sure, extravagant spending, unencumbered consumption and grandstanding are privileged behaviors. On the one hand, they nurture states' domestically focused political ambitions for longevity, domination and social control;[25] on the other hand, they respond to externally focused interests, to catch up to (or even supersede) the West, and thus (hopefully) earn international recognition. As their own subjects insist, Gulf rulers are motivated by personal enrichment and pandering to western powers so as to retain their acceptance and their business.[26]

Insofar as the lure of modernity and the cry for recognition are concerned, GCC states mimic the West, and follow its lead in deepening the ecological crisis. In fact, GCC states' over-the-top efforts reveal the underbelly of modernity itself: how mastering nature does not liberate humanity from ecological constraints, but rather, speeds up the race toward biological limits. Furthermore, such hyper-modernity exposes a contradiction at the heart of Climate Inc., namely, that the same practices that brought about climate change are relied upon to solve climate change! In short, in an attempt to provide pioneering models for a more livable future – based on the promise of modernity and the imperatives of ruling oil-rich, dynastic states – Gulf monarchies have simply reaffirmed the same carbon-entrenched structures of power and modes of existence, with their economistic and consumerist orientations, which are the font of the climate challenge.

In trying to imitate the West and undertaking projects to placate their subjects, Gulf rulers have been fairly successful so far. To be sure, they have not *become* the West, but rather, as Homi Bhabha (1984, 127) puts it, they are a "partial presence." Nor does their domestic politics fully account for their pet mega-projects; surely, sudden access to fantastic wealth in the absence of effort plays a significant contributing role in inspiring grand plans. However, Gulf rulers have gotten much of what they wished for, but it turns out that such yearnings hold as much peril as they do promise. GCC states have put modernity on steroids to pursue their goals and in doing so, they have provided a litmus test for modernity's potential to address climate change effectively and chart an ecologically sound future. The results call for caution in all similar efforts.

To "heal the earth," as a Qatari interlocutor once put it, "the soul must first be healed."[27] A normative framework, driven by a vision that prioritizes human welfare, acknowledging that the latter is intimately connected to and dependent upon the protection of the natural environment, should be elaborated and guide behavior. This would require, no doubt, a new consciousness – a radical rethinking of human community, of relationships and priorities, but also, of resource use and wealth circulation practices. It would require, at a minimum, a willingness to go beyond Climate Inc., unleash political imagination, and explore more inventive, alternative conceptual terrain. Despite a preoccupation with trying to mimic the West and consolidate their rule, GCC regimes can actually offer resources for such exploration. Buried beneath the thick modernist façade, Gulf peoples enjoy indigenous ethical and religious-cultural traditions that may prove ripe for informing a world severely destined to an unsustainable future. Reimagining climate change calls for unearthing these traditions and reviving their relevance in the service of a livable world.[28]

Acknowledgements

Field research for this study was conducted with generous support from the Carnegie Corporation of New York, which named me "Carnegie Scholar" (2008–10). I thank, as well, the following individuals whose comments on earlier drafts of this chapter have been very helpful: Neve Gordon, Jeannie Sowers, Paul Wapner, John Waterbury, Erika Weinthal.

Notes

1   See Munif (1987) for a fictional account of the impact of the encounter on Gulf Arab society. Fanon (1966) argues that to be acknowledged by the colonial master, the colonized dons the white master's masks. His efforts notwithstanding, he fails to gain the recognition he seeks and he ends up schizophrenic.

Bhabha (1984, 126) suggests that the colonizer encourages the colonized subject to try to be like him, but mimicry results in ambiguity; what it produces is "almost the same, but not quite."

2   See, for example, Kanna (2011).

3   For one spectacular example, consider the recreation of the city of Venice (Italy), with its canals, gondolas, foot-bridges and loggias, in Villagio Mall in Doha, Qatar.

4   Patrimonial practices, for the purposes of self-enrichment and societal quiescence, have been cited by the 'resource curse' literature as characteristic of rentier states. In the case of Arabian Gulf monarchies, however, such practices pre-date the inception of the oil-based economy, but have been significantly expanded and refined since then. See, for example, Vassiliev (1998, 303–6, 333–6) and Crystal (1990).

5   The GCC is comprised of Bahrain, Kuwait, Oman, Qatar, Saudi Arabia, and the United Arab Emirates.

6   In a private communication (17 November 2014), Jeannie Sowers suggested that these statistics are misleading: oil exports count in per capita carbon emissions, but those fuels are consumed elsewhere. Hence, small populations with large fossil fuel exports are over-counted (see note 14 below). Note that the 'resource curse' literature has said little about the negative effects that behaviors associated with classic rentier states have on environmental sustainability.

7   As stated by one of my Qatari interlocutors, a sociologist and statistician, "there is no way to be environmentally friendly here" (Doha, 29 February 2012).

8   For the GCC states, excluding Bahrain, hydrocarbons comprise 70–90 percent of government revenues; excluding Bahrain and the UAE, they comprise 66–95 percent of national exports (USEIA undated). In recent decades, rising oil and gas prices have facilitated lucrative foreign investments and the creation of savings funds, which in turn, have added significantly to state revenues (Seznec 2012).

9   In terms of oil and gas reserves, respectively, three GCC states rank among the top seven countries in the world for each category (USEIA undated). As for population size, apart from Saudi Arabia which has about 20 million, the GCC states each have between 230,000 and 2.5 million nationals.

10 Kuwait, for example, with a total population of 2.7 million, of which nationals, the main beneficiaries, are roughly 40 percent, spent as much as $22 billion in 2012 – almost 20 percent of government revenues – on subsidies alone, without the cost of healthcare, education, and housing (Kuwait Times 2013).

11 Interviews: Doha, 4 March 2012; Kuwait, 5 May 2012; Muscat, 11 February 2012.

12 Interviews: Riyadh, 28 March and 2 April 2012.

13 On urban development as symbolic capital see Kanna (2005) and Nagy (2000). Gardner (2014, 349) refers to the "mega-features of the urban landscape" in Qatar and its neighbors as the "symbolic capital by which these states assert their position in the vanguard of a cosmopolitan rendition of modernity." See, as well, Menoret (2014, 61–101). On the transformation of Mecca see, among others, al-Adawy (2013).

14 In 2009–12, Qatar – at 44 metric tons – had the highest per capita CO_2 emissions in the world; Kuwait was fourth (30.3 metric tons), UAE sixth (22.6), Bahrain eighth (20.7), Saudi Arabia thirteenth (16.1). It is interesting to note that the United States was twelfth (17.2 metric tons) and Canada fourteenth (15.3) (World Bank 2014b). Again, see Jeannie Sowers, *supra*, note 6. She goes on to say that what matters for climate change are both aggregate annual

emissions and historical contributions since industrialization, which in both cases, Gulf contributions are scant. Furthermore, once domestic consumption is subtracted from aggregate exports, then insofar as the composition of their economies is concerned, their share is even less.

15 Woertz (2013a, 76) notes that while subsidies provided 50 percent of the cost for fertilizers, pumps, agricultural machinery and animal feed, and 30 percent for dairy and poultry equipment, the government covered the entire cost of importing cattle.

16 According to one estimate, the direct costs of the program's subsidies from 1984 to 2000 were equivalent to 18 percent of the kingdom's oil revenues during that same period (Elhadj 2008).

17 Insofar as climate change is concerned, it is noteworthy that aquifer drawdown has been found to contribute to the rise in sea levels (Wada *et al.* 2010).

18 Furthermore, recent efforts of Saudi companies, which had been involved in farming at home, to prospect for lucrative farming opportunities in distant lands – in Africa and/or Asia, for example – could present another set of negative effects, both human and environmental (Pearce 2012; Woertz 2013b, 195–207).

19 As reported in Luomi (2012, 106), according to the World Wildlife Fund's Ecological Footprint Index, that "measures stress per capita on the use of natural and ecological resources within a country's borders," the UAE has "held the world's highest ecological footprint" from 2000, when calculations started, until 2012, when Kuwait and Qatar overtook the federation.

20 Author's interviews with administrators and technocrats at Masdar City, Abu Dhabi, November 7, 2013.

21 *Ibid.*

22 *Ibid.* Two problems, related to technology and know-how, became apparent: first, the extreme heat and dust in the natural environment impaired the efficiency of solar panels; second, wind turbines could not be placed because of the proximity of the airport (Luomi 2012, 125–7).

23 Interviews, Masdar City, Abu Dhabi, November 7, 2013.

24 Ouroussoff (2010) writes that Masdar represents "the crystallization of another global phenomenon: the growing division of the world into refined, high-end enclaves and vast formless ghettos ..." Masdar is the epitome of "a self-sufficient society, lifted on a pedestal and outside the reach of most of the world's citizens."

25 Gardner (2014, 361–2) suggests that the enclave character of "supermodern" projects favors domination.

26 "These countries are run like investment companies" (interview, Kuwait, 6 May 2012); "Sovereignty from colonialism was not really achieved and our rulers are puppets of the colonial powers. What we have are governments trying to modernize and westernize, but also show the west that they're being obedient and they are just like them" (interview, Doha, 22 February 2012); "insatiable greed, love of money, and total disregard for the common good characterize the state" (interview, Riyadh, 5 April 2012).

27 "The main problem is with our mentality: the soul of society has been snatched away for the appearance of modernity" (Interview, Doha, 29 February 2012).

28 For discussions about Islamic law as a resource for "healing the earth" and promoting environmental sustainability, see Johnston (2012) and Jenkins (2005).

000

References

al-Adawy H 2013 Mecca's creeping capitalism *The Independent* 4 February (www.independent.co.uk/voices/comment/meccas-creeping-capitalism-8479827.html) accessed 7 July 2015

Alusi A, Eccles R, Edmondson A and Zuzul T 2011 *Sustainable Cities: Oxymoron or the Shape of the Future?* Working paper 11-062 Harvard Business School, Cambridge MA 20 March (www.hbs.edu/faculty/Publication%20Files/11-062.pdf) accessed 12 August 2014

Bhabha H 1984 Of mimicry and man: the ambivalence of colonial discourse *October* 28 (spring) 125–33

Crystal J 1990 *Oil and Politics in the Gulf: Rulers and Merchants in Kuwait and Qatar* Cambridge University Press, Cambridge

Elhadj E 2008 Saudi Arabia's agricultural project: from dust to dust *MERIA* 12(2) (www.gloria-center.org/2008/06/elhadj-2008-06-03) accessed 3 September 2014

Fanon F 1966 *Black Skin, White Masks* Grove Press, New York

Gardner A 2014 How the city grows: urban growth and challenges to sustainable development in Doha, Qatar" in Sillitoe P ed *Sustainable Development: An Appraisal from the Gulf Region* Berghahn Press, Oxford 343–66.

Hertog S 2010 *Princes, Brokers, and Bureaucrats: Oil and the State in Saudi Arabia* Cornell University Press, New York

Jenkins W 2005 Islamic law and environmental ethics: how jurisprudence (*usul al-fiqh*) mobilizes practical reform *Worldviews* 9(3) 338–64

Johnston D L 2012 Intra-Muslim debates on ecology: is Shari'a still relevant? *Worldviews* 16 218–38

Jones T 2010 *Desert Kingdom: How Oil and Water Forged Modern Saudi Arabia* Harvard University Press, Cambridge MA

Kanna A 2005 The "state philosophical" in the "land without philosophy": shopping malls, interior cities, and the image of Utopia in Dubai *Traditional Dwellings and Settlements Review* 16(11) 59–73

Kanna A 2011 *Dubai: the City as Corporation* University of Minnesota Press, Minneapolis MN

Kumetat D 2009 *Climate Change in the Persian Gulf: Regional Security, Sustainability Strategies and Research Needs* Paper prepared for Conference Climate Change, Social Stress and Violent Conflict 19–20 November Hamburg

Kuwait Times 2013 Kuwaiti PM warns gravy train about to fly off rails *Kuwait Times* 28 October

Luciani G 2005 From private sector to national bourgeoisie: Saudi Arabian business in Aarts P and Nonneman G eds *Saudi Arabia in the Balance* New York University Press, New York 144–82

Luomi M 2012 *The Gulf Monarchies and Climate Change: Abu Dhabi and Qatar in an Era of Natural Unsustainability* Hurst, London

Mahdavy H 1970 Patterns and problems of economic development in rentier states: the case of Iran in Cook M A ed *Studies in the Economic History of the Middle East* Oxford University Press, Oxford 37–61

Masdar Abu Dhabi Future Energy Company 2009 *Today's Source for Tomorrow's Energy* [Brochure] Masdar Abu Dhabi Future Energy Company, Abu Dhabi

Menoret P 2014 *Joyriding in Riyadh: Oil, Urbanism, and Road Revolt* Cambridge University Press, New York

Mubadala Development Company 2007 Mubadala launches the world's first city targeting zero-carbon and zero-waste [Press release] 8 May (www.mubadala.com/en/news/mubadala-launches-world%E2%80%99s-first-city-targeting-zero-carbon-and-zero-waste#sthash) accessed 22 August 2014

Munif A 1987 *Cities of Salt [Mudun al-Malḥ]* Vintage Books, New York

Nagy S 2000 Dressing up Downtown: urban development and government public image in Qatar *City and Society* 12(1) 125–47

Ouroussoff N 2010 In Arabian desert, a sustainable city rises *International Herald Tribune* 25 September

Pacific Institute 2013 Freshwater withdrawal by country and sector (2013 update) *The World's Water* (Worldwater.org/wp-content/uploads/sites/22/2013/07/ww8-table2.pdf) accessed 10 December 2013

Pearce F 2012 Saudi Arabia stakes a claim on the Nile *National Geographic Daily News* 30 November (http://news.nationalgeographic.com/news/2012/12/121217-saudi-arabia-water-grabs-ethiopia) accessed 14 September 2014

Reiche D 2010 Renewable energy policies in the Gulf countries: a case study of the carbon-neutral "Masdar City" in Abu Dhabi *Energy Policy* 38 378–82

Ross M L 1999 The political economy of the resource curse *World Politics* 51 297–322

Rueter G 2012 Desert Eco-City is more glitz than substance *Deutsche Welle* 28 November (www.dw.de/desert-eco-city-is-more-glitz-than-substance/a-16408150) accessed 15 August 2014

Seznec J 2012 The sovereign wealth funds of the Persian Gulf in Kamrava M ed *The Political Economy of the Persian Gulf* Columbia University Press, New York 69–93

Stillwell B and Lindabury S 2008 *Masdar* Final project for City and Regional Planning 3840, Green Cities December

USEIA undated *International Energy Data and Analysis* United States Energy Information Administration (www.eia.gov) accessed 12 December 2013

Vassiliev A 1998 *The History of Saudi Arabia* Saqi Books, London

Wada Y, Ludovicus P H, van Beek C M, van Kempen J, Reckman W T M, Vasak S and Bierkens M F P 2010 Global depletion of groundwater resources *Geophysical Research Letters* 37 L20402

Woertz E 2013a *Oil for Food: the Global Food Crisis and the Middle East* Oxford University Press, Oxford

Woertz E 2013b Poor Gulf: inequality and the lack of statistics Gulf Research Center 11 April (http://grc.net/?frm_action=view_newsletter_web&sec_code=grcanalysis&frm_module=contents&show_web_list_link=1&int_content_id=80 683) accessed 19 September 2014

World Bank 2014a World development indicators (http://data.worldbank.org) accessed 8 July 2015

World Bank 2014b CO_2 emissions per capita (databank.worldbank.org/data/reports.aspx?Code=EN.ATM.CO2E.PC&id) accessed 8 July 2015

Yom S 2011 Oil, coalitions, and regime durability: the origins and persistence of popular rentierism in Kuwait *Studies in Comparative International Development* 46 217–41

6 Overcoming food insecurities in an era of climate change

Hilal Elver

Point of departure

Perhaps today's biggest single question about the future is whether we will have enough to eat in a very hot and crowded planet in the coming decades. Any future scenarios on food systems in the age of climate change should take account of the steadily increasing world population and the enormous negative impact of this growth on vital natural resources such as land, water and seeds, which are the three most important elements of food production. Since the 2007 hike in global food prices, the United Nations Food and Agricultural Organization (FAO) and the Intergovernmental Panel on Climate Change (IPCC) have reported on the danger of new food crises, and significant negative impacts of current agricultural practices on climate and vice versa. In the last few years, an enormous amount of energy was spent by civil society and scientific institutions to discuss the impact of climate change on food security, alerting governments and policy makers to the coming danger. At recent Conference of the Parties (COP) meetings of the United Nations Framework Convention on Climate Change (UNFCCC) in Lima and Paris, food security side events were the most well-attended meetings by civil society and actors, highlighting a growing chasm between the issues that powerful state actors are concerned with and the issues that are important to those who have to live with the day-to-day consequences of climate change.

The relationship between climate change and food systems is very complex. While climate change has a negative impact on agriculture, agriculture and food systems are also accelerating climate change. Increases in food production mean more GHG emissions, and therefore an acceleration of climate change, which brings more extreme weather events, which can also affect food production.

The dominant agricultural practice, large-scale industrial agriculture, which is at the heart of the global food system and dominates all aspects of food production and consumption, is fundamentally harmful to the environment, dangerous to human health, and responsible for accelerating human induced climate change. Notwithstanding the damage caused by the current approach, proponents of large-scale industrial agriculture continue to present it as the solution to climate-related challenges to agriculture by proposing high tech responses including bioengineered, drought resistant crops, technologically sophisticated irrigation systems, and genetically modified seeds, which are designed to be high yielding and thus work against food scarcity. As food production becomes more challenging as a result of climate change, Big Agriculture is becoming even more confident and demanding in advancing its industrial model.

In this chapter, I argue that reimagining agriculture and food systems in an age of climate change requires moving away from supply-oriented production models and into an alternative paradigm. In order to do that, first I will provide an overview of the ways in which climate change adversely impacts food systems. In the second part, I will discuss the impact of the mainstream food system on climate change. In the third part, I will present alternative approaches to food systems in an age of climate change. I argue that we should look beyond large-scale industrial agriculture and instead look to a different vision of farming by supporting and promoting small-holder farmers, local food initiatives, and agroecology on a global scale. There are many examples of this emergent alternative model around the world, including organic, biodynamic, bee-friendly, and community-supported food systems. People-centered agriculture can not only maintain food security, but it also offers a new model of community and human relations that could also have broader social impacts on issues such as employment and internal migration from rural to urban areas.

Following an analysis of alternative food production systems, I will introduce the human rights-based approach in global climate change governance. The human rights-based approach is an important and necessary paradigm shift in dealing with climate justice. The current climate change regime exacerbates social and economic injustices, pushing those who are already vulnerable in society further to the edge. A profound culture shift is necessary to respond to the new problems of climate change, beyond simple mitigation and adaptation strategies, if we are to meaningfully respect peoples' human rights and guarantee the sustainability of the earth's resources. A truly climate resilient society should embrace such approaches not as an alternative but, in fact, as the only way to ensure the future of the planet and its human population.

The adverse impact of climate change on food security

The IPCC has noted with high confidence in its Fifth Assessment Report that climate change will potentially affect all components of food security, including availability, accessibility, utilization and food system stability (Porter *et al.* 2014, 488). The IPCC has a well-deserved reputation for being a conservative and careful intergovernmental body; however, in its last report published in April 2014, with input from more than 300 scientists around the world, it did not hesitate to use bold language to express concerns related to food security.

The impacts of global climate change on food systems are expected to be widespread, complex, geographically and temporally variable, and profoundly influenced by socioeconomic conditions. Historical studies and integrated assessment models provide evidence that climate change will affect agricultural yields and earnings, food prices, reliability of delivery, food quality, and, notably, food safety as a result of increased flooding in lowland areas, greater frequency and severity of droughts in semiarid areas, and excessive heat conditions. Although a great deal remains unknown about how multiple stresses may combine to further impact the climate and food production, low-income producers and consumers of food will be more vulnerable to climate change owing to their comparatively limited ability to invest in adaptive institutions and technologies under increasing climatic risks.

Moreover, climate change is undermining food security and the right to food, with disproportionate impacts on those who are most vulnerable to its effects and who have contributed least to the problem. Unless considerable efforts are made to improve people's resilience, the risk of hunger could increase by 20 percent by 2050, with an estimated 600 million more people affected by 2080 as a direct result of climate change (WFP 2014). The negative impacts of climate change on food security, such as declining crop yields, are expected to become more likely as early as 2030. Even if by 2050 greenhouse gases (GHG) emissions are reduced to below half of 1990 levels, the expected global temperature rise will pose a serious risk to human survival. Rising temperatures make it more difficult to expand the world grain harvest fast enough to keep up with the record pace of demand. According to crop ecologists, for every degree the temperature rises above the normal average during the growing season, farmers can expect a 10 percent decline in grain yields (Brown 2012, 57).

Although the effects of changes in climate on crop yields are likely to vary greatly from region to region, anticipated changes are expected to have large and far-reaching effects predominantly in the developing world. Official statistics predict that poor farmers in developing countries will be especially vulnerable to these impacts of climate change because of their geographic exposure, low incomes, greater reliance on agriculture and limited capacity to seek alternative livelihoods (Altieri 2002). For these vulnerable groups, even minor changes in climate can have disastrous impacts on their lives and livelihoods. Implications can be very profound for subsistence farmers located in remote and fragile environments, where yield decreases are expected to be very large, as these farmers depend on crops that are especially likely to be negatively impacted by climate change, such as maize, beans, potatoes and rice.

Besides rising temperature with changing climate, the world is experiencing more natural disasters that threaten global food security and political conflicts arising as a result of climate-induced food shortages. Large disaster-prone countries like China and India are particularly vulnerable to climate change, which is concerning given that historically these two countries have struggled to produce enough food to feed their large populations. In 2010, a Russian heat wave prompted an export ban on wheat that wreaked havoc on international markets. Price increases particularly affected wheat-importing countries in the Middle East and contributed to massive social unrest, culminating in the Arab Spring. The following year, a severe drought in the Greater Horn of Africa led the number of people in the region in need of food assistance to double in a period of six months (De Schutter 2012).

The IPCC report warned that crops could see yields decline 2 percent per decade, at the same time that demand for food from a growing population with increased appetites is projected to increase by 2 percent each year. Food demand is accelerating at a faster rate than population growth, in part due to the increase in GDP worldwide: as populations get wealthier, they eat more (Oxfam 2012). Moreover, not only do wealthier people consume more food, they also consume more meat and dairy products in particular, as well as produce more waste. This has historically been the case in the developed world; however, emerging economies such as China, India and Brazil are catching up.

There is little doubt that extreme weather will intensify and aggravate future food prices in the years ahead (Gillis 2012). Food items carry a large portion of the consumer price index of developing countries. Therefore, developing countries, especially heavily populated ones like China and India, are much more vulnerable to the fluctuation of staple food prices. Middle class households in the developed world, spend between 10 to 20 percent of the family budget on food, while this ratio climbs to an astounding 75 percent or more in developing countries. In countries like the United States, drought will have a major impact on global food prices, which in turn have important implications for both food supply and demand, because the United States is the world's biggest exporter of grains. Moreover, the global dependence on US exports of wheat and corn is predicted to grow as climate change increases the likelihood of extreme droughts in many parts of the world, including North America.

Options to expand food production by bringing more land under cultivation are limited. Forty percent of the entire surface of our planet is currently being used for agriculture and 47 percent of the remaining land is underdeveloped, consisting of forests, high mountains, tundra and deserts. Therefore, there is not a lot of remaining, arable land that can be used for agriculture (Emmott 2014). Even if there was, there may not be an available source of fresh water or the soil may be so depleted of nutrients that not even an increase in fertilizer would help (Economist 2011).

Emission reduction and climate stabilization are essential to any long-term solution for global agriculture (Ackerman and Stanton 2013, 11);

within a few decades, business-as-usual climate change would reach levels at which adaptation is no longer possible even at very dangerous zones. Avoiding that fate will require a reduction of between 40 to 70 percent of greenhouse gas emissions by mid-century, which means embarking on a revolution of the way in which we produce and consume food and energy (New York Times 2014). Alarmingly, the former co-chair of the IPCC said: "The world has only about 15 years left in which to begin to bend the emissions curve downward. Otherwise, the costs of last-minute fixes will be overwhelming. We cannot afford to lose another decade. If we lose another decade, it becomes extremely costly to achieve climate stabilization" (New York Times 2014).

How do we mitigate greenhouse gas emissions and feed the world?

Agro-pessimism

Although climate change is a threat multiplier that applies to all aspects of our lives, the complex relationship between climate change and food systems requires further investigation as agriculture and food systems are an important driver of climate change. Direct GHG emissions from agriculture include methane (CH_4) emissions from flooded rice fields and livestock, nitrous oxide (N_2O) emissions from the use of organic and inorganic nitrogen fertilizers, and carbon dioxide (CO_2) emissions from the loss of organic carbon in soil as a result of agricultural practices in croplands, and increased grazing intensity in pastures (HLPE 2012, 68). Crop and livestock agriculture accounts for about 15 percent of total global emissions today (Bailey *et al.* 2014).

Agriculture and food production also cause indirect emissions that are accounted for in other sectors such as industry, transport, and energy supply, from the production of fertilizers, herbicides, pesticides, and from energy consumption for tillage, irrigation, fertilization, harvest, and transport, all of which contribute 60 percent of total food system emissions, with significant regional variation. Land use change, much of which is driven by expansion of agricultural areas under cultivation, adds another 15 to 17 percent. Moreover, future income and population growth will increase agricultural emissions dramatically unless low-emissions growth strategies for agriculture are found (Molla 2014; Vermeulen, Campbell and Ingram 2012). All told, the global food system is the largest contributor to the production of GHG emissions.

Besides GHG emissions, negative consequences of agricultural production include loss of biodiversity, soil degradation and depletion in ground and surface water availability as agriculture globally consumes 60 to 70 percent of fresh water resources. Desertification and soil degradation that result from this are major threats for food security of the planet.

A strong "agro-pessimism" – a fear that humankind will not be able to feed itself except by destroying the environment – has developed, and this has been used to further the interests of large agribusiness corporations by highlighting the challenges we face in an alarming manner[1] and proposing agribusiness as the only solution to these challenges. While this may result in increased sales (Bittman 2013), it is certainly not the way to eradicate hunger and solve food insecurity, while reducing GHG emissions. Emphasizing the supply side of global food systems is common, but it generally undermines any nuanced understanding of the demand side of food policies. Unfortunately, increasing net food production does not solve the issue of hunger, given that hunger is not a result of food shortages but rather is about economic and social inaccessibility. The world has long produced enough calories to adequately feed the global population with a production output of around 2,700 calories per day per human. Not only is this sufficient to meet the needs of the current global population of seven billion, it is enough to meet the United Nations projection of a population of nine billion in 2050 (Bittman 2013).There are hungry people not because food is lacking, but because they cannot afford to buy it. It is also worth noting that a third of all calories produced goes to feed animals, and another 5 percent are used to produce biofuels, and as much as a third are wasted at various points along the food chain.

Are genetically modified crops a remedy to eliminate hunger and respond to climate change?

Proponents of using science and technology to enhance food production contend that the future of civilization depends on our ability to expand food production efficiently. The use of chemicals for fertilization and for pest and disease control, the induction of chemical or radiation-induced mutations in plants to improve yields, and the mechanization of agriculture are among the techniques that have increased the amount of food that can be grown on each acre of land by as much as 10 times in the last 100 years. Promoters of bioengineering claim that these extraordinary increases must be doubled by 2050 if we are to provide adequate nutrition to an expanding population. Furthermore, as people become more affluent, they are demanding diets that are richer in animal protein, which will require more robust feed crop yields to be maintained and expanded (Federoff 2011). In 2010, crops modified by molecular methods were grown in 29 countries on more than 360 million acres. Of the 15.4 million farmers growing these crops, 90 percent are poor, with small operations. The reason farmers turn to genetically modified crops is simple: yields increase, costs decrease, and profits rise (Federoff 2011).

Undoubtedly, during the last few decades, advances in technology enabled steady gains in land productivity while environmental degradation and increased population created difficulties for farmers to produce enough food to meet demands. Indeed, world grain yield per acre has tripled since 1950. However, this era of ever-increasing productivity appears to be coming to an end in some of the more agriculturally-advanced countries, where farmers are already using all available technologies to raise yields.

Larger farmers and "agro-businesses" have employed a largely scientific approach to farming as evidenced by the fact that the most popular agricultural technologies that have been taken up are based on genetic engineering, rather than ecosystem-oriented, low-technology agroecological methods. However, the use of genetically modified crops (GMC) is not without controversy. Proponents of GMCs believe that they provide the only solution to the challenge of increasing food production and are frustrated with regulations that they see as costly and burdensome and prevent their further use. They claim that the technology has significantly improved and has a track record of safety. The US Environmental Protection Agency (EPA) however, insists on requiring a significant amount of data on GMCs, claiming that it could inflict serious damage in the absence of an adequate monitoring and regulatory system.

In the United States, only a handful of GMCs are currently approved, including soybeans, corn, canola and cotton, all of which are commodity crops mainly used for feed or fiber, and were developed by big biotechnology companies. About 94 percent of soybeans, 72 percent of corn and 73 percent of the cotton grown in the US now use GM-tolerant herbicides, according to the US Department of Agriculture. According to the GMC industry, only large corporations possess the money needed to deal with the regulatory procedures imposed by the EPA and FDA (Food and Drug Administration). Proponents of GMCs believe that crop modification methods are not dangerous and offer the only realistic means to achieve food security and environmentally sustainable agriculture. They seek to reduce the present heavy regulatory burden so as to reduce the price tags for high tech companies.

The opposing argument also has strong followers. Longtime Indian activist Vandana Shiva has tirelessly mounted resistance against multilateral biotechnology companies and agribusiness operations in India, encouraging support instead for small-scale family farming (Shiva 2010). A report from Friends of the Earth International reveals that the claims made by the biotech industry that GMCs can combat climate change are both exaggerated and premature (Friends of the Earth International 2010a), and rather, GMCs actually increase carbon emissions while failing to feed the world. This is because GMCs are responsible for huge increases in the use of pesticides in the US and South America, which in turn intensifies fossil fuel use. The cultivation of GM soy to feed factory-farmed animals is also contributing to widespread deforestation in South America, causing massive GHGs emissions. Millions are being spent by governments on GMCs, which are being promoted as an unproblematic solution to climate change. The GMC corporate world is even hoping that it could be funded in the future through the UN climate emission reduction Clean Development Mechanisms (CDM) (Friends of the Earth International 2010b).

Paradigm shift

To achieve food security for all, it is imperative that global agriculture and the food system are reformed in such a way that they:

- are more resilient to the impacts of climate change and other shocks and crises, such as food price volatility, the ongoing economic crisis, and depletion of natural resources;
- contribute less to global climate change; and
- ensure the right to food of people through appropriate levels of production as well as through distribution and equitable access.

Shifting from the current, supply oriented, fossil fuel intensive industrial model of agriculture to agroecology, which supports local food movements and smallholder farmers, while maintaining sustainability is a necessary first step. Second, some of the mitigation and adaptation policies of the current climate change regime that compete with food security and accessibility in the developing world should be avoided altogether. Third, there is a need for a legal and political solution. Promoting a human rights-based approach to climate governance is the only alternative to current mainstream climate change diplomacy that continues to prioritize market based solutions rather than protect the most vulnerable. This must be a prerequisite to climate justice. Human rights approaches and mechanisms in climate change diplomacy will respect, protect and fulfill the right to food for all while reducing GHG emissions.

From climate smart agriculture to agroecology

Multinational corporations, aided by developed country governments, are vying to increase their control of land, seeds, markets and labor where agricultural lands are still available, and current farming practices are deemed not sufficiently "efficient and scientific." The majority of this change is aimed at developing countries. Donors, development agencies and multilateral financial initiatives continue to push a one-size-fits-all industrial model of agriculture, with agribusiness investment increasingly being seen as the only way to address hunger and poverty in times of climate change. Within this context, the concept of "climate smart agriculture" (CSA), a concept first articulated in 2009 and subsequently developed in 2010 by the FAO (FAO 2010), has been proposed as an alternative to industrial agriculture. According to its proponents, CSA increases productivity in a sustainable way, contributes to resilience, and reduces GHG emissions while enhancing the achievement of national food security and development goals. However, these claims are questioned by several NGOs and peasant organizations, who argue that CSA is fundamentally flawed in a number of ways. They claim that the absence of measurable criteria make it impossible to ascertain claims of sustainability. Further, they point out that CSA exists outside of a rights-based framework and therefore the right to food is not represented in a meaningful way. There is also a very limited understanding of resilience and, overall, a misplaced focus on climate change mitigation strategies, combined with a complete failure to recognize historical responsibility of the developed countries in relation to GHG emissions. Most importantly, there is a lack of clarity around the concept of CSA that could be misleading, offering leeway for socially and environmentally detrimental practices to be captured within its definition (CIDSE 2014).

One such initiative is the new Global Alliance for Food Security and Nutrition, a voluntary initiative, leveraging policy changes to help corporations increase their control of agricultural markets and resources in Africa. While bodies such as the World Committee on Food Security (CFS) and the UNFCCC are appropriate and legitimate forums for tackling the challenges of food security and climate change, the Alliance has pushed for its own initiatives, establishing a roadmap during the UNSG Climate Summit in September 2014 in order to support CSA as a response to climate change. The three aspirational outcomes it developed include: sustainable and equitable increases in agricultural productivity and income, greater resilience of food systems and farming livelihoods and reduction and/or removal of greenhouse gas emissions associated with agriculture, wherever possible. While these goals are indeed laudable, no details are given as to how the end goal to be reached other than simply pointing to CSA as a solution for all.

Among other questionable features, the Alliance lacks both transparency and a governance structure that guarantees social and environmental safeguards – two things that are crucial in any governance framework designed to tackle issues so fundamental to human rights as food and the environment. It places corporations in the powerful position of having access to decision making related to food systems over African countries, yet provides no adequate accountability and monitoring mechanisms to ensure legitimacy, coherence and transparency of their proposed involvement in agriculture in the region (CIDSE 2014). Through this initiative, the industrial model of agriculture is yet again being pursued at the expense of small-scale farmers who, in Africa, produce 70 percent of the continent's food on less than 15 percent of available agricultural land, largely through agroecological sustainable agricultural methods. Africa can feed itself with sustainable farming, despite the rules being rigged in favor of industrial agriculture (Global Justice Now 2015).

Studies show that agroecology increases food productivity and yields at a level comparable to, or better than, corporate-controlled agriculture. Agroecology also leads to better opportunities for women, increased income, employment, agricultural biodiversity, health and nutrition, at the same time as mitigating the impacts of climate change. Agroecology encompasses the science of ecological principles as applied to food systems, the practices and techniques of sustainable farming, and a movement that addresses the social, economic and political aspects of food systems (Wezel *et al.* 2011). Agroecological methods also improve opportunities for local control, emphasize the use of local resources, local knowledge, and take into account the ways in which food is produced. Agroecology recognizes how cultivating and sustaining the "cultural" dimensions of growing crops are central to providing food in the age of climate change. Unlike big agro-industrial approaches, the agroecology narrative supports traditional farmers, seed savers, food communities, farmers markets, community supported agriculture, slow and local food eating. It represents a complete shift in the way that we understand food, its production and respect of ecosystem.

There are many good agroecological practices, frameworks, guidelines, models and alternatives to overcome hunger in the face of climate change, which already exist and could help shape our food system, both in the global North and South. Around the world, peasant organizations, pastoralists, fisher folk, indigenous peoples, women and civil society groups are forming food sovereignty movements, which give communities control over the way food is produced, traded and consumed (Nyéléni 2007). Food sovereignty provides the framework within which agroecological systems and techniques should be developed. What distinguishes agroecology is the focus on a low-input and sustainable approach to farming. Research consistently shows that agroecology leads to better use of resources, better ways of growing food while producing as much food as or more than industrial farming, and upholding agriculture's social and environmental functions. But the benefits of agroecology go beyond productivity and increasing yields, and include promoting human rights to food, reducing the gender gap, increasing employment and income, increasing agricultural biodiversity, improving health and nutrition, and more importantly addressing climate change (Global Justice Now 2015, 6).

Agro ecology, climate change and resilience

Research has shown that many small farmers employing agroecological methods have successfully minimized crop failure through increased use of drought tolerant local varieties, water harvesting, mixed cropping, agroforestry, soil conservation practices and a series of other traditional techniques (Altieri and Koohafkan 2008). The only insurance mechanism available to these farmers is derived from the use of inventive self-reliance, experiential knowledge, and locally available resources (Altieri 2002). Observations of agricultural performance after extreme climatic events in the last two decades have revealed that resiliency to climate disasters is closely linked to the high level of on-farm biodiversity, a typical feature of traditional farming systems. Based on this evidence, various experts have suggested that rescuing traditional management systems combined with the use of agroecologically based management strategies, such as bio-diversification, soil management and water harvesting, may represent the only viable path to increase the productivity, sustainability and resilience of peasant-based agricultural production under predicted climate scenarios (Altieri and Nicholls 2013).

Crop rotation, improved grazing, cropland and manure management, maintaining and restoring the fertility of soils, conserving energy and water use and year-round crop cover can all help to sequester carbon dioxide and reduce agriculture's GHG emissions and reduce its impact on the environment. Between 40 and 65 percent of GHG emissions from agriculture could be mitigated by converting a certain proportion of conventional farms to organic farming (Niggli *et al.* 2009), because organic farming systems can sequester more carbon dioxide than industrial farms, and sustainable farming in general tends to require fewer carbon intensive external inputs, such as chemical fertilizers (ITC and FiBL 2007). It has also been shown that soils managed using organic methods can hold water better and produce more yields than conventional farming systems in conditions of drought or heavy rainfall.

Agroforestry has also been shown to help reduce farmers' exposure to climate-related risks. Planting "fertilizer trees" can help the soil retain moisture during droughts, as well as providing additional income through firewood and offering a less risky investment than chemical fertilizers in the event of crop failure. It also has important social benefits; in western Kenya, agroforestry has benefited women in particular who have access to a stable source of cooking fuel and income from firewood, which has been shown to help reduce their vulnerability to climate change (Thorlakson, Neufeldt and Dutilleul 2012).

Most of the food consumed today in the world is derived from peasant-bred locally adapted plant varieties mostly grown without agrochemicals (ETC 2009). 1.5 billion smallholders, family farmers and indigenous people on about 350 million small farms occupying no more than 20 percent of the world's arable land contribute no less than 50 percent of the global agricultural output for domestic consumption (ETC 2009). Some estimate that approximately 50 percent of these peasants use resource conserving farming systems – a testament to the remarkable resiliency of traditional agro-ecosystems in the face of continuous environmental and economic change – while contributing substantially to food security at local, regional and national levels (Toledo and Barrera-Bassols 2008, cited in Altieri and Nicholls 2013).

Moreover, the use of traditional, agroecological farming methods has a long history: most developing countries have a significant peasant population embedded in hundreds of ethnic groups with a history that can be traced back more than 10,000 years practicing traditional agriculture. Most forms of traditional agriculture are place specific, evolving in time in a particular habitat and culture, but many share common agroecological methods which have been shown by scientists to enhance stability and resiliency of farming systems. The realization of the contribution of indigenous and peasant agriculture to food security in the midst of scenarios of climate change as well as economic pressures has enabled the concepts of food sovereignty and agroecologically based production systems to gain much worldwide attention in the last two decades (Altieri and Toledo 2005). Two recent major international reports (IAASTD 2009; de Schutter 2010) state that in order to feed nine billion people in 2050, we urgently need to adopt the most efficient farming systems and recommend a fundamental shift towards agroecology as a way to boost food production and improve the situation of the poorest. Both reports, based on broad consultations with scientists and civil society and industry representatives, contend that small-scale farmers can double food production within 10 years in critical regions by using agroecological methods already available.

Despite the ecological and cultural significance of traditional agriculture and the wealth of accumulated knowledge and experience of indigenous farmers in the management and use of natural resources in the midst of change, very few efforts have been devoted to elucidate the mechanisms that explain why traditional agroecosystems have stood the test of time (Koohafkan and Altieri 2010). Such principles can establish the agroecological foundations for thousands of small farmers to design resilient systems thus avoiding excessive yield and economic losses when affected by droughts or hurricanes.

Most of the examples of traditional agroecosystems focus on the ecological resiliency of such systems or their speed of recovery from climatic disturbances. Little has been written about the social resilience – the ability of communities to withstand external shocks to their social infrastructure – of the rural communities that manage such agroecosystems (Adger 2000). Clearly, agroecological strategies that enhance the ecological resiliency of farming systems are a necessary but not sufficient condition to achieve sustainability. The ability of groups or communities to adapt in the face of external social, political, or environmental stresses must go hand in hand with ecological resiliency.

Local practices

Small-scale farmers and agroecological practices also play a central role in conserving crop diversity and developing varieties of plants adapted to a range of weather conditions, including drought. In 2010, a drought in Guangxi, in southwest China, destroyed many of the modern hybrid crop varieties while the better adapted traditional varieties, such as drought and wind resistant maize, were able to survive (Swiderska *et al.* 2011). Villages involved in participatory plant breeding programs were able to recover better after the drought because they had more of their own seed varieties, whereas other villages, which had grown hybrid seeds in the past, struggled due to a shortage of hybrid seeds on the commercial market.

In Kenya, many farmers have returned to their traditional crop varieties and are planting different varieties together to reduce the risk of crop failure (Swiderska *et al.* 2011). As a result, farmers have made themselves more resilient to the impacts of climate change, more independent of commercial seed breeders, and able to avoid using expensive chemical inputs, which are required with modern hybrid seeds (Swiderska *et al.* 2011). In South Africa, farmers started noticing seasonal temperature changes, which help to predict drought, and have begun adapting pre-emptively by planting short-season and faster growing crops, as well as planting more drought-resistant crop varieties, increasing irrigation and planting trees to help mitigate the effects of climate change (Komba and Muchapondwa 2012).

Locally developed varieties of rice in West African countries such as Ghana, Guinea Bissau, Sierra Leone and Togo have been shown to be extremely adaptable and "robust" because they have been bred over generations specifically to cope with difficult ecological and social conditions (Mokuwa *et al.* 2013). These "farmer rice varieties" are often more productive than imported varieties of rice, can grow with less inputs than modern varieties and require less maintenance (SciDev 2013). When the 2009 hurricane in West Bengal turned large amounts of farmland into salty ponds, only traditional rice varieties thrived – the most high-yielding modern varieties of rice were useless on the salty soil (Deb 2009).

Further, researchers have shown how farms based on agroecological principles can be more resilient to the impacts of natural disasters like hurricanes. Farms that used sustainable agricultural methods in Nicaragua, Honduras and Guatemala suffered considerably less damage from Hurricane Mitch in 1998 than conventional farms. Sustainable farms had up to 40 percent more topsoil and had suffered less economic loss than neighboring conventional farms (Holt-Giménez 2002). In Chiapas, Mexico, coffee-based farms that had more plant diversity also suffered less damage from Hurricane Stan in 2005 than more conventional plantations (Philpott *et al.* 2008). In Cuba in 2008, monoculture farms suffered greater losses (95%) from the impact of Hurricane Ike than highly diverse agroecologically managed farms, which suffered only 50 percent losses. Agroecological farms were also able to recover faster after the hurricane (Rosset *et al.* 2011).

Yet despite all of these effective practices, governments, development agencies, donors and policy makers are still focusing on large-scale, high input solutions, which marginalize small scale farmers because of existing political biases, trade rules and policies. This limits the ability of governments to support small-holder farmers and agroecological practices, attract investment for agroecology and supply sufficient research funding (Global Justice Now 2015, 7).

From global food systems to local food movement

Food systems are changing as a result of globalization and urbanization. Market liberalization and foreign direct investment are leading to changes in food consumption patterns, nutrition and health outcomes, economic disparities associated with food production and the livelihoods of small-holder farmers who are more vulnerable to the volatility of food prices. Multinational food corporations also play a powerful role in this process, as they monopolize the process of food consumption and impact our under-standing of what to eat, when and how much. Competition for market share of food purchases benefits powerful players such as large multina-tional fast food and supermarket chains to the detriment of small local agents, traditional food markets and merchants selling "street food" as well as other food items. Consumers are often drawn to supermarkets on the basis that they bring with them significant improvements in standards of food quality and safety at competitive prices and convenience.

These changes in food systems affect availability and access to food through changes to food production, procurement and distribution systems and the food trade environment. This is bringing about a gradual shift in which a universal food culture has emerged, with consequent changes in dietary consumption patterns and nutritional status that vary with the socio-economic strata. Indeed, lower socio-economic population groups drift towards poor-quality, energy-dense but cheap and affordable foods (FAO 2004).

At the same time, a lack of sustainability in food production is a key threat to resilience and needs to be addressed by changing the way we produce food so as not to generate large contributions to GHG emissions, debilitate our natural resources, and make us sick. Having access to all types of food all the time, in such large quantities and at a relatively cheap cost is a new problem.

Identifying and supporting food production and distribution practices that are more resource efficient, local and seasonal, and have fewer envi-ronmental externalities should be a high priority. Considering the diversity of environmental and social settings in which food production takes place, solutions for improving sustainability will differ. Examples of effective community based adaptation include improving water management prac-tices by building infrastructure for more efficient irrigation systems and small scale water capture, storage and use, adopting practices to conserving soil moisture, organic matter and nutrients, using short cycle varieties and setting up community based seed and grain banks. Farmers and food producers alone cannot adapt successfully to climate change. They need to be supported by governments and the private sector, and there is also an important role for civil society organizations.

One of the most viable options for every society is shifting food systems and eating habits based on local availability. New farmland-mapping research projects in the United States show that more than 90 percent of the population of the US could eat food grown or raised within 100 miles of their homes. This helps local economies, uses less fossil fuel by avoiding long distance transportation and makes agriculture more sustainable. Researchers found surprising potential in major coastal cities. For example, New York City could feed only 5 percent of its population within 50 miles but as much as 30 percent within 100 miles, while the greater Los Angeles area could feed as much as 50 percent within 100 miles.

The popularity of "farm to table" has skyrocketed in the past few years as people become more interested in supporting local farmers and getting fresher food from sources they know and trust. Even large chain restaurants are making efforts to source supplies locally, knowing that more customers care where their foods come from. The most recent US 2014 Farm Bill supports local production because there are profound social and environmental benefits from eating locally, as well as improvement of efficiencies in the food energy water nexus.

Diet can also make a difference. Moving from an animal-based diet to a plant-based diet can also change the percentage of people who can eat locally (Campbell 2015). Local food around San Diego can support 35 percent of the people based on the average US diet, but as much as 51 percent of the population if people switched to plant-based diets. The proportion of livestock products in a diet is one of the key drivers of GHG emissions. Slowing the global growth in consumption of livestock products will help to slow the growth of agricultural and food sector emissions. However, many livelihoods depend on livestock, and animals are very valuable since they can digest cellulose and agricultural residues. Furthermore, in developing countries where indigenous diets include animal protein, high quality protein from livestock products such as milk, meat and eggs will help to improve nutrition. Based on careful evaluation of regional, climatic and cultural changes, altering consumption patterns and food preparation practices is important to provide food security in many circumstances.

During recent decades the composition of the standard American diet in the US has become markedly less healthy, and these changes, in combination with an increasingly sedentary lifestyle, have resulted in an epidemic of non-communicable diseases. In the US, 35 percent of the adult population suffers from cardiovascular disease, 9.3 percent has diabetes, and 40 percent of the population will be diagnosed with cancer during their lifetime. The epidemic of non-communicable diseases is an important contributor to increasing U.S. health care costs to almost $3 trillion per year, representing 18 percent of the total US GDP in 2014, and 20 percent by 2022. The toll of these diseases can be greatly reduced by adopting a healthy lifestyle, including healthy diets (WCRF/AICR 2007; WHO/FAO 2003). Research has shown that this can result in significant reductions in diseases including diabetes, heart disease and obesity and reductions in both health care costs as well as GHG emissions (Cleveland *et al.* 2015). Given the urgency of mitigating emissions over the short term in order to avoid catastrophic climate change, the mitigation potential of diet change should be investigated more thoroughly for incorporation into national, state and local climate policies (Cleveland *et al.* 2015).

Reduction of food losses and waste

Food waste has a considerable environmental impact, with the vast amount of food that ends up in landfills adding to global warming as a result of increased methane emissions. This food waste represents a missed opportunity to improve global food security, but also to mitigate environmental impacts and resources use from food chains. A recent FAO study (FAO 2013) found that the global volume of food wastage is estimated to be 1.6 gigatonnes (Gt) of "primary product equivalents," while the total wastage for the edible part of food is 1.3 Gt. When compared to total global agricultural production for both food and non-food uses, of about 6 Gt, one can see that food waste is equivalent to more than half of world annual cereal production (FAO 2011). Food wastage ranks as the third top source of GHG emissions after the US and China. Globally, the blue water footprint – the consumption of surface and groundwater resources – of food wastage is about 250 km^3, which is equivalent to the annual water discharge of the Volga river, or three times the volume of lake Geneva. In order to produce the current volume of food that is wasted, almost 1.4 billion hectares of land is required, which represents close to 30 percent of the world's agricultural land area. Finally, there are impacts on biodiversity as negative impacts of monocropping and agriculture expansion into wild areas are compounded (FAO 2013).

The loss of land, water and biodiversity, as well as the negative impacts of climate change represent huge costs to society that are yet to be quantified. The direct economic cost of food wastage of agricultural products, excluding fish and seafood, based on producer prices only is about US$750 billion, which is equivalent to the GDP of Switzerland (FAO 2013). With figures so significant, it seems clear that a reduction of food waste at global, regional, and national levels would have a substantially positive effect on natural and societal resources. Food waste reduction would not only avoid pressure on scarce natural resources but also decrease the need to raise food production by 60 percent in order to meet the estimated 2050 population demand.

Food waste varies significantly by country and region. In developing countries, food waste and losses principally occur during the early stages of the food value chain and can be traced back to constraints on harvesting techniques and deficient storage facilities. In developed countries, however, food is mainly wasted or lost at a later stage in the supply chain, with the behavior of consumers having a significant impact (UNEP 2009). This is especially true in the United States, where 40 percent of food goes uneaten, and according to even most conservative estimates, Americans waste 160 billion pounds of food each year (Gunders 2012). The rate of food loss in the United States far exceeds that of much of the rest of the world, with the average American consumer wasting 10 times as much as food as the average consumer in Southeast Asia. One key contributor to wasting food is confusing and unregulated food expiration dates (NRDC 2013).

As a result of all of this, the High-level Panel of Experts on Food Security and Nutrition of the Committee on World Food Security stresses the importance of reducing food waste (HLPE 2014). Innovative ideas for tackling food waste are needed in order to do so. One of the goals established by the Zero Hunger Challenge, launched by the UN Secretary-General at the United Nations Conference on Sustainable Development, is to achieve zero loss or waste of food by minimizing the losses which occur during storage and transport by retailers and consumers, empowering consumer choice through appropriate labeling, encouraging commitment by producers, retailers and consumers of all nations, and achieving progress through financial incentives, collective pledges, locally relevant technologies and changed behavior. While the challenge does not rely on legally binding obligations, it offers States an opportunity to review current policies in relation to food waste.

Legal solutions: the right to food approach to climate change

Although the climate change regime has clearly recognized the threat climate change poses to food security, it has thus far been reluctant to implement a human rights-based approach. The gaps in the climate change regime have already been identified, particularly in relation to human rights implications of the Clean Development Mechanism and reducing emissions from deforestation and forest degradation in developing countries (REDD), as well as other measures on energy, biofuels and adaptation (Roht-Arriaza 2009–10; Cameron 2010; Paderson 2011). Nevertheless, the response measures of climate change mitigation and adaptation of the UNFCCC, at best undermine human rights if not contribute to outright violations.

For a long time, the IPCC Assessment Reports did not acknowledge the human right to food in its discussion of food security and climate change. As mentioned, this changed in April 2014 with the report of Working Group II of the IPCC. The Report highlights the current and future impacts of climate change on people in the context of food security, health, access to water and personal security. The Report also clarifies that while people all over the world are vulnerable to the impacts of climate change, the poor and marginalized are most vulnerable. This confirms earlier statements from the Human Rights Council that climate change undermines human rights including the right to life, the right to adequate food, the right to water, the right to health, the right to adequate housing, and the right to self-determination.

The UN Human Rights Council is the only UN organization that insists on promoting human rights-based approach in climate change policies, indicating the necessity of "special attention to vulnerable and disadvantaged groups, especially in areas under immediate threat." Indeed, it is "the rural hungry whose livelihood is intimately tied to the food sector who are most at risk from … climate-exacerbated fluctuations in the global food system." The climate change regime's failure to focus on the human right to food has meant that the international community has not focused on these groups in establishing adaptation and mitigation measures,[2] leaving many in developing countries defenseless.

It is imperative that any action to address climate change should not further undermine human rights, but rather protect and respect them. This can be achieved with a climate justice approach: climate justice links human rights and development to achieve a human-centered approach, safeguarding the rights of the most vulnerable and sharing the burdens and benefits of climate change and its resolution equitably and fairly. Climate Justice Principles are founded in legal and moral imperatives of human rights and respect for the dignity of the person, making them the indispensable foundation for action on climate justice (Mary Robinson Foundation 2013).

The principles of rights-based approaches include (i) respecting people's right to participate in decision-making processes that affect their lives; (ii) understanding and addressing the root causes of poverty and suffering; (iii) emphasizing the equal dignity and worth of all people and promotion of tolerance, inclusion, nondiscrimination and social justice; and (iv) holding all development actors accountable for respecting, protecting and fulfilling human rights (De Schutter, Robinson and Shine 2013). A rights-based approach could provide both practical, conceptual, and more importantly, a moral framework to UNFCCC for effective action especially in time of "voluntary commitments." The negotiations leading up to the COP 21 in Paris in December 2015, where the objective is to achieve a legally binding universal agreement on climate change, are an opportunity to ensure the adoption of a human rights-based approach that identifies and satisfies the most pressing needs of vulnerable persons.

Conclusion

Profound societal change is needed to shift from the current business as usual attitude to a responsible global policy that will respect, protect and fulfill human rights, understand the immediate needs of vulnerable people and societies, and push governments and corporations to behave responsibly. Further, we need to move beyond the current industrial approach to agriculture and beyond "food security" to "agroecology." This is the only way we can ensure harmony with our community and our planet and continue to provide food to a hungry planet whose population is increasing. This is not a utopian, romantic or even radical alternative, but rather a simple truth that is often lost among the strong resistance of the large agro-business lobby that is increasingly monopolizing our food systems. It's telling that even imagining an alternative seems to be a radical shift; however a change of this magnitude is not only an idea whose time has come, it is a practical shift that is crucial in the era of climate change. Indeed, the most important task of policymakers at this moment in time is to overcome the challenge to food security caused by climate change: the future of our planet and our ability to inhabit it is at stake.

Notes

1   See, for example, *The Economist*, August 26, 2010, which uses headlines such as: "World population will reach 9 billion in 2050," followed by: "world grain output will have to rise by half and meat production must double to meet demand."
2   See, for example the following UN resolutions: 2008 Resolution 7/23; 2009 Resolution 10/4; 2011 Resolution 18/22.

References

Ackerman F and Stanton E A 2013 *Climate Impact on Agriculture: A Challenge to Complacency?* February Tufts University, Medford MA (www.ase.tufts.edu/gdae/publications/working_papers/index.html)

Adger W M 2000 Social and ecological resilience: are they related? *Progress in Human Geography* 24 347–64

Altieri M 2002 Agroecology: the science of natural resource management for poor farmers in marginal environments *Agriculture, Ecosystem and Environment* 93 1–24

Altieri M and Koohafkan 2008 *Enduring Farms: Climate Change, Smallholders and Traditional Farming Communities* Environment and Development Series 6 Third World Network, Malaysia

Altieri M and Nicholls C I 2013 The adaptation and mitigation potential of traditional agriculture in a changing climate *Climatic Change* 120(3) 1–2

Altieri M and Toledo 2005 Natural resource management among small scale farmers in semi-arid lands: building on traditional knowledge and agroecology *Annals of Arid Zone* 44 365–85

Bailey R, Froggatt A and Wellesley L 2014 Livestock – climate change's forgotten sector: global public opinion on meat and dairy consumption Research paper December Chatham House, London (www.chathamhouse.org/sites/files/chathamhouse/field/field_document/20141203LivestockClimateChangeBaileyFroggattWellesley.pdf)

Bittman M 2013 How to feed the world *The New York Times* 4 October (www.nytimes.com/2013/10/15/opinion/how-to-feed-the-world.html?pagewanted=all&_r=0)

Brown L 2012 *Full Planet Empty Plates: The New Geopolitics of Food Security* W W Norton, New York

Cameron E 2010 Human rights and climate change: moving from an intrinsic to an instrumental approach *Georgia Journal of International and Comparative Law* 38 673–716

Campbell E 2015 The potential for local croplands to meet US food demand *Frontiers in Ecology and Environment* 13(5) 244–8

CIDSE 2014 *Climate Smart Agriculture: The Emperor's New Clothes?* Discussion paper CIDSE, Brussels (www.cidse.org/articles/item/640-climate-smart-agriculture.html)

Cleveland D, Hallström E, Gee Q, Donnelly N and Scarborough P 2014 The potential for reducing greenhouse gas emissions from health care via diet change in the US in Schenck R and Huizenga D eds *Proceedings of the 9th International Conference on Life Cycle Assessment in the Agri-Food Sector 8–10 October 2014, San Francisco* American Center for Life Cycle Assessment, Vashon WA 233–40

Deb D 2009 Valuing folk crop varieties for agroecology and food security *Independent Science News* 26 October (www.independentsciencenews.org/unsustainable-farming/valuing-folk-crop-varieties)

De Schutter O 2010 *Report of the Special Rapporteur on the Right to Food* United Nations General Assembly A/65/281 United Nations, New York (www.srfood.org/images/stories/pdf/officialreports/20101021_access-to-land-report_en.pdf)

De Schutter O 2012 Famine isn't an extreme event, it's the predictable result of a broken system *The Guardian* 30 January

De Schutter O, Robinson M and Shine T 2013 *Human Rights: Their Role in Achieving Climate Justice and Food Nutrition Security* Thematic Papers, Mary Robinson Foundation (www.mrfcj.org/media/pdf/HNCJ-rights.pdf)

Economist 2011 Crisis prevention *The Economist* 24 February (www.economist.com/node/18229412)

Emmott S 2014 *10 Billion* Penguin Books, London.

ETC 2009 *Who Will Feed Us? Questions for the Food and Climate Crisis* Comunique #102 ETC Group, Ottawa

FAO 2004 *Globalization of Food Systems in Developing Countries: Impact on Food Security and Nutrition* FAO Food and Nutrition Paper 83 Food and Agriculture Organization, Rome (www.fao.org/3/a-y5736e.pdf)

FAO 2007 *Adaptation to Climate Change in Agriculture, Forestry and Fisheries: Perspective, Framework and Priorities* Food and Agriculture Organization, Rome

FAO 2010 *"Climate Smart" Agriculture: Policies, Practices and Financing for Food Security, Adaptation and Mitigation* Food and Agriculture Organization, Rome (www.fao.org/docrep/013/i1881e/i1881e00.htm)

FAO 2011 *Global Food Losses and Food Waste – Extent, Causes and Prevention* Food and Agriculture Organization, Rome

FAO 2013 *Food Wastage Footprint: Impacts on Natural Resources* Food and Agriculture Organization, Rome (www.fao.org/docrep/018/i3347e/i3347e.pdf)

FAO 2014 *The State of Food Insecurity in the World 2013: The Multiple Dimensions of Food Security* Food and Agriculture Organization, Rome (www.fao.org/docrep/018/i3434e/i3434e.pdf)

Federoff N V 2011 Engineering food for all *The New York Times* 18 August (www.nytimes.com/2011/08/19/opinion/genetically-engineered-food-for-all.html)

Friends of the Earth International 2010a *Who Benefits from GMCs? The Great Climate Change Swindle* September 117 Friends of the Earth International,

London (https://www.foeeurope.org/sites/default/files/publications/who_benefits_full_report_2010.pdf)

Friends of the Earth International 2010b *GMCs Failing to Tackle Climate Change* 23 February Friends of the Earth International, London (www.foei.org/press/archive-by-subject/food-sovereignty-press/gm-crops-failing-to-tackle-climate-change) accessed November 2014

Gillis J 2012 Climate Change and the Food Supply *New York Times* 6 September (http://green.blogs.nytimes.com/2012/09/06/climate-change-and-the-food-supply)

Global Justice Now 2015 *From the Roots Up: How Agroecology Can Feed Africa* February Global Justice Now, London (www.globaljustice.org.uk/sites/default/files/files/resources/agroecology-report-from-the-roots-up-web-version.pdf)

Gunders D 2012 *Wasted: How America Is Losing Up to 40% of Its Food from Farm to Fork to Landfill* Issue Paper IP:12-06-B Natural Resources Defense Council, New York (www.nrdc.org/food/files/wasted-food-ip.pdf)

HLPE 2012 *Food Security and Climate Change* Report by High Level Panel of Experts on Food Security and Nutrition of the Committee on World Food Security, Rome (www.fao.org/3/a-i3901e.pdf)

HLPE 2014 *Food Losses and Waste in the Context of Sustainable Food Systems* Report by High Level Panel of Experts on Food Security and Nutrition of the Committee on World Food Security, Rome (www.fao.org/3/a-i3901e.pdf)

Holt-Giménez E 2002 Measuring farmers' agroecological resistance after Hurricane Mitch in Nicaragua: a case study in participatory, sustainable land management impact monitoring *Agriculture, Ecosystems and Environment* 93(1) 87–105

IAASTD 2009 *Agriculture at a Crossroads: The Synthesis Report* ed McIntyre B D Herren H R Wakhungu J Watson R T International Assessment of Agricultural Knowledge, Science and Technology for Development, Washington DC

ITC and FiBL 2007 *Organic Farming and Climate Change* International Trade Centre and Research Institute of Organic Agriculture, Geneva (www.fibl.org/fileadmin/documents/shop/1500-climate-change.pdf)

Komba C and Muchapondwa E 2012 *Adaptation to Climate Change by Smallholder Farmers in Tanzania* ERSA Working Paper 299 Economic Research Southern Africa, Cape Town (www.econrsa.org/system/files/publications/working_papers/wp299.pdf)

Koohafkan P and Altieri M A 2010 *Globally Important Agricultural Heritage Systems: A Legacy for the Future* Food and Agriculture Organization, Rome

Mary Robinson Foundation 2013 *Principles of Climate Justice* Mary Robinson Foundation, Dublin (www.mrfcj.org/pdf/Principles-of-Climate-Justice.pdf)

Mokuwa A, Nuijten E, Okry F, Teeken B, Maat H, Richards P and Struik P C 2013 Robustness and strategies of adaptation among farmer varieties of African rice (*Oryza glaberrima*) and Asian rice (*Oryza sativa*) across West Africa *PLoS ONE* 8(3) e34801

Molla R 2014 How much of world's GHG emissions come from agriculture? *The Wall Street Journal* 29 September (http://blogs.wsj.com/numbers/how-much-of-worlds-greenhouse-gas-emissions-come-from-agriculture-1782)

New York Times 2014 Running out of time *New York Times* 20 April (www.nytimes.com/2014/04/21/opinion/running-out-of-time.html?action=click&contentCollection=Opinion&region=Footer&module=MoreInSection&pgtype=article)

Niggli U, Fließbach A, Hepperly P and Scialabba N 2009 *Low Greenhouse Gas Agriculture: Mitigation and Adaptation Potential of Sustainable Farming Systems* April Food and Agricultural Organization, Rome (ftp://ftp.fao.org/docrep/fao/010/ai781e/ai781e00.pdf)

NRDC 2013 *The Dating Game: How Confusing Food Date Labels Lead to Food Waste in America* Report R13-09-A Natural Resources Defense Council, New York (www.nrdc.org/food/files/dating-game-report.pdf)

Nyéléni 2007 Declaration of the Forum for Food Sovereignty, Nyéléni (http://nyeleni.org/spip.php?article290) accessed 22 November 2014

Oxfam 2012 *Extreme Weather, Extreme Prices: The Cost of feeding a Warming World* Oxfam Issue Briefing September Oxfam, Oxford (www.oxfam.org/sites/www.oxfam.org/files/20120905-ib-extreme-weather-extreme-prices-en.pdf)

Padersen O 2011 The Janus head of human rights and climate change: adaptation and mitigation *Nordic Journal of International Law* 80 403–49

Philpott S M, Lin B, Jha S and Brines S 2008 A multi-scale assessment of hurricane impacts on agricultural landscapes based on land use and topographic features *Agriculture, Ecosystems and Environment* 128(1) 12–20

Porter J R, Xie L, Challinor A J, Cochrane K, Howden S M, Iqbal M M, Lobell D B and Travasso M I 2014 Food security and food production systems in *Climate Change 2014: Impacts, Adaptation, and Vulnerability. Part A: Global and Sectoral Aspects. Contribution of Working Group II to the Fifth Assessment Report of the Intergovernmental Panel on Climate Change* Cambridge University Press Cambridge 485–533

Roht-Arriaza N 2009–10 "First, do no harm": human rights and efforts to combat climate change *Georgia Journal of International and Comparative Law* 38 593

Rosset P M, Sosa B M, Jaime A M and Lozano D R 2011 The Campesino-to-Campesino agroecology movement of ANAP in Cuba: social process methodology in the construction of sustainable peasant agriculture and food sovereignty *Journal of Peasant Studies* 38(1) 161–91

SciDev 2013 Local rice makes the grade in West Africa *SciDevNet* (www.scidev.net/global/biotechnology/news/local-rice-makes-the-grade-in-west-africa.html) accessed May 2015

Shiva V 2010 *Biotechnology and World Food Supplies* (www.schumachercollege.org.uk/community/open-evening-with-vandana-shiva-2010) accessed October 2014

Swiderska K, Reid H, Song J, Li J, Mutta D, Ongugo P, Pakia M, Oros R and Barriga S 2011 The role of traditional knowledge and crop varieties in adaptation to climate change and food security in SW China, Bolivian Andes and Coastal Kenya Paper presented at the UNU-IAS workshop on Indigenous Peoples, Marginalised Populations and Climate Change: Vulnerability, Adaptation and Traditional Knowledge Mexico July (http://pubs.iied.org/pdfs/G03338.pdf)

Thorlakson T, Neufeldt H and Dutilleul F C 2012 Reducing subsistence farmers' vulnerability to climate change: evaluating the potential contributions of agro-forestry in western Kenya *Agricultural Food Security* 1(15) 1–13

UNEP 2009 *The Environmental Crisis. The Environment's Role in Averting Future Food Crises* United Nations Environment Programme, Nairobi

Vermeulen S, Campbell B M and Ingram J 2012 Climate change and food systems *Annual Review of Environment and Resources* 37 195–222

WCRF/AICR 2007 *A Challenge for the Meat Processing Industry* World Cancer Research Fund, London

Wezel A, Bellon S, Doré T, Francis C, Vallod D and David C 2011 Agroecology as a science, a movement and a practice *Sustainable Agriculture* 2 27–43

WFP 2014 *Two Minutes on Climate Change and Hunger: A Zero Hunger World Needs Climate Resilience* World Food Programme, Rome (http://sv.wfp.org/sites/default/files/sv/file/fact_sheet_-_climate_change_and_hunger.pdf)

WHO/FAO 2003 *Diet, Nutrition and the Prevention of Chronic Diseases* Report of a Joint WHO/FAO Expert Consultation WHO Technical Report Series no. 916 World Health Organization, Geneva

7 Reimagining climate engineering

The politics of tinkering with the sky

Simon Nicholson

The rise and rise of climate engineering

In the fall of 1965, US President Lyndon B. Johnson's White House published a report titled *Restoring the Quality of Our Environment* that analyzed the drivers and impacts of industrial pollution (Environmental Pollution Panel 1965). A short section, tucked away in an appendix, was devoted to the specific challenge of "atmospheric carbon dioxide." It makes for quite extraordinary reading.

For one thing, the passage, even buried as it was at the end of the report, shows quite clearly that the basic science of climate change was well understood by the mid-1960s by scientists with access to the highest levels of the United States government, giving lie to the notion that climate change is some recently emergent puzzle with which the world has had insufficient time to grapple.

Second, and more directly on point, the "atmospheric carbon dioxide" section of the report is notable for the kinds of responses the authors thought worthy of consideration. In particular, the fact that increasing atmospheric CO_2 content could be "deleterious from the point of view of human beings" was, the report's authors suggested, reason enough to begin research into "deliberately bringing about countervailing climatic changes" (Environmental Pollution Panel 1965, 127).

What the report's authors referred to as "countervailing climatic changes" we now call *climate engineering* or *geoengineering*. Climate engineering has become an umbrella term for a wide array of imagined large-scale technological responses to climate change. Now, to be clear, these are not the kinds of technological responses that have been typical fodder in climate change circles – new forms of renewable energy as a mitigation strategy, say, or advanced systems of dykes and sea walls to help coastal regions adapt to rising waters. Instead, climate engineering covers an array of technologies of a wholly different character, aimed at intervening in basic earth system functions, sometimes in quite dramatic and quite new ways.

In the *Restoring the Quality of Our Environment* report, the authors speculated about tackling climate change by increasing the albedo of the world's oceans by spreading reflective particles over large portions and by attempting to change the atmospheric energy balance by changing the composition of high-altitude cirrus clouds (Environmental Pollution Panel 1965, 127). Dozens of additional high-tech countermeasures of a similar ilk have been proposed by other individuals and groups, before and since. Other well-known potential climate engineering schemes range from dumping large amounts of iron into the world's oceans in the hopes of promoting great carbon-inhaling blooms of phytoplankton, to introducing sulfate particles into the stratosphere in an effort to reflect some amount of incoming solar radiation, to creating artificial trees that capture carbon dioxide directly from the air.

Many of these and other climate engineering proposals can sound, frankly, outlandish. Indeed, such ideas have long been considered so beyond the pale that until just a few short years ago any reference to climate engineering was considered taboo, dismissed, as David Victor once put it, as "a freak show in otherwise serious discussions of climate science and policy within mainstream climate circles" (Victor 2008, 323). Times, though, have changed. Talk of climate engineering is gaining steam, as evidenced by a string of new research programs, academic publications, and attention by scientific bodies and government agencies (for a timeline of activities related to climate engineering, see FCEA 2015).

Greater consideration is now being paid to climate engineering for a complex mix of reasons. For one thing, there is a growing set of high-profile scientists clamoring for some kind of robust response to climate change, who point to what they see as a relative paucity of action spurred by international and domestic political processes. At the same time, and as will be examined in more detail below, this call by scientists coincides with powerful social, cultural, and economic forces that favor some kind of large-scale technological response to climate change over other forms of action.

The future for climate engineering, and whether the kinds of technologies now under discussion will ever leave the drawing board, is still uncertain. There is much at stake. This is because climate engineering proposals offer great promise but also much peril. Sorting among the options ahead requires clear, careful assessment.

The particular purpose of this chapter, in keeping with the others in the volume, is to contribute to the examination of the climate options before us by interrogating the taken-for-granted assumptions that are made about, in this case, climate engineering. More narrowly, my intent here is to point out and unpack potential dangers associated with the dominant ways climate engineering is being described and discussed.

As a starting point, one potential way to think about climate engineering is that it enables a wholesale, largely positive reimagining of the climate change solution set. Developing a capacity to engineer the climate adds a new set of tools to the toolkit. These tools, say some proponents, will buy time for other forms of response to be further developed and to take hold.

It is possible to imagine, in other words, a wholly beneficial use of climate engineering technologies, to be researched and deployed in strategic coordination with existing and new approaches to mitigation of greenhouse gas production and adaptation to climate change's effects.

Having a new tool, though, does not alone guarantee a positive result. A hammer, for instance, can be used to drive in a nail or to break a bone. Hammers can also serve as potent distractions if the job at hand really demands a screwdriver (as the old saying goes, "if all you have is a hammer, every problem looks like a nail").

Hammers may seem to have little in common with sulfate particles in the stratosphere or iron dumped in the oceans. As technological artifacts, though – as products of imagination and will that serve to extend humanity's reach – they are alike in some basic ways. One fundamental commonality is that while we can imagine many beneficial uses of any given technology, the ultimate impact is not wholly predetermined nor ever set in stone. This is because technological pathways are, to use the language of Langdon Winner, "inherently political," meaning that they are subject to all manner of contestation (Winner 1986). Whether a technology is used for good or bad ends partly rests on the choices of particular actors at particular moments. At the same time, the available ends are baked, to some degree, into the technology itself. (A hammer serves as an effective weapon because of its heft and mass, and its fit in one's hand). And, importantly, the ends to which technologies are directed are themselves products of shared imagination and framing. The ways in which we discuss and understand particular technologies, this is to say, privilege particular forms of use.

In the climate engineering discussion, one framing stands above the others. This is the idea that climate engineering is a kind of "Plan B," meaning that climate engineering serves as "an alternative fall-back option that can be reached for if plan A fails" (Corry 2014, 5). Put differently, climate engineering offers an escape hatch in the event that mitigation is not enough.

The biggest problem with this dominant frame is that the Plan B notion can quickly elide into thinking and talking about climate engineering as a sort of "get out of jail free" card. When climate engineering is seen in this way, not as one set of responses among many but rather as some kind of ready alternative pathway to established ways of tackling climate change, then the whole enterprise becomes irretrievably technocratic, raising the specter of dangerous path dependencies and technological lock-in (Cairns 2014). The framing is also damagingly dichotomous – we either "succeed" in tackling climate change via Plan A (existing mitigation measures), which to date, for reasons discussed elsewhere in the volume, has been insufficient, or we throw our lot behind Plan B, the climate engineering *deus ex machina*.

The present volume's editors have established the challenges inherent in a "hardening of the categories" – an encrustation of understandings and practices – when it comes to climate change. Climate engineering is itself coming to be understood in a circumscribed, limiting fashion, as a way to evade the failing mainstream climate regime. This is foolhardy thinking. Climate engineering is not, in fact, a Plan B. At best, it's a kind of Plan A+, or Plan A.5. Certain climate engineering strategies may, under certain conditions, and if developed and deployed with appropriate caution and humility, augment other forms of response. Understanding the true promises and perils of climate engineering requires breaking free from the Plan B framing. This means that if climate engineering is to ultimately serve some beneficial purpose, it requires a reimagining of the climate engineering project.

The climate engineering landscape

At the start of any discussion of climate engineering it is important to issue a reminder that such a catch-all term can obscure as much as it reveals. There is a huge range of various approaches with quite different characteristics that fall under the climate engineering umbrella. As such, an important first step in unpacking the climate engineering conversation is to disaggregate the overarching category, to avoid sweeping generalizations.

Disaggregation begins with the drawing of a distinction, as most do in conversations about climate engineering, between imagined carbon dioxide removal (CDR) approaches and those that might be aimed at solar radiation management (SRM) (see, for instance, Committee on Geoengineering Climate 2015a, 2015b). Proposed CDR schemes seek to draw CO_2, and, perhaps, other greenhouse gases out of the atmosphere, and to then hold those gases in long-term benign storage or to put them to productive use. In contrast, SRM involves letting CO_2 buildup in the atmosphere but regulating the amount of sunlight hitting the planet or otherwise altering the planet's overall thermal energy budget.

Drawing a distinction between CDR and SRM is important because their respective, associated technologies raise very different technical, ethical, and governance questions. There are also important distinctions to be drawn *within* each of the categories. Adding iron to the oceans and adding biochar to soils are both CDR techniques, but they are quite different in terms of the risks they pose. At the same time, there is value to be found in maintaining the over-arching "climate engineering" label or something like it, to indicate essential commonalities. I will have more to say about each of these points later in the chapter.

The CDR/SRM division is now common in reports and other writings about climate engineering. The most recent, fifth assessment report of the Intergovernmental Panel on Climate Change, for instance, gave, for the first time in the IPCC's history, some substantial attention to both broad categories of climate engineering approach. (As an aside, the fact that the authors of the IPCC report decided to look at climate engineering says something important about the movement of climate engineering from the fringes toward the mainstream of the climate change conversation.)

CDR received treatment in the report of the IPCC's Working Group III, the group tasked with considering climate change mitigation options (IPCC 2014). The working group ended up examining more than 1,000 separate greenhouse gas emission pathways, using models to consider the impacts of different assumptions and trends out to the year 2100. Their analysis concluded that most scenarios that would stabilize emissions at between 430 and 480 ppm CO_2eq – a level of CO_2eq that would likely keep the world from warming more than 2°C on average above pre-industrial levels – would require *global net negative emissions* in the second half of the century.

Consider that phrase for a moment: net negative emissions. The world's premiere scientific body tasked with looking at climate change is suggesting that finding ways to suck vast amounts of carbon and other greenhouse gases out of the atmosphere will likely be *necessary* to avoid a breach of the 2°C guardrail agreed to by the international community. In this way, the interaction of negotiated international targets with the systems whereby climate science are examined, articulated, and translated for the policy world and public is working to ensure that CDR is becoming a mainstream proposition.

As previously mentioned, a range of different CDR schemes have received consideration, from the seeding of the world's oceans with iron to the enhanced weathering of naturally occurring silicates. Newly emerged as the most prominent idea, in the wake of the attention given to it in the recent IPCC report, is bioenergy with carbon capture and storage (BECCS). Basically, a large-scale BECCS program would entail transforming some significant portion of global energy production such that it could be powered by bioenergy, through, for instance, the growing of vast amounts of biomass and its conversion into liquid biofuels or its burning at biomass fuel-power stations. The bioenergy production system would then need to be paired with a carbon capture and sequestration system that would capture carbon emissions at the source of release and convert them for long-term storage, perhaps deep underground in chasms left vacant by the removal of oil and gas deposits.

Such a proposal certainly seems immensely attractive on its face. After all, what is not to like about any idea that would address the "source" of climate change, if the "source" is taken to be the amount of CO_2 and other greenhouse gases in the atmosphere? (This is an analytic assumption that I'll return to).

Yet BECCS, on the magnitude required, would be a truly heroic industrial undertaking. Back-of-the envelope calculations have suggested that capturing and burying carbon on the scales needed to match the IPCC's negative emissions pathways would require development of a network of pipelines, railways, and the like on the scale of the current infrastructure for the world's entire oil and gas industry (personal correspondence with Professor Wil Burns). More sophisticated analysis, in the wake of the IPCC report, has indicated that, following the IPCC pathways, BECCS would have to account for something like 5–25 percent of the level of CO_2 emissions present in 2010 annually by 2050 (Fuss *et al.* 2014).

Such sobering calculations point out some of the chief challenges inherent in CDR schemes. They would, for the most part, appear to be massively expensive and would work, if they could be made to work, only over very long time scales. Those are not reasons alone to dismiss CDR ideas out of hand. They are, though, reason enough to be skeptical about any suggestion that CDR offers a quick fix.

Let us turn attention, then, to SRM approaches. One way, at least in theory, that the atmospheric warming associated with increasing concentrations of greenhouse gases could be abated would be by deflecting or scattering some amount of incoming solar radiation. Some models have suggested that the warming associated with a doubling of atmospheric CO_2 concentrations above pre-industrial levels could be offset by reducing the amount of incoming solar radiation by something like 1.8 percent (MacCracken *et al.* 2013). Now, taking explicit and coordinated actions that would, in effect, dim the sun would be no small undertaking. It is, though, entirely imaginable with existing or near-future technologies. In fact, it is taking place today via human activities. The burning of sulfur-laden coal in ever-greater quantities by the world's emerging powers, in particular, has been credited with introducing reflective particles into the air in such quantities that the world's temperature is being held cooler than without such intervention, so that fossil fuel use, the major driver of anthropogenic climate change, is itself responsible for a massive SRM experiment (Kaufmanna *et al.* 2011).

The goal of most imagined SRM schemes would be to increase planetary albedo – the earth's reflectivity. This could be achieved via a variety of means, from enhancing the reflective character of the wakes of ocean-going ships, to artificially whitening clouds, to installing mirrors in space. The most talked about scheme, already mentioned above, involves introducing a layer of reflective particles – sulfur dioxide would be a good candidate – into the stratosphere. A reflective layer of sulfur dioxide particles in the upper atmosphere would mimic an effect that accompanies volcanic eruptions. The eruption of Mount Pinatubo in the Philippines in 1991, for instance, ejected an estimated 22 million tons of sulfur dioxide into the atmosphere, with the effect that global average temperatures fell by an estimated 0.5°C for the following two years (Self 2006).

There are technical barriers to such a scheme. It is conceivable, though, and some rough calculations have suggested it would be relatively cheap. Nobel Prize-winning atmospheric chemist Paul Crutzen suggested, in a 2006 article widely credited with helping to break the scientific taboo against consideration of climate engineering, that a sulfate injection scheme could be developed and implemented for $25–50 billion a year (Crutzen 2006). A more recent estimate by a team of scientists led by Alan Robock has suggested that fitting sulfur tanks and hoses onto existing military jet aircraft could enable a scheme to get up and running for something like $1–3 billion a year (Robock *et al.* 2009).

As was the case with the CDR technologies described above, the appeal of sulfate aerosol spraying, the most talked-about SRM scheme, should be obvious, if for different reasons. For relatively little money and over a relatively short time horizon, modelers suggest that one of the signature effects of climate change, global average temperatures, could be brought under control. What is not to like?

Is tinkering with the climate a realistic or hubristic response?

The prospects for climate engineering are more complicated, however, than might be taken from the quick outline above. There are, as one might expect, potential downsides along with the upsides. In fact, there is a long and complex catalogue of risks that attach to climate engineering, which I have elsewhere suggested can usefully be organized into three categories: material, political, and existential (Nicholson 2013).

In sorting through the risks associated with climate engineering, and in seeking to accurately assess whether or not particular climate engineering ideas should be developed or deployed, framing matters. Here, let us pick up again on the "Plan B" framing that was introduced earlier.

The idea that climate engineering might serve as some kind of Plan B in the event that political and social responses to climate change fail to bear fruit has been around for as long as there has been serious scientific discussion of climate engineering. Paul Crutzen, for instance, in his seminal 2006 paper making the case for consideration of sulfate aerosol injection, called the work of policy makers attempting to formulate a plan to address climate change "grossly unsuccessful" (Crutzen 2006, 212). That assessment opened the way, in his analysis, to consideration of another, alternative, technological form of response. In this way, climate engineering is understood as a backstop should Plan A fail us.

The United Kingdom's Royal Society followed with a major and much anticipated report in 2009, titled *Geoengineering the Climate: Science, Governance and Uncertainty* (Royal Society 2009). In the report's foreword, Lord Rees, President of the Royal Society, wrote of climate engineering emerging as a product of the "pressure to consider a 'plan B,'" a pressure that, in his estimation, would surely mount should greenhouse gas emissions continue to rise.

A quick online search reveals many thousands of scholarly and popular sources that utilize the plan B framing. This should be no surprise. It is, after all, an easy and compelling way to think and talk about the opportunities offered by climate engineering. There are important reasons, however, that the Plan B framing should be set aside. One reason is that the Plan B framing elides into a belief that technological miracles wait in the wings.

"Plan B," as Olaf Corry has explained, "must initially be a less preferred option than plan A but *must also be assumed to be feasible if and when the preferred option fails*" (quoted in Kreuter 2015, 19; emphasis added). To propose a Plan B assumes that the Plan B can be pulled off. Moreover, if Plan B can be successful, why devote any more time to Plan A?

The dominance of the Plan B framing is shaping the climate engineering conversation in important ways. Notably, it constrains the sorts of questions that can be asked and answered about the climate engineering project. When it comes to risks, there is a good deal of attention paid to the physical or material challenges associated with climate engineering schemes, as problems to be overcome on the way to a managed climate. A good deal of attention is also being paid to governance challenges, in this case to imagine control of the political processes that will guide development and potential deployment of climate engineering technologies.

However, the Plan B frame allows insufficient attention to critical *existential* questions. I will argue below that abandoning Plan B framing offers new ways of seeing climate engineering, beyond the strictures of Climate Inc.

Again, it is important not to conflate all types of potential climate engineering, but instead, when talking about risks and costs, to look at the risks that attach to specific imagined technological options. So, for the purposes of the next few paragraphs, let us look very briefly at a handful of the material and political risks associated with sulfate aerosol injection, the most talked about and examined of the SRM options, before turning to give more extensive consideration to the category of existential risks.

Material risks abound when it comes to the idea of introducing sulfates into the stratosphere. Most basically, what if things go disastrously wrong? Some computer modeling exercises have suggested, for instance, that changing planetary albedo via this SRM method could upset global rainfall patterns, undermining food security and triggering the dieback of essential forest cover. If that were to eventuate, the "cure" might be worse than the underlying malady. Sulfate particles also remain suspended in the atmosphere for only a limited period of time. Modeling simulations suggest that any cessation of a sulfate aerosol injection program, after it had begun, could lead to a sudden "pulse" of warming caused by the building up of greenhouse gases in the intervening years – a pulse that would be more catastrophic than the more gradual warming experienced absent the project.

These kinds of concerns connect directly with a host of potential political risks. If a sulfate aerosol injection scheme needed to be run for some extended period of time, and perhaps indefinitely, what kinds of mechanisms of international cooperation could be brought to bear? Who would get a voice? Who would get their figurative hand on the new global thermostat? And who would take the blame if things did not go to plan? In thinking about that last point, University of Oxford professor Steve Rayner has remarked that if India had embarked on a go-it-alone sulfate aerosol injection scheme a few years prior to the floods that devastated large swathes of Pakistan in 2011 and 2012, it would have been almost impossible to convince Pakistani military officials that the Indian state was not responsible for their suffering (quoted in Barker 2013, 24). It is one thing to experience a disaster as a natural event; quite another to experience disaster as a real or perceived consequence of the actions of another.

The above is just a sampling of the kinds of intragenerational material and political risks that might be considered when examining the potential of climate engineering responses. A number of scholars and reports have pored over these and other risks in detail, and still others have given attention to *intergenerational* issues that arise via consideration of sulfate aerosol injection, in particular (Burns 2011). In common across both categories of risk, when viewed through the Plan B frame, is the underlying assumption that each potential risk can be identified, catalogued, probed, and ultimately surmounted. Hence the call by some for research agendas that focus exclusively on domestic or international climate engineering governance, or that call for investigation of particular scientific or engineering puzzles that must be overcome before sulfate aerosol spraying could be deployed.

Plan B framing and existential risks

I am guilty in the section immediately above of a little exaggeration for effect. The governance and physical science debates and conversations around climate engineering are not given their entire shape by the Plan B frame, and so are a good deal more nuanced and interesting than I am suggesting above. Still, the point holds. The Plan B frame narrows the range of questions that receive sustained attention even as it runs together with the promise of coming technological miracles. Problematizing the Plan B frame is essential, then, to open space for consideration of a third, existential category of risk, and for the understandings of an additional set of challenges associated with climate engineering.

By "existential risk," I should be clear that I am *not* here speculating about threats to all existence that flow from consideration of climate engineering. Instead, I am drawing, in a crude way, on the philosophical tradition of existentialism to suggest that examination of strategies like climate engineering may impact how individuals view themselves in relation to one another and the natural world, and that this in turn may influence how people view the nature of climate change.

A less torturous way to say this is as follows: *the embrace of a particular understanding of climate engineering – the kind of understanding that is encouraged by the Plan B framing – may close off other forms of response to climate change.*

One aspect of the argument is that full-throated advocacy and wholehearted embrace of a climate engineering agenda could, as many others have pointed out, produce a kind of "moral hazard" that draws attention away from mitigation. The logic here is that, if geoengineering looks at all like an option beyond mitigation, then many may suggest abandoning efforts to reduce GHGs. Such a hazard is a critically important consideration, and is a good reason in itself to be wary of a Plan B framing.

At the same time, a point that has received much less attention is that climate engineering may work against other forms of response in another way, by reinforcing some of the very social, political, and ideational dynamics that have given rise to climate change in the first place. It is far easier, after all, for powerful elites to package and sell a technological fix than for publics to imagine and bring about large-scale social, economic, political, and technological transformation. Many people would rather, in the face of illness, be offered a pill than submit to lifestyle change. By the same token, climate engineering can readily be sold as the climate change pill – the magic elixir that makes the problem go away. Like many pills, it addresses merely the symptoms of climate change without addressing the root causes. Furthermore, it leaves existing political, economic, and cultural structures of power intact.

My overarching theme here is that problem diagnosis matters. How a problem is understood drives the search for, and colors what counts as, a reasonable response. To say, for instance, as many have started to do, that CDR technologies would tackle the "causes" of climate change is a troubling move. For one thing, this kind of argument draws an unnecessary and false equivalence between activities aimed at keeping greenhouse gases from ever entering the atmosphere and those aimed at pulling them out. In other words, CDR and greenhouse gas mitigation come to be seen as correspondent approaches. Yet the slippery slope beckons. If Plan B offers the same outcomes as Plan A, and if Plan B means that I don't have to change anything about how I live my life, why bother with Plan A? Why work to keep fossil fuels buried beneath the earth if new technologies will inject the byproducts of combustion back into the ground? Likewise with SRM: why bother reducing CO_2 emissions and working to restructure societies if we can simply blanket the planet with reflective particles? Plan B, in other words, comes to be seen increasingly as Plan A.

In this way we start to see that the Plan B framing can lead to a sense that climate engineering offers control without consequences. As Mike Hulme has noted, conventional routes for understanding and responding to climate change all tend to be "variants on the idea of 'engineering' – geo-engineering, political engineering and social engineering – *and all of them with connotations of global control and mastery of the climatic future*" (Hulme 2008, 12; emphasis added). This is treacherous territory. So long as climate engineering is driven by an impulse to master, there is a ready potential that it will operate as an extension of, and serve to preserve, the very forces that have driven us into the age of climate warming.

The framing challenge even extends to the concept of "risk" that is prevalent in the climate engineering conversation (and so many others), and that I am using here to organize thinking about material, political, and existential challenges. The world used to impose *hazards*. Now, we humans face *risks*. The difference is that hazards are imprecise and incalculable dangers while risks can appear as specific possibilities that can be discerned and controlled. The concept of risk offers the modern age a powerful contemporary language and set of tools for coming to terms with uncertainty. It should never be forgotten, though, that the concept is a loaded one. It carries the weight of its history, even as it purports to shed light on things to come. Michael Mayerfeld Bell and Diane Bell Mayerfeld have put it this way:

> Consider the connotations of the word "risk." Using the term immediately conjures up numbers and calculations in a way that words like hazard and concern and danger do not. Risk is imbued with the image of science, of studies that have been done or could be done. Risk turns witchcraft into statistics. Risk turns subjective uncertainties into objective probabilities, sanctified by the iron laws of mathematical logic and scientific method.
>
> (Bell and Mayerfeld 1999, 2)

Climate change imposes massive risks that we attempt to overcome via the development of risky climate engineering responses, with each climate engineering response itself the bearer of further risks to be identified and managed. It is an interesting analytical conundrum, particularly when to think that risk is something that can be totally rationalized is, according to social theorists like Ulrich Beck, one of our age's chief pathologies (Beck 1992). Control is an elusive goal given the complexities involved with climatic intervention. Any framing of climate engineering that rests on deeply unreasonable expectations about technical mastery, and that assumes away the political dimensions of technological development and deployment, should be carefully avoided. The multiplicity of geoengineering dynamics cannot easily be broken down into discrete layers of calculated risk that can be controlled for, since the uncertainties, scale, and intensity involved defy analytical precision, disaggregation, and faith in complete human comprehension.

Yet some who are arguing for consideration of climate engineering appear excited by the idea of humanity's more firmly seizing control of the planet's most basic functioning. At the very end of an otherwise measured book on climate engineering, David Keith, a figure well-known in climate engineering and broader climate change circles, takes on a somewhat triumphalist tone, when he suggests,

> About a million years after inventing stone cutting tools, ten thousand years after agriculture, and a century after the Wright Brothers flight, humanity's instinct for collaborative tool building has brought us the

ability to manipulate our own genome and our planet's climate. ... We may use these powers for good or ill, *but it is hard not to delight in these newfound tools* as an expression of collaborative human effort to understand the natural world.

(Keith 2013, 173–4; emphasis added)

Such a strong view in favor of the promise of technological advance is present in other parts of the conversation about appropriate responses to climate change. Michael Shellenberger and Ted Nordhaus, for instance, have, with the establishment of their "Breakthrough Institute," crafted a clearinghouse for a technologically optimistic environmental narrative. In a piece titled "Evolve," they warn against an "ecotheocracy" that privileges low-tech forms of response to environmental crises, arguing instead for a "modernization theology" that encourages the unleashing of humanity's technological prowess in the service of human wellbeing and environmental protection (Nordhaus and Shellenberger 2011). More recently, Nordhaus and Shellenberger have come together with David Keith and a range of other prominent writers and thinkers to propose a new "ecomodernist manifesto," premised on developing a "good Anthropocene" via technological mastery (Asafu-Adjaye *et al.* 2015).

It is easy to spin a story of technology-driven progress, ever forward and upward. Technological advance is based on increasingly sophisticated mastery of material and natural processes. Technological advance also generates aggregate material wealth, and with wealth comes investment in new rounds of technological advance that, the thinking goes, will solve current problems, including those created by the last set of technological advances. Whatever the problem, technology will save us. On this basis, the dominant vision in the search for a sustainable world has become, according to commentators such as philosopher of technology Aidan Davison (2001), a sort of global technocratic biospheric management. This vision is one in which the unintended environmental consequences of technical actions are met with ever more sophisticated technological solutions, and, ultimately, in which the whole of nature is to be brought under a human yoke.

The Plan B framing around climate engineering flows from and is supportive of this kind of grand techno-optimism. It suggests that a techno-fix is waiting in the wings when and if other efforts fail. In turn, the Plan B framing gives rise to what Rose Cairns has characterized as "cognitive lock-in," creating false choices between the various options that lie before us (Cairns 2014, 651). Cognitive lock-in, as Cairns points out, can be linked to "socio-technical lock-in," whereby a faith in the future prospects for climate engineering technologies sets us on the path to their production, and "carbon lock-in," whereby a focus on climate engineering works to "shore up current dependence on fossil fuels" (Cairns 2014, 649).

All of this serves to render climate engineering the exclusive domain of scientists and technocrats. We are, by this view, stuck on the path to a technological future that can only be understood and shaped by the experts who have a grip on efficiency's knowledges:

> [In the dominant essentialist vision of technology] the development of technology is seen to obey an autonomous and value-neutral logic in which science-bound, technical elites (engineers, city-planners, physicians, architects etc.) realize ever more effective and reliable means to attain the necessary, incontrovertible goals of modern society. As such, existing technology at any particular moment in time appears to have a self-evident rationality and necessity which repels the very possibility of authentic ethical choice and political debate.
>
> (Doppelt 2001, 156)

The ways that we think clearly play some significant role in shaping the realities of social life. In this case, Plan B framings of climate engineering would have us believe that the routes by which climate change can be comprehended and responded to are the exclusive domain of technical experts. Now, Plan B proponents may well reply that the job of scientists and engineers is merely to provide options, and that it is up to politicians and perhaps society at large to determine whether or not climate engineering interventions are warranted or desirable. The trouble with that line of argument is that much of the *appeal* of climate engineering lies in its being a technical response that can circumvent the messiness of social engagement. We need a Plan B, after all, because the Plan A of international agreement-making and the like has not proved an adequate response. The political effect of this view is to exclude from decisions about technology the voices of lay-people – indeed, the voices of those very people who are most affected by technological change.

Finally, there is another, more prosaic aspect to the uses to which climate engineering might be put. It should come as no surprise, for instance, that dozens of patent applications for potential climate engineering technologies have already been filed by corporate actors. It should also come as no surprise that private companies may distort the use of climate engineering in pursuit of short-term financial gain. As author Robert Olson (2014) has put it:

> What can stop the drive for shareholder profits from leading to inappropriate engineering deployments? Would companies undermine mitigation efforts by influencing governments to allow engineering technologies to qualify for carbon credits or to meet emissions reduction targets?
>
> (Olson 2014, 1)

Climate engineering, in other words, could ultimately serve Climate Inc. in two senses: first by fitting neatly into established understandings of climate change as a problem and what it means to mount a response; and second by providing profit and increased power to the very actors and institutions that have the strongest vested stake in the status quo.

Can climate engineering eschew mastery?

Here, then, is the crux of the matter. Can there be forms of climate engineering that are not premised wholly and solely on human mastery over nature, and that therefore do not reinforce the destructive power of Climate Inc.? Put differently, must climate engineering remain insulated within a Plan B mentality that requires technological hubris, subscription to a narrative of mastery, and delegating decision making to experts? Or might there be a Plan A+ or Plan A.5 frame that could integrate aspects of the climate engineering spirit without having to embrace the entire socio-technological package?

One important thing that I have not made especially clear to date and that is important to keep in mind is that climate engineering technologies are still almost entirely speculative. There has been much talk but, to this moment, still little focused research that would allow assessment of the efficacy or practicality of any specific climate engineering proposals. This is an essential point, because climate engineering, in common with other complex emerging technological forms, is often written, talked, and thought about as though it were already here, rather than as a distant and at this point mostly hypothetical and abstract undertaking.

This means that climate engineering is, to borrow language from philosopher of technology Andrew Feenberg, still an "ambivalent" technological form (Feenberg 1999). By this, I mean, following Feenberg, that any particular engineering idea or approach or technology is not just something that can jump out of the ether, fully formed. Nor is the climate engineering conversation or the potential development or deployment of climate engineering technologies completely locked in to any particular set pathway (though Rose Cairns' points about lock in, noted above, help us to understand that certain paths forward are in the process of being privileged over others). Despite significant path dependence, there is some room for maneuver at this crucial, early stage of the climate engineering discussion. As Feenberg reminds us, our technological future is "not a destiny but a scene of struggles. It is a social battlefield … on which civilization's alternatives are debated and decided" (Feenberg 1991, 12). To widen the bandwidth of struggle requires imagination. It involves, specifically, reimagining climate engineering, especially in ways that reveal the ends toward which it is directed.

The battle that is being played out via the proxy of climate engineering is over very different understandings of what climate change is and what should be done in response. One increasingly dominant way involves defining climate change as a matter of *greenhouse gases*, and carbon dioxide in particular. Humanity is burning fossil fuels and changing land-use patterns in ways that are leading to more and more CO_2 production. At the same time, various other activities are adding methane, nitrous oxides, chlorofluorocarbons, and other greenhouse gases to the atmosphere. Climate change, by this view, is a nasty side effect of industrial life, best overcome by the application of ever more elaborate technological fixes. Tackling climate change any other way would be disastrous. Climate change is a problem to be solved, and, as has been outlined above, climate engineering can be packaged and sold in such a way that it appears to offer the fix.

But climate change is assuredly much more than a CO_2 problem. At the very least, we should be talking about climate change as a fossil fuel combustion problem, which means that it's best conceived as a global energy system(s) and transportation problem. It is tempting to go still further and suggest that climate change is symptomatic of deeply troublesome global economic, social, and political arrangements, such that an effective response to climate change starts with a reimagining of some of the most entrenched and taken-for-granted aspects of modern industrialized life. (This broader orientation informs many of the other chapters of this volume.)

This gives rise to a second, increasingly marginalized way to think about climate change. By this second reckoning, climate change is about *limits*. It is about fashioning forms of existence that allow human thriving within the biophysical constraints imposed by the planet's ecology. Down this path lies the search for high prosperity / low consumption forms of life and livelihood, for greater meaning and new understandings of virtue, and alternative economic, political and cultural systems of value that align humanity's striving with the needs of the planetary systems of which we are an inseparable part. Climate change is now a planetary feature, with the human task being to find ways to craft responses that, to quote architect William McDonough, allow for the flourishing of the "children of all species ... for all time" (McDonough and Braungart 2002, 186). Climate engineering, at least when conceived as a Plan B that largely holds in place the status quo, seems wholly incompatible with this kind of understanding of climate change. Luckily, Plan B need not provide the only frame for thinking about climate engineering. Alternative orientations offer ways of adopting aspects of climate engineering that pose less danger and, more importantly, encourage moving beyond the status quo. Climate engineering can escape the strictures of Climate Inc.

Some climate engineering measures, for instance, are what Robert Olson has called "soft" geoengineering strategies (Olson 2012). These are strategies that could be deployed locally, that appear relatively environmentally benign, that could be pulled back if deemed harmful, and that could still have measurable impact on some impacts associated with climate change. Olson suggests, for example, installing white roofs and making paved areas in urban centers more reflective to reduce urban heat island effects while also imparting a very slight cooling effect by increasing planetary albedo. He also discusses injecting highly reflective "microbubbles" into reservoirs – an act that would have the co-benefit of reducing evaporation from bodies of still water and that could be turned off instantly if any untoward effects were to be encountered.

Taking climate engineering out of Climate Inc. involves more, though, than small-scale strategic acts. It can also include incorporating the aspiration toward greater compassion and justice that some proponents of climate engineering express. A number of thinkers insist on pursuing climate engineering out of concern that, despite significant global mitigation efforts, at some point in time climate change may prove unacceptably punishing to the poor and marginalized. In such a situation, they suggest, it might be immoral not to deploy climate engineering technologies. Those advancing such a perspective do not consider climate engineering a Plan B for the wealthy or for the world at large, but specifically as a moral obligation to those who traditionally find themselves on the receiving end of hardship and injustice. As I see it, we would do well to embrace such concern and exercise it beyond climate engineering enterprises. Caring about the poor and exploited, especially within the corridors of would-be climate engineers and those who would seek to govern their activities, offers a chance to include measures aimed at greater justice in international negotiations, domestic mitigation and adaptation, and cultural appreciations for the consequences of climate change. To be sure, and as should be obvious, climate engineering does not possess a monopoly on thinking about climate justice. In fact, most SRM and CDR schemes are tone-deaf to it and there is a broader climate justice movement that is generally opposed to climate engineering (see Chapter 9, this volume). But, to the degree that calls for greater compassion and justice are emerging *within* the climate engineering literature, this should be welcomed. Ironically, it could be the case that greater research into climate engineering may provide a forum in which clearer articulations of climate justice might materialize. This will only happen, however, if we relax the commitment to seeing climate engineering as Plan B and rather incorporate it into the broader attempt to address climate change as a global social question, rather than as a giant techno-management issue.

An additional and related way that discussions about climate engineering might contribute is through analyses of the political, economic, and cultural contexts for research and possible deployment. Climate engineering or "geoengineering" is about technically altering, as the terms suggest, the entire earth. It involves modifying atmospheric and terrestrial features and functions of the planet itself. From a governance perspective, ideally no single person, group, or region should decide how and when to adopt it. Rather, such decisions should be matters of international cooperation with the greatest amount of democratic input. Moving toward such cooperation and global solidarity represents a good in its own right and certainly a worthwhile endeavor for any responsible and effective response to climate change. In this sense, the world should embrace discussions of climate engineering that seek to advance collaborative and ultimately innovative forms of global governance.

From an economic perspective, climate engineering requires devoting financial resources toward a common good rather than simply a narrow, parochial national or personal interest. Exploring the economic requirements of geoengineering, then, invites novel thinking about economic relations and the purpose of economies in general. Might it be that considering how to pay for climate engineering spawns new ideas about how to share the world's economic wealth in more generous and collaborative ways?

Finally, climate engineering can offer alternative cultural sensibilities. Climate engineering reminds us that we live on one planet and that working for climate protection is a universal effort. It breaks down boundaries of concern, affiliation, and identity. To be sure, climate change itself calls for such cosmopolitanism but so far the world's mitigation and adaptation efforts have yet to instill a planetary type consciousness. As discussions of climate engineering become more real and as people consider the stakes and scope of planetary-wide schemes – putting at risk the only home our species has – the possibility exists that a unifying responsiveness may emerge and give shape to new forms of cultural relations. Put differently, that humanity might alter the globe itself in a desperate attempt to stave off climate change might provide urgency and instruction in recognizing the reality of socio-ecological interdependence.

These opportunities stand ready to be capitalized upon. However, they will remain unrealizable in the current framing of climate engineering. As long as climate engineering continues to be packaged and sold as some kind of Plan B, as a purely technological fix to be held in humanity's back pocket and rolled out in case of emergency, we risk squandering genuine opportunity. Thus, rather than think in terms of dichotomous choices – Plan A or B – we need to forge a more nuanced and sophisticated framework, one in which climate engineering becomes part of a broader, more inclusive, and more deliberative exercise in exploring responses to climate change. Climate engineering thus must be in conversation with mitigation and adaptation schemes. It must be a voice involved at all levels of climate response. It would be a mistake to allow climate engineering the privilege to inhabit its own, insulated realm of consideration to the side of current climate efforts. It is not a Plan B. It is not separate from everything else that is being done on behalf of a safer climate.

One final point needs to be made here. Climate engineering cannot be Plan B not only because the world needs its contributions to the larger conversation but also, and arguably more importantly, there is no Plan A against which to situate itself. Climate engineering arose partly because international and domestic efforts have been failing to address climate change. The engines of climate intensification continue to roar and, in many senses, are accelerating. No plan, method, model, strategy, or blueprint exists for promising responses. There is no coherent trajectory at present and we must recognize this. Thus, it is time to stop thinking in either/or terms, especially since neither side of the dichotomy – Plan A or B – really exists. Our job is to fashion collective ways to address climate change. At the heart of this involves focusing not on the symptoms – for example, higher temperatures that *might* be lowered through planetary engineering – but causes – the political, social, and economic dynamics that give rise and drive extractivist, consumptive cultures. To get at these, more fundamental causes, requires reimagining climate engineering outside the straightjacket of Plan B and, as other chapters in this book suggest, reimagining climate change itself.

This kind of talk may come across as politically naïve. There have, after all, been few signs that the world is ready to take reasoned and strategic action in the face of any aspect of climate change, and good reason to believe that the actors and forces looking to hold in place the status quo will wield climate engineering in the service of that end. It is hard, on that basis, to imagine that the introduction of climate engineering will make things any better, and plenty of good reasons to believe that having climate engineering receive serious consideration will make things a good deal worse. Such is the view of, for instance, the ETC Group, a Canadian NGO. The leadership of ETC sees any talk of climate engineering as dangerous. Climate engineering is, to their view, a false solution and a dreadful distraction. Further, any consideration of or speculation about climate engineering normalizes the conversation, they say, and normalization speeds climate engineering's eventual arrival (ETC Group 2010).

My own view is somewhat different. In engaging with the world as it is, rather than as one might wish it to be, it is essential to realize that climate engineering is far too enticing and powerful a notion to be shoved aside. Climate engineering is not going away. No new taboo will be erected that forces the climate engineering genie entirely back into its bottle. Desperation is too strong a motivator. And so for me the question is not climate engineering or no climate engineering. The question becomes, are there forms of climate engineering, and ways of conducting the conversation about climate engineering approaches, that can bring out the best in humanity's climate response? Climate engineering is emerging as a key site of political struggle. But the struggle is not just over whether or not climate engineering is a good idea – a bipolar, "to geoengineer or not to geoengineer" debate. Instead, it is a more complex, nuanced struggle, which has to do with the role of engineering within the broader set of responses to climate change, and the particular character of engineering options that might see development or deployment.

It will require extraordinary vigilance to ensure that climate engineering technologies are not advanced as some kind of false solution. The task ahead is to push the climate engineering conversation in productive rather than destructive directions. This can best happen to the degree that climate engineering is subjected to careful, early, and well-crafted social oversight.

The need for active civic engagement with climate engineering

Climate engineering is not some fiendish plot hatched by a group desperate to ward off real action on climate change. It could well serve the same function, though, by distracting us from other, more beneficial actions. Climate engineering certainly fits neatly with current dominant ways of understanding and responding to climate change, by telling us that climate change is a discrete and manageable "problem" that can be tackled via technological means.

And yet, at the same time, climate engineering is not something that can be written off or ignored. I have asked here, can *any* engagement with climate engineering be productive? The answer is, it depends; it rests on how the conversation is engaged. The argument set out above is that consideration of climate engineering is now inevitable, so that the task of those interested in climate politics and political action becomes to *ensure* that the climate engineering conversation is a productive one.

As the chorus of voices calling for consideration of climate engineering continues to grow in size and volume, as it is bound to do, it will become ever more important for a wider array of actors to engage productively in the conversation. Climate engineering is not some aberrant, marginal response to climate change. It is, instead, the expected response of a culture that partly looks to technological solutions to complex societal challenges. Other approaches exist. These need to be heard to guide the direction of climate engineering research and incorporate such forays into the broader challenge of addressing climate change.

References

Asafu-Adjaye J, Blomqvist L, Brand S, Brook B, Defries R, Ellis E, Foreman C, Keith D, Lewis M, Lynas M, Nordhaus T, Pielke R Jr, Pritzker R, Roy J, Sagoff M, Shellenberger M, Stone R and Teague P 2015 *An Ecomodernist Manifesto* (www.ecomodernism.org) accessed 15 May 2015

Barker M 2013 Let's play God: the scientific experiments that might save the world (or destroy it …). *The Independent* 20 October (www.independent.co.uk/environment/green-living/lets-play-god-the-scientific-experiments-that-might-save-the-world-or-destroy-it-8884386.html)

Beck U 1992 *Risk Society: Towards a New Modernity* Sage Publications, London

Bell M M and Mayerfeld D B 1999 *The Rationalization of Risk* Iowa State University, Ames IA

Burns W C G 2011 Climate geoengineering: solar radiation management and its implications for intergenerational equity *Stanford Journal of Law, Science and Policy* 4 39–55

Cairns R C 2014 Climate geoengineering: issues of path-dependence and socio-technical lock-in. *Wiley Interdisciplinary Reviews: Climate Change* 5(5) 649–61

Committee on Geoengineering Climate 2015a *Climate Intervention: Carbon Dioxide Removal and Reliable Sequestration* Committee on Geoengineering Climate: Technical Evaluation and Discussion of Impacts, National Academy of Sciences, Washington DC

Committee on Geoengineering Climate 2015b *Climate Intervention: Reflecting Sunlight to Cool Earth* Committee on Geoengineering Climate: Technical Evaluation and Discussion of Impacts, National Academy of Sciences, Washington DC

Corry O 2014 Questioning the Plan-B framing of climate engineering: political feasibility and emergency measures Paper presented at the Climate Engineering Conference 2014 (CEC14) 18–21 August Berlin

Crutzen P 2006 Albedo enhancement by stratospheric sulfur injections: a contribution to resolve a policy dilemma? *Climatic Change* 77(3–4) 211–20

Davison A 2001 *Technology and the Contested Meanings of Sustainability* State University of New York Press, Albany NY

Doppelt G 2001 What sort of ethics does technology require? *Journal of Ethics* 5(2) 155–75

Environmental Pollution Panel 1965 *Restoring the Quality of Our Environment* The White House, Washington DC

ETC Group 2010 *Geopiracy: The Case Against Geoengineering* Communiqué 103 ETC Group, Ottawa

FCEA 2015 Climate engineering timeline Forum for Climate Engineering Assessment (http://dcgeoconsortium.org/climate-geoengineering-timeline) accessed 15 May 2015

Feenberg A 1991 *Critical Theory of Technology* Oxford University Press, New York

Feenberg A 1999 *Questioning Technology* Routledge, London

Fuss S, Canadell J G, Peters G P, Tavoni M, Andrew R M, Ciais P, Jackson R B, Jones C D, Kraxner F, Nakicenovic N, Le Quéré C, Raupach M R, Sharifi A, Smith P and Yamagata Y 2014 Betting on negative emissions *Nature Climate Change* 4 850–53

Hulme M 2008 The conquering of climate: discourses of fear and their dissolution *The Geographical Journal* 174(1) 5–16

IPCC 2014 *Mitigation of Climate Change: Contribution of Working Group III to the Fifth Assessment Report of the Intergovernmental Panel on Climate Change* Cambridge University Press, Cambridge

Kaufmanna R K, Kauppi H, Mann M L and Stock J H 2011 Reconciling anthropogenic climate change with observed temperature 1998–2008 *Proceedings of the National Academy of Sciences* 108(29) 11790–93

Keith D 2013 *A Case for Climate Engineering* MIT Press, Cambridge MA

Kreuter J 2015 *Technofix, Plan B or Ultima Ratio? A Review of the Social Science Literature on Climate Engineering Technologies* Institute for Science, Innovation and Society Working Paper Series Oxford University, Oxford

MacCracken M C, Shin H-J, Caldeira K and Ban-Weiss G A 2013 Climate response to imposed solar radiation reductions in high latitudes *Earth System Dynamics* 4 301–15

McDonough W and Braungart M 2002 *Cradle to Cradle: Remaking the Way We Make Things* North Point Press, New York

Nicholson S 2013 The promises and perils of geoengineering in Assadourian E *State of the World 2013: Is Sustainability Still Possible?* Island Press, Washington DC 317–31

Nordhaus T and Shellenberger M 2011 Evolve *Orion* 2 (https://orionmagazine.org/article/evolve)

Olson R 2012 Soft geoengineering: a gentler approach to addressing climate change *Environment* 54(5) 29–39

Olson R 2014 *A Venture into Geoengineering* Forum for Climate Engineering Assessment, Washington DC

Robock A, Marquardt A, Kravitz B and Stenchikov G 2009 Benefits, risks, and costs of stratospheric geoengineering *Geophysical Research Letters* 36(19) L19703

Royal Society 2009 *Geoengineering the Climate: Science, Governance and Uncertainty* Royal Society, London

Self S 2006 The effects and consequences of very large explosive volcanic eruptions *Philosophical Transactions A* 364(1845) 2073–2097

Victor D 2008 On the regulation of geoengineering *Oxford Review of Economic Policy* 24(2) 322–36

Winner L 1986 *The Whale and the Reactor: A Search for Limits in an Age of High Technology* University of Chicago Press, Chicago IL

8 Climate of the poor

Suffering and the moral imperative to reimagine resilience

Paul Wapner

In the early 1990s, politicians, scientists, and environmental activists debated the merits of adaptation as a strategy for responding to climate change. Proponents argued that measures like building seawalls, burying electric lines, and developing drought resistant crops were essential to accommodate ourselves to a warmer future. To do otherwise was irresponsible. In contrast, critics feared that adaptation would be a dangerous distraction. They argued that adaptation might provide a false sense of security and thus possibly undermine mitigation efforts. In their view, adaptation was the height of irresponsibility as it represented surrender to a climate changed world (Gore 1992; Revkin 2002). In economic language, adaptation represented a "moral hazard."

Despite heated debate, within only a few years, the critical voices grew silent as meteorological events rendered their viewpoints anachronistic. A string of record-breaking temperatures, devastating storms, rapidly melting ice caps, and untimely droughts across the globe made clear that the opening chapters of the climate age were upon us and thus it would be unethical and reckless not to take action to minimize the harm global warming was bringing in its wake. By the time the Intergovernmental Panel on Climate Change (IPCC) published its third assessment in 2007, the matter was settled. In no uncertain terms, the IPCC called for aggressive adaptation measures in addition to mitigation efforts (IPCC 2007). It recognized that we had entered a new phase: climate change was not a future possibility but a present reality whose effects could no longer be avoided.

In this chapter I suggest that we are in the opening chapters of a third phase of climate change, one that requires us to move beyond not just mitigation but also adaptation – two mechanisms at the core of Climate Inc. This third phase recognizes that no matter how much we mitigate and adapt to climate change, the world has pumped so much carbon into the atmosphere that irreversible, punishing climate change is inescapable. Thus, we no longer have the luxury of trying only to avoid or minimize the effects of climate change; we now have to learn how to live in a warmer world. And key to this involves learning how to live necessarily with widespread suffering. Today, tens of thousands of people and untold other species are having their lives ripped out from under them because of climate change and we know that this will only get worse. Climate Inc., which focuses fundamentally on a combination of mitigation and adaptation strategies, remains largely silent about widespread suffering. It assumes that we can dodge, one way or another, the climate bullet. It ignores the reality of having to live with pervasive pain.

What does it mean to live with widespread climate suffering? Can the world respond meaningfully to it? If so, what would such a response look like and how would it fit into broader local, national, and international strategies to address climate change? This chapter explores the politics of climate suffering. At its core, it seeks to find an appropriate response to climate hardship. Mitigation was a response to the buildup of greenhouse gases. Adaptation was a response to an inability to reduce atmospheric carbon concentrations. What is the proper response to suffering? Is there a promising policy measure or orientation appropriate for the current age of widespread climate hardship?

In the pages that follow, I advance the idea of "radical resilience" as a meaningful rejoinder. Resilience usually means the ability to withstand exogenous assaults and bounce back to pre-existing conditions. With regard to climate change, it conventionally involves building nimble structures and communities that can withstand climate assaults and return to a semblance of the status quo. In contrast, *radical* resilience eschews the status quo. It sees the existing conditions as the cause or at least intensifier of widespread climate suffering and thus seeks to transform it. Put differently, radical resilience places suffering at the center of its considerations and employs it as a tool for both analyzing and prescribing ways to respond to climate challenges. This chapter argues for reimagining climate change by going beyond Climate Inc.'s commitment to mitigation and adaptation and adding radical resilience to the menu of policy choices.

Climate change and suffering

Today, global average temperatures are higher than they have been in 4,000 years and every ecosystem is showing signs of climate stress. Everything on earth that is frozen is melting; historic droughts are drying up essential agricultural lands; floods due to rising sea levels and ocean surges are inundating previously protected cities; biodiversity is plummeting as ecotones shift toward the poles; and intensifying storms are tearing apart houses, businesses, and electrical grids. We have become familiar with this litany of climate calamities as it now represents the horizon within which we live. Indeed, climate change is a system-altering phenomenon that is throwing entire organic and human infrastructures out of whack. Mitigation and adaptation efforts – the core strategies for responding to climate change for the last two decades – have reached their limits. It is clear that climate change consequences cannot easily be prevented or prepared for. We have entered a new phase of climate change that demands strategies that transcend attempts to stop or simply adjust to a warmer world.

In 1997, in what is now considered the first phase of the Kyoto Protocol, countries agreed to reduce their greenhouse gas emissions by 5 percent below 1990 levels (this was considered simply an opening bid toward mitigation since scientists called for reductions of 80 percent below 1990 levels to stabilize the climate; Gupta *et al.* 2007, 776). Over the past two decades, initiatives have expanded the use of renewables like wind, solar, and hydroelectric and the greater use of more traditional fuels like nuclear power and natural gas has led to significant energy intensity reductions for some countries and actual emissions reductions in others (Clark 2012). Furthermore, the 2015 Paris meetings represented another major commitment as countries went on record to reduce greenhouse gas emissions by sizeable amounts. Despite such efforts and pledges, mitigation has done little to alter climate change's trajectory and shows little sign of being able to do so given even the most forward looking commitments to date. When Kyoto was signed, world CO_2 emissions stood at 24.4 billion tons. Today, they stand at 34 billion tons (USEPA 2015). Kyoto and its aftermath have done little to slow world carbon emissions. Furthermore, having agreed in Copenhagen in 2009 to ensure that global temperatures should not rise more than 2° Celsius – a figure that was widely seen as the absolute maximum to avoid the most devastating ecological feedbacks – countries are increasingly recognizing that within the context of current political and economic realities even this target may no longer be an option.

Adaptation efforts are harder to measure but provide little additional comfort. Individual countries have invested in information technologies aimed at predicting severe weather events and assessing the vulnerability of large-scale energy, water, and food systems. Additionally, some states have made actual infrastructural adjustments to accommodate increased flooding and more intensified storms, and mandated that local governing bodies establish emergency response capabilities. At the global level, the United Nations has established a number of funds to finance adaptation and every significant international negotiation related to climate change addresses adaptation to some degree. Such efforts specifically target least developed countries (UNFCCC 2014; Climate Funds Update undated; Adaptation Fund Board 2013, 28). Notwithstanding such efforts, adaptation protects a precious few from the ravages of stronger storms, longer droughts, and higher temperatures. Not only have the poor or otherwise marginalized been left out of most adaptation considerations, the entire effort has yet to be scaled up to enable much of humanity to dodge the disasters associated with climate change, and there are serious questions about whether adaptation can ever reach a globally meaningful scale.

The shortcomings of mitigation and adaptation make clear that we have entered a new phase of climate change. Environmental intensification is now a way of life. We can keep telling ourselves that the climate will some-how stabilize if we can simply double down on our Climate Inc. efforts by mitigating more or putting in place more adequate and abundant adapta-tion measures. But this ignores what is happening before our eyes. We are living in a climate changed and changing world. It is too late to stop accel-erating change and to evade widespread hardship for the current as well as future generations – at least within any reasonable timeframe. Along with our mitigation and adaptation efforts that aim at stopping or avoiding climate pain, we must also adopt ways of confronting climate suffering.

The (under) study of climate suffering

To date, policymakers, scholars, activists, and others have largely ignored climate suffering. To be sure, they have reported anecdotes from the front-lines of climate hardship and have rehearsed the litany of climate dangers (as I have done above). But they have not taken seriously the reality of climate pain and have thus left it under-analyzed and under-theorized. This is partly because researchers have failed to notice the political dimension of suffering. They have seen suffering as a residual category – something that happens *after* political efforts are already expended. Put differently, climate suffering is simply what happens when mitigation and adaptation fail. First we try to mitigate climate change; then we try to adapt to those changes we cannot avoid; finally, we simply suffer. Suffering, as such, is merely the last, unavoidable experience in a line of human effort. Thus, it lacks political definition insofar as power relations seem to be out of the picture and there is little collectively to be done about it.

Most of us tend to think of climate hardship as a homogeneous experi-ence. Catastrophes like Katrina and Sandy, the heat waves that have ravaged Europe and more recently India, the intensified flooding that has inundated the Philippines, and the punishing droughts that have devastated Australia in recent years seem to hit people equally. They do not discrimi-nate between income levels, cultures, race, or varied political systems. If you are in the eye of the storm or the belly of the drought zone, you are affected. Period. The homogeneous quality of the experience suggests that questions of power and sociological distinctions – which are clearly relevant for addressing mitigation and adaptation responsibilities – are inappropriate for making sense of climate suffering. There is no politics for that which affects people equally.

This orientation comes from seeing the effects of climate change simply as biophysical facts of life. Humans may be the cause of climate change – and, indeed, some are more implicated than others – but people have no influence over the ecological dynamics once the process is underway and thus over who will be affected and to what degree. Climate change, in this sense, plays no favorites. It is a matter of indifferent bio-chemical mechan-ics. The anonymous character pushes politics further into the background insofar as it then renders the sensed experience of hardship a matter of individuality. That is to say, while the cause of climate hardship arises out of public circumstances, once the effects land on the body, etch into the mind, or stir the emotions, they enter a private space often seen as inaccessible to political analysis and response.

Such an understanding blinds itself to the widespread evidence showing how the poor and the politically weak are disproportionately on the receiving end of climate change. The poor and disadvantaged not only tend to live on the most fragile land, in the most tenuous shelters, and among the thinnest of official safety networks; they also have the least amount of resources to deploy in adjusting to changed conditions. For the poorest of the poor, life is often a struggle to secure basic needs. As Paul Farmer writes, the most impoverished have only a tenuous "hold on survival" (Farmer 1997, 262). For the less destitute, poverty involves a dearth of capabilities and a narrowly circumscribed spectrum of life chances (Sen 1999; Nussbaum and Sen 1993). This makes the poor the most defenseless against and susceptible to climate suffering. Indeed, almost every instance of weather-related tragedies even mildly associated with climate change – for example, hurricane Sandy in the US, Typhoon Haiyan in the Philippines, and the flooding of Bhola Island in Bangladesh – found the poor disproportionately affected (World Meteorological Organization 2006; Parenti 2011; UNDP 2014). The poor are the least able to evacuate threatened and then ravaged areas, the last to receive sustained relief, and the least able to rebuild the physical circumstances of their lives after catastrophe strikes. This fits a broader pattern of environmental injustice and reminds us that climate suffering is not some private, individualized, idiosyncratic experience that just happens to accompany climate change, but a political reality in which power determines the socio-economic pattern of environmental pain (Bullard 1999, 2005; Lerner 2012).

The political aspect of climate suffering comes into even sharper relief when one notices that the emotional and intellectual experiences of climate hardship result not simply from geographical or exogenous biophysical forces or even patterns of collective experience, but include the social construction of people's interior landscape. As Kleinman, Das, and Lock point out, suffering takes place in "nested contexts of embodiment" that partly determine the felt quality of one's physical and existential experience (Kleinman *et al.* 1997, xix). Through media representations of climate suffering, mobilization of different forms of emergency response, and institutional requirements for refugee status, medical attention, and financial restitution, the actual experience of climate suffering itself is politically and socially framed. Discourses of climate hardship instrumentalize one's inner experience. For instance, today people understand themselves as climate "refugees," "insurance beneficiaries," and/or "victims" based on social categories of climate disaster that are driven and perpetuated by the current regime of Climate Inc.

The absence of scholarly and policy attention to climate suffering has not only left the politics of climate hardship un-analyzed, it has also helped fuel the de-politicization of climate policies and response strategies. Ghettoized into the private sphere and understood as merely an idiosyncratic reaction to a natural phenomenon, suffering is not about structures of power or politics per se but matters of medical and emergency response. As such, it involves solely the somatic and psychological dimensions of enduring hardship.

This is why, as I argue, mitigation and adaptation are incomplete as strategies for addressing climate change. Aimed at preventing climate suffering, they are speechless in response to climate pain once it inevitably arrives. That is, they each aim to avoid or minimize the experience of climate hardship to a degree that they then offer no insight into how to soldier or otherwise live through the physical, emotional, and intellectual pain of climate suffering.

Radical resilience

Radical resilience recognizes and embraces the political dimensions of climate suffering. It deliberately interprets climate pain through political categories and seeks to identify opportunities to transform current ways of life, social conditions, and political arrangements that drive climate change and splice humanity into haves and have-nots such that people unjustly experience fundamentally different degrees of climate hardship.

Mitigation and adaptation seek to preserve the status quo. Mitigation does so by defining climate change as an emissions problem and working to reduce and eventually stop the buildup of greenhouse gas concentrations in the atmosphere. Its aim, in other words, is not social or political change per se but mechanical. If we moved to a post-carbon world through some technological innovation, market adjustment, or incremental behavioral change that did not alter structures of power, mitigation would be a success. It implicitly values the status quo of our carbon world and seeks to preserve it by solving a specific problem. Climate change is not a civilizational or fundamentally political challenge rather it is a circumscribed mechanistic dilemma in need of a bounded solution.

Likewise, adaptation preserves the status quo by mimicking it. Measures like erecting sea walls, genetically modifying crops to withstand enduring droughts, and changing regulatory codes so buildings can tolerate excessive heat or punishing storms, for instance, act as accouterments to existing socio-political and economic conditions rather than as transformative agents. In fact, they specifically work to maintain existing systems by blunting or accommodating the most painful and potentially damaging climate assaults. Furthermore, as a number of authors have observed, most adaptation schemes seek not merely to protect current power relations but deepen them (Adams 2013; Klein 2014, 8–9). As corporations position themselves to be the providers of "climate ready crops" and private security services benefit from offering at-risk police services and infrastructures, the power relations of Climate Inc. are perpetuated rather than challenged and altered. Adaptation, in other words, simply grafts accommodations onto contemporary societies rather than leverage widespread change.

Such adjustment is part of even the most forward-looking form of adaptation, namely, resilience. As it is conventionally understood, resilience implies the ability to withstand exogenous assault and bounce back to a pre-existing state of affairs. Many liken it to a reed that can maintain integrity by bending with the wind without snapping. In the context of climate change, resilience refers to the ability of infrastructures and institutions to endure flooding, extreme temperatures, intensified storms, and so forth. In this sense it is the conceptual foundation of adaptation. Today, engineers are designing steel to bend with higher winds and asphalt to expand and contract with extreme temperatures. Pharmacologists are developing medicines and vaccines to protect farm animals from climate-induced, vector-borne diseases. Communities are producing more products locally to withstand the dislocations associated with extreme weather. In such cases, the idea is to create more nimble systems that can absorb climate effects and bounce back. According to Walker and Salt, climate resilience is the "capacity to experience shocks while retaining the same function, structure and identity – without shifting to a new regime" (Walker and Salt 2006, cited in Goldstein 2012, 129). It involves being able to "absorb perturbations without being undermined" (Randolph 2012, 129), or receive an exogenous jolt and return to preexisting conditions. As the 2013 draft National Climate Assessment puts it, resilience is the "capability to anticipate, prepare for, respond to, and *recover* from significant multi-hazard threats with minimum damage to social well-being, the economy and the environment" (NCADAC 2013, 985; emphasis added).

Conventional understandings of resilience are important for orienting adaptation strategies but are incomplete when thinking about climate change in general. This is where *radical* resilience comes in. Radical resilience takes the concept of nimbleness further by adding a sense in which one does not simply bend and then recover or return to preexisting conditions, but evolves into a new set of conditions. It entails transitioning from one state of affairs to another. Radical resilience is akin to Nassim Taleb's notion of "antifragile" (Taleb 2012). For Taleb, antifragility is a state in which things gain from disorder or, put differently, thrive through disruption and pressure. It is about learning, adjusting, and transforming. According to Taleb, antifragility involves absorbing shocks not to bounce back to a pre-existing state, but to get better.

There is an incipient literature focused on this more radical notion of resilience. It recognizes that nimbleness can actually, ironically, postpone necessary changes that can advance widespread and long-term protection against climate change. Focused less on technological capability and emergency response, it emphasizes things like community learning, building capacity among previously neglected groups, constructing networks for collaboration, embracing uncertainty, and sharing stories of vulnerability to generate social mobilization (Zellner *et al.* 2012; Randolph 2012). This literature implicitly seeks the alteration of existing power relations since power structures tend to resist rather than advance change. From a different angle, the literature celebrates the possibility of new virtues arising that can breed greater compassion and concern for the less fortunate and pave the way for meaningful socio-economic and political change (Thompson and Bendik-Keymer 2012). Although it does not use the phrase, this literature provides a ground for appreciating radical resilience and its appropriateness as a response to climate suffering.

Taking suffering seriously

Radical resilience contravenes Climate Inc. in that it understands and honors the political dimensions of climate suffering and uses this understanding to craft more transformative responses to climate change. There is no question that suffering is a consequence of climate change. It happens as temperatures soar, oceans rise, and storms strengthen, and people and other creatures endure the negative consequences. Radical resilience recognizes how politics comes into play in defining and treating victims of climate suffering (as discussed above) and, in taking this seriously, devises responses that aim to shift the power relations having to do with the lived experience of climate pain. Radical resilience also, however, takes seriously the suffering that precedes and actually produces climate change in the first place. It notices how existing economic, political, and cultural systems that fuel climate change generate widespread pain across various social strata. They create and perpetuate severe inequalities, exploitations, and injustices that are simply part of contemporary collective life. In this sense, radical resilience sees climate travails not simply as the result of an alteration in the status quo (i.e. climate change) but a function *of* the status quo. That is, climate suffering is not some effect emerging from a beneficent system, but the expression of an unjust and exploitative system. Far from resulting solely *from* climate change, suffering also fundamentally *drives* it. Climate change is the atmospheric expression of a system of suffering.

In her most recent book, Naomi Klein helps explain this wider view of suffering. She does so through her description of contemporary societies as "extractive." According to Klein, extractivism is a resource-depleting model of economic growth and development employed by governments across the ideological spectrum wherein the earth and its people are treated as objects to be used rather than honored, nurtured, or embraced:

> Extractivism is a nonreciprocal, dominance-based relationship with the earth, one purely of taking. It is the opposite of stewardship, which involves taking but also taking care that regeneration and future life

continue. Extractivism is the mentality of the mountaintop remover and the old-growth clear-cutter. It is the reduction of life into objects for the use of others, giving them no integrity or value of their own – turning living complex ecosystems into "natural resources," mountains into "overburden" (as the mining industry terms the forests, rocks, and streams that get in the way of its bulldozers). It is also the reduction of human beings either into labor to be brutally extracted, pushed beyond limits, or, alternatively, into social burden, problems to be locked out at borders and locked away in prisons and reservations. In an extractivist economy, the interconnections among these various objectified components of life are ignored; the consequences of severing them are of no concern.

(Klein 2014, 169)

Extractivism, thus understood, is the ultimate form of exploitation. It marginalizes people, renders the nonhuman world as ontologically inferior, and objectifies life so that the powerful can perpetuate and systematize legal, cultural, economic, and political conditions of privilege.

Extractivism and its violences and injustices sit at the center of climate change. All along the climate change chain – excavation, processing, transportation, and the burning of fossil fuels as well as the buildup of atmospheric carbon concentrations – one finds debasement. Take mining. Many people near coalmines, oil refineries, or hydraulic fracturing facilities are living with contaminated water, polluted air, and despoiled landscapes, while distant others enjoy the advantages produced by such hardship. In these cases, the privileged displace the costs and burdens of fossil fuel use to those who are too poor or otherwise political weak to avoid such pain. At work is not simply the machinations of market economics but the moral arrogance of belittling those who live downstream. The same pattern pertains to the burning of fossil fuels. Not only are most coal burning plants, oil refineries, and natural gas facilities far from affluent neighborhoods, but, as mentioned, the poor disproportionately experience severe climate effects. Living on fragile lands and in substandard structures and lacking the means to protect themselves from climate-related incidents, the poor are implicitly on the receiving end of the buildup of CO_2 concentrations in the atmosphere.

One sees this, by the way, not only within certain countries but also between them. For instance, Nepal has contributed virtually nothing to current climate challenges. Almost all its power is hydroelectric or biomass and its per capita energy use is, relative to other countries, infinitesimal. With 60 percent of its people living on less than two dollars a day, a tenuous system of rain-fed agriculture, and a typography that has many living on fragile lands, Nepal is the fourth most vulnerable country to climate disruptions (Maplecroft 2010). In recent years, the country has been ravaged by landslides and mountain flooding (including glacier lake outbursts) due to erratic and powerful rains, scorching heat and droughts in the plains, and intensified storms that have weakened and, in many cases, crippled much of its infrastructure – conditions that many associate with climate change (see, for example, Yang 2013). Nepal is the victim of a climate extractive mindset (Wapner 2014).

Extractivism is not simply about taking from the poor and politically weak, it also involves robbing future generations. Fossil fuel reserves build up over geologic time yet the world is using them at breakneck speed with little regard about their availability to future generations. To be sure, warnings about peak oil were certainly exaggerated but it is clear that fossil fuels are, for all intents and purposes, finite. At some point in time – and it will certainly be after the world experiences runaway climate change – oil, gas, and coal reserves will tap out. Using them in such profligate ways and in such enormous amounts is to unfairly extract them from future generations.

The same pattern, of course, holds for greenhouse gas emissions. Climate change is already being felt throughout the world but we know that current droughts, floods, and so forth only harbingers of a warmer world. As emissions continue to rise, successive generations will be on the receiving end of intensified, climate-related disasters. By choosing to burn fossil fuels (and cut down trees, graze cattle, and so on) present generations are making the choice to enjoy associated benefits while transferring costs across time to future generations. They are mining the future.

Climate extraction hurts not simply people but also the more-than-human world. Mining fossil fuels rips apart landscapes, pollutes waterways, and thus literally destroys habitat for plants and animals. Even the most environmentally sensitive quarrying degrades air, water, and soil. Extractivism takes its toll deep into the earth's crust, far across its oceans, high into its skies, and into the very membranes of living beings that must suffer contamination from the mining and burning of fossil fuels. Climate extraction also includes deforestation not only because forests must be cleared to locate, remove, and transport shale oil, tar sands, and natural gas, but also because deforestation releases roughly 3 billion tons of carbon into the atmosphere each year and thus is part of the climate extractivist complex (Union of Concerned Scientists undated). Like those humans living downstream from climate extractivist practices, nature is silent in its suffering. The production of climate change fundamentally involves power as an anthropocentric mindset encourages humanity to treat nature with abandon.

Politics operates not only at the causal end of climate hardship for the more-than-human world but also, as should be obvious, in the consequences. Hotter temperatures, changes in humidity, and newly emerging seasonal fluctuations are shifting biomes across the planet and undermining the ecological base of many creatures. To be sure, some animals and plants can migrate across ecosystems in search of accommodating conditions. But many others lack mobility and most are unable to cross highways, cities, and other manufactured features of the human-changed landscape. In fact, many now identify climate change as a primary cause of species extinction and this represents a further example of extractive practice (CHGE undated; Convention on Biological Diversity undated).

Nonhuman species and those people most vulnerable to displacement across time and space share the same status and condition. They are the voiceless, poor, politically powerless, and disregarded of the world – the "global residuum," as Mike Davis (2006) puts it. Future generations, for instance, do not vote, buy and sell goods, or otherwise lodge public preferences. Likewise, the marginalized, from whom industries grab resources and who lack material protection, have little influence on public affairs. In fact, they are usually the victims of other people's decisions. And of course nonhuman creatures not only find themselves undeserving of moral worth but also lack the capacity for political expression. In all three cases, power differentials structure relationships and assume patterns of injustice. The most disturbing thing is that these patterns, which reveal climate inequality, are not unique to fossil fuels or even environmental issues in general. They are part of, and in fact intimately constitute, the contemporary world (Wapner and Matthew 2009).

Climate Inc., with mitigation and adaptation as its poster children, is either blind to or, for convenience sake, ignores contemporary societal injustices and hardships. This is unsurprising given its circumscribed aim to focus on climate protection but it also indicates how deeply extractivism and suffering are woven into contemporary regimes. Power differentials and widespread pain are often hidden from view. They are part of, what Edward Said calls, the "normalized quiet of unseen power" (Said 2001, quoted in Nixon 2011, 34). This correlates with Galtung's (1969) notion of structural violence or, more recently, Nixon's (2011) understanding of slow violence. According to Nixon, slow violence is "violence [that] is neither spectacular nor instantaneous, but rather incremental and accretive, its calamitous repercussions playing out across a range of temporal scales" (Nixon 2011, 2). This is exactly what is happening as the privileged and underprivileged go about their lives often unaware of the accretive brutality that courses through and imprints itself upon the very bodies of those living (or soon to be living) downstream.

Mitigation and adaptation miss this wider, more intimate type of violence and therefore suffering. So focused on the legitimate horrors of climate change, they ignore the pervasive repulsions of contemporary life that produce climate change in the first place and that mark the lives of those living on the frontlines of climate intensification. Mitigation and adaptation, as insurers of the status quo, have little room to consider, let alone respond effectively to, climate suffering. Suffering remains a residual category invisible to Climate Inc. yet capable of harboring injustices that perpetuate the engines of climate change.

Toward climate justice

How does one move forward? How can one take climate suffering seriously and conscientiously respond? What does it mean to move beyond mitigation and adaptation? Is there really any responsible place beyond efforts to avoid or adjust to climate change? Here is where radical resilience comes in. Radical resilience offers a trajectory that questions Climate Inc. It provides a way to address the injustices that give rise to and are produced by climate change. In this last section, I would like to provide a few examples of radical resilience with the aim of showing that climate suffering need not be left out of political analysis and action but can meaningfully direct efforts. I should mention at the outset that the following examples are merely illustrative not empirically uncontestable or conceptually airtight. The hope, however, is that they can provide some sense of how the imagination can help move us beyond Climate Inc.

The first example has to do with using radical resilience to distinguish between technological choices. Many people have been advocating for nuclear power as a substitute for fossil fuels. Nuclear energy emits no greenhouse gases and is thus seen as a partial answer to our climate woes. A number of countries rely heavily on nuclear power and the nuclear option represents a promising direction for countries seeking to reduce their reliance on fossil fuels. What does radical resilience offer for thinking about nuclear power?

Radical resilience, remember, aims at transformation. It responds to exogenous pressures not by resisting change or bending with force and then working to aright itself, but by capitalizing on outside pressures to establish better conditions. Radical resilience in the context of climate change involves building communities that can absorb and bend with climate shocks with the aim of creating conditions more amenable to addressing climate suffering. Nuclear energy largely fails the test of radical resilience since it requires hard technologies operated by centralized entities and thus does little to change existing power relations. Nuclear energy keeps in place the inequalities and perpetuates the injustices associated with the systems that brought us climate change in the first place and does nothing to alter those societal hierarchies that sustain exploitative practices. To be sure, nuclear energy represents a form of mitigation, in that it reduces carbon emissions, and offers a way of moving to a post-carbon economy. But, without the ability to transform broader power relations and operating by mining uranium, it accentuates the extractivist mindset. It fails to open up genuinely new trajectories toward a future of significantly less suffering.

In contrast, consider solar energy. Unlike nuclear power, solar energy illustrates a type of radical resilience. Solar energy uses soft technologies and, most importantly, promises to decentralize energy production and use. It potentially can break up concentrations of economic power and make people less beholden to large energy companies that are fundamentally committed to selling fuel. Unlike coal, oil, and gas reserves, the sun shines everywhere. Potentially, anyone can utilize its energy. To be sure, solar technology is presently expensive and thus embracing solar in the short-term accentuates structures of economic power. However, this is beginning to change and there is nothing necessary about capturing solar energy that requires concentrations of political and economic power. The price of solar energy has dropped significantly over the past few decades (solar energy costs went from US$76.67 per watt in 1977 to US$0.613 per watt in 2013; Clean Technica 2014). Additionally, millions of villages in the least developed parts of the world are adopting some type of inexpensive, photovoltaic or solar water heating system each year (McDonnell 2014). Below the radar of price and numbers of users, solar has distributional potential in that consumers need not rely on external providers but become their own generators of energy. In this sense, solar plays a key part today in, what is called, "distributed energy" – off-grid, small-scale devices that can provide electricity and, sometimes, thermal energy, directly to consumers (USDE undated).

Aside from being carbon-free in its operation and decentralizing in terms of power distribution, solar also represents a step away from an extractivist mentality. We no longer need to reach into the earth and steal its fossilized life or uranium deposits but can cultivate a reciprocal relationship with the endless renewable capacity of the sun. Solar is not about purely taking, as Klein would say, but involves stewardship in that it harmonizes with rather than lording over ecosystemic dynamics. It is a form of radical resilience because it is building an ability to adapt to a post-carbon future through means that promise to transform contemporary power relations. While imperfect, the introduction of solar can reduce suffering by contributing less to climate change and offering individuals and communities the ability to take greater control over energy production and use by localizing power generation.

A second example contrasts radical resilience with adaptation (recognizing that resilience is a form of adaptation). Recently, scientists have been calling for more research into and some piloting of geoengineering schemes. Geoengineering involves altering the biophysics of the planet to blunt the harmful effects of global warming. Ideas include pumping sulfates into the atmosphere to scatter sunlight and thus reduce the amount of heat hitting the planet, introducing sunshades to reflect sunlight, fertilizing the oceans with iron to grow more phytoplankton that would absorb CO_2, and capturing and sequestering carbon. These may sound fantastical and even, to some, desirable. But we should recognize that geoengineering is not about reducing emissions or otherwise calling for changing current behavior. Rather, it promises that society can continue on its fossil fueled path without having to endure rising temperatures. Moreover, many of its proponents tell us that it is cheap. Geoengineering promises to moderate temperatures at a fraction of the financial costs of most large-scale mitigation measures.

(To be sure, advocates always say that geoengineering should not replace efforts to reduce emissions and that it is only a "last resort," but one should recognize the fundamental distinction between trying to solve climate change and simply postponing it [see Chapter 7, this volume]).

Geoengineering is a type of adaptation insofar as it promises to accommodate us to an increasingly carbon rich world. It offers a technological response that can blunt the experiential effects of climate change even if the biophysical mechanisms are still at work. The problem with geoengineering, from the perspective of climate suffering, is that it offers nothing in the way of transformative leverage. Existing power relations can remain intact; fossil fuel companies need not alter their portfolios or otherwise switch practices; the poor will continue to be poor and experience the hardships of slow violence. Geoengineering, in other words, simply extends the status quo and remains tone deaf to the suffering laced through contemporary systems and ripe for alteration in a climate age.

In contrast to geoengineering, aid to the developing countries represents an alternative adaptive response and, since it has the potential to alter power relations, is closer to a form of radical resilience. Ever since developing countries called for a New Economic Order, the world has clearly understood the devastating effects of global economic inequality. Colonial strictures established imperialist relations and the North performed sustained extraction on the South. (This is not to say, of course, that all of the South's problems – even all its economic ones – stem from Northern exploitative economic practices. It simply recognizes how the modern world economy established itself on core-periphery relations based on an extractive mindset.) Development aid can transform this relationship. If done fairly and sensitively – rather than using development aid as another tool to deepen dependency – it has the potential to empower the South to take more control over its destiny, democratize its regimes, and otherwise alter relations of power such that extraction need not continue. Furthermore, it has the potential to do this while it is helping poorer nations withstand the worst effects of climate change. Adaptive development aid is not your typical "build higher sea walls." Rather, it infuses the developing world with climate-associated capacity and thereby uses climate change as an opportunity to reduce the suffering that accompanies severe economic inequality, alter life chances throughout the world, and shift geopolitical power imbalances.

These examples point to a final promise of radical resilience. Throughout this chapter, I have discussed radical resilience as an alternative or at least add-on to mitigation and adaptation. I introduced it as a way to address climate suffering and thus distinguished it from the two other approaches that simply see suffering as a residual consequence of failed mitigation and adaptation. Such distinction, while analytically useful, is conceptually and practically imprecise. Climate suffering is not a residual category that comes after mitigation and adaptation. Rather, it fundamentally influences the other two. How people experience or imagine climate suffering will have a tremendous impact on their commitment to and choice of mitigation and adaptation strategies. Put differently, how people live through the traumas of climate intensification not only determines the quality of their pain, but also influences their attitudes toward mitigation and adaptation. Indeed climate suffering is already sending people in different mitigation and adaptation directions.

For some people and states the experience or specter of climate hardship appears so traumatic that it inspires them to pursue survivalist strategies. This involves walling themselves off from others in anticipation of food riots, waves of refugees, and collapsing infrastructure. Today, Chinese firms are buying up agricultural land in Africa, India is completing a containment wall along its Bangladesh border to stem climate refugees, and people throughout the developed world are investing in generators, water purification systems and even guns to insulate themselves from the expected chaos associated with climate change (Malley 2011; Brown 2009; Tidwell 2011). Such moves fit one strand of the social science and popular literature which suggests that collective hardship leads to competitive tendencies (see, for example, Friedman 2005; Nordhaus and Shellenberger 2007).

In other cases, the experience and fear of climate hardship is less frightening or at least leads to less desperate measures. In these instances, people and states are pursuing communal forms of adaptation aimed at building networks of care that seek collective rather than fragmentary experience. They are, to put it differently, choosing to throw in their lot with others, and live through climate change together. Today, countries like Norway, Sweden and Germany are integrating climate threats into overseas development aid to help others adapt to a changing climate (Briggs and VanDeveer 2011) and towns like Totnes, England, and Hardwich, Vermont are designing social structures of resilience to endure the worst effects of climate change as whole communities committed to perpetually pursuing greater equality and justice within and outside their borders (McKibben 2010; Transition Town Totnes 2011). Such efforts accord with an alternative social science literature that suggests people often become more benevolent and altruistic in the face of communal hardship (see, for example, Scary 2011; Solnit 2009).

The difference between these two reactions is not written in the nature of a singular climate experience but turns on how different people make sense of climate harm – how they interpret their own brushes with climate hardship, senses of vulnerability, and predictions about the future. By attending to such understandings and experiences of climate suffering, radical resilience is not simply a last resort measure aimed at ameliorating climate hardship – a kind of compensation for those living on the frontiers of climate suffering – but a transformative strategy that shapes the entire configuration of climate responses. Put differently, radical resilience can tip the balance between survivalist and cooperative mitigation and adaptation strategies. It can encourage more compassionate forms of mitigation and adaptation insofar as it offers the possibility of ushering in more just, humane conditions.

Conclusion

This chapter argues that mitigation and adaptation, as we conventionally understand and practice them, can no longer monopolize how we respond to climate change since we are now in the opening chapters of climate suffering. No matter how much we have tried hitherto to stop or avoid climate change or how much we intend to do so in the future, large numbers of people and untold species are already and will continue to suffer. I introduced the idea of radical resilience as a way to develop a political strategy that could speak meaningfully to this latest phase of climate reality and therewith reimagine our current regime of Climate Inc. If mitigation aims to address climate change as an emissions problem and adaptation works to minimize damage because so little mitigation progress has been made, radical resilience emerges as a response to climate suffering. It accepts climate hardship and embraces it as an opportunity to transform existing arrangements. In this sense, it seeks not to maintain or even slightly reform the status quo but, as the word radical implies, it works to alter the very roots of social, political, and economic conditions. It recognizes that suffering is both a consequence of climate change and, importantly, a cause. As mentioned, climate change is the atmospheric expression of a system of suffering. When we learn how to stop exploiting or extracting from each other (including from our relations of the more-than-human world), we will not only finally step onto the trail toward climate protection but will also make progress toward becoming more human.

References

Adams V 2013 *Markets of Sorrow, Labors of Faith: New Orleans in the Wake of Katrina* Duke University Press, Durham NC

Adaptation Fund Board 2013 *Report of the Nineteenth Meeting of the Adaptation Fund Board* AFB/B.19/6/Rev. 1. Adaptation Fund, Bonn (www.adaptation-fund.org/sites/default/files/AFB%2019%20Rev.1%20report.pdf) accessed 14 February 2015

Briggs C and VanDeveer S 2011 Europe, climate change, and inter-national security: transatlantic and global dimensions in Moran D ed *Climate Change and Regional Security* Georgetown University Press, Washington, DC 141–51

Brown L R 2009 *Plan B 4.0: Mobilizing to Save Civilization* W W Norton, New York

Bullard R 1999 Anatomy of environmental racism and the environmental justice movement in Bullard R *Confronting Environmental Racism: Voices from the Grassroots* South End Press, Cambridge MA 15–40

Bullard R 2005 Environmental justice in the 21st century in Bullard R ed *The Quest for Environmental Justice: Human Rights and Politics of Pollution* Sierra Club Books, San Francisco CA 19–42

CHGE undated Climate change and biodiversity loss (www.chgeharvard.org/topic/climate-change-and-biodiversity-loss) accessed 1 July 2015

Clark D 2012 Has the Kyoto protocol made any difference to carbon emissions? *The Guardian* Environment Blog 26 November (www.guardian.co.uk/environment/blog/2012/nov/26/kyoto-protocol-carbon-emissions) accessed 14 February 2015

Clean Technica 2014 13 charts on solar panel cost and growth trends 4 September (http://cleantechnica.com/2014/09/04/solar-panel-cost-trends-10-charts) accessed 1 July 2015

Climate Funds Update undated Adaptation fund (www.climatefundsupdate.org/listing/adaptation-fund) accessed 14 February 2015

Convention on Biological Diversity undated Climate change and biodiversity (www.cbd.int/climate) accessed 1 July 2015

Davis M 2006 *Planet of Slums: Sinister Paradise* Treason Press Pamphlets, Canberra

Farmer P 1997 On suffering and structural violence: a view from below in Kleinman A Das V and Lock M eds *Social Suffering* University of California Press, Berkeley CA 261–83

Friedman B M 2005 *The Moral Consequences of Economic Growth* Knopf, New York

Galtung J 1969 Violence, peace, and peace research *Journal of Peace Research* 6(3) 167–91

Goldstein B E 2012 *Collaborative Resilience: Moving through Crisis to Opportunity* MIT Press, Cambridge MA

Gore A 1992 *Earth in the Balance: Ecology and the Human Spirit* Houghton Mifflin, Boston MA

Gupta S, Tirpak D A, Burger N, Gupta J, Höhne N, Boncheva A I, Kanoan G M, Kolstad C, Kruger J A, Michaelowa A, Murase S, Pershing J, Saijo T and Sari A 2007 Policies, instruments and co-operative arrangements in Metz B, Davidson O R, Bosch P R, Dave R and Meyer L A eds *Climate Change 2007: Mitigation. Contribution of Working Group III to the Fourth Assessment Report of the Intergovernmental Panel on Climate Change* Cambridge University Press, Cambridge 745–807

IPCC 2007 *Climate Change 2007: Impacts, Adaptation and Vulnerability. Contribution of Working Group II to the Fourth Assessment Report of the Intergovernmental Panel on Climate Change* Parry M L, Canziani O F, Palutikof J P, van der Linden P J and Hanson C E eds Cambridge University Press, Cambridge

Klein N 2014 *This Changes Everything: Capitalism versus the Climate* Simon and Schuster, New York

Kleinman A, Das V and Lock M 1997 Introduction in Kleinman A, Das V and Lock M eds *Social suffering* University of California Press, Berkeley CA ix–xxvii

Lerner S 2012 *Sacrifice Zones: The Front Lines of Toxic Chemical Exposure in the United States* MIT Press, Cambridge MA

Malley M 2011 Indonesia in Moran D ed *Climate Change and Regional Security* Georgetown University Press, Washington DC

Maplecroft 2010 Advisory services 21 October (http://maplecroft.com/about/news/ccvi.html) accessed 25 September 2014

McDonnell T 2014 There's a place in the world that is fighting poverty with solar power *Mother Jones* 15 September (www.motherjones.com/environment/

2014/09/these-tanzanian-villages-dont-have-plumbing-they-have-solar-power) accessed 1 July 2015

McKibben B 2010 *Earth: Making a Life on a Tough New Planet* Time Books, New York

NCADAC 2013 *Draft Climate Assessment Report* National Climate Assessment and Development Advisory Committee, Washington DC (http://ncadac.globalchange.gov) accessed 14 February 2015

Nixon R 2013 *Slow Violence and the Environmentalism of the Poor* Harvard University Press, Cambridge MA

Nordhaus T and Shellenberger M 2007 *Break Through: From the Death of Environmentalism to the Politics of Possibility* Houghton Mifflin, Boston MA

Nussbaun M and Sen A 1993 *The Quality of Life* Oxford University Press, New York

Parenti C 2011 *Tropic of Chaos: Climate Change and the New Geography of Violence* Nation Books, New York

Randolph J 2012 Creating the climate change resilient community in Goldstein B E ed *Collaborative Resilience: Moving through Crisis to Opportunity* MIT Press, Cambridge MA 127–48

Revkin A 2002 Climate talks shift focus to how to deal with changes *New York Times* 3 November

Scary E 2011 *Thinking in an Emergency* W W Norton, New York

Sen A 1999 *Development as Freedom* Oxford University Press, New York

Solnit R 2009 *A Paradise Built in Hell: The Extraordinary Communities that Arise in Disasters* Viking, New York

Taleb N 2012 *Antifragile: Things that Gain from Disorder* Random House, New York

Thompson A and Bendik-Keymer J eds 2012 *Ethical Adaptation to Climate Change: Human Virtues of the Future* MIT Press, Cambridge MA

Tidwell M 2011 Weathering the weather: a climate-change activist prepares for the worst *Washington Post* Opinions 26 February

Transition Town Totnes 2011 *Transition in Action: Totnes 2030: An Energy Descent Action Plan* Transition Town Totnes, Totnes

UNDP 2014 *Human Development Report 2014* United Nations Development Programme, New York (http://hdr.undp.org/en/2014-report/download) accessed 14 February 2015

UNFCCC 2014 *Focus: Adaptation* United Nations Framework Convention on Climate Change (http://unfccc.int/focus/adaptation/items/6999.php) accessed 14 February 2015

Union of Concerned Scientists undated Deforestation and global warming (www.ucsusa.org/global_warming/solutions/stop-deforestation/deforestation-global-warming-carbon-emissions.html#.VZMEK6bjZ_8) accessed 1 July 2015

USDE undated *Distributed Energy* Office of Electricity Delivery and Energy Reliability, United States Department of Energy (http://energy.gov/oe/technology-development/smart-grid/distributed-energy) accessed 2 July 2015

USEPA 2015 Global greenhouse gas emissions data United States Environmental Protection Agency, Washington DC (www.epa.gov/climatechange/ghgemissions/global.html) accessed 14 February 2015

Wapner P 2014 Climate suffering *Global Environmental Politics* 14(2) 1–6

Wapner P and Matthew R 2009 The humanity of global environmental ethics *Journal of Environment and Development* 18(2) spring 203–22

World Meteorological Organization 2006 *Statement on Tropical Cyclones and Climate Change* WMO International Workshop on Tropical Cyclones (IWTC-6) San Jose, Costa Rica (www.wmo.int/pages/prog/arep/tmrp/documents/iwtc_statement.pdf) accessed 14 February 2015

Yang L 2013 Power outage in Nepal reaches 14 hours per day *Xinhua* 19 January (http://news.xinhuanet.com/english/world/2013-01/19/c_132114071.htm) accessed 14 February 2015

Zellner M, Hoch C and Welch E 2012 Leaping forward: building resilience by communicating vulnerability in Goldstein B E *Collaborative Resilience: Moving through Crisis to Opportunity* MIT Press, Cambridge, MA 39–60

9 Reimagining radical climate justice

John Foran

Introduction

The science is not in question: climate change is here now, not in the future (IPCC 2013) and it is already having devastating effects on people's lives (IPCC 2014). That's the bad news, of course.

Even worse, the massive social, economic, and political inequalities already generated by neoliberal capitalism would seem to set the social and natural worlds on a collision course which the elites cannot win – even on their own terms – without destroying the basis for all human life. To put it bluntly, the climate crisis is perilous, our 500-year-old economic system cannot see us through it safely, the window for resolving this dilemma is closing inexorably, and the forces arrayed against our common survival are strong, *very* strong.

The good news is that there's a global climate justice movement that is growing in numbers, reach, strength, and inventiveness. This movement is impossible to encompass easily because it consists of literally thousands of organizations at every level – community, city, bio/region, nation, and the global – interlinked in a vast network of networks.[1] But it *is* here, and more crucially, represents a fundamental critique of business-as-usual global capitalism, what in this volume is referred to as Climate Inc. By placing justice at the center of climate change activism, it offers the possibility of addressing the root causes, rather than the symptomatic expressions, of climate change. Climate change is certainly a technological, economic, and governmental challenge but beyond this, and more fundamentally, it is a matter of widespread and deep injustice. From the mining of fossil fuels by low-paid workers performing dangerous tasks and the contamination that saturates extraction sites and power plants (usually visited upon the poor and politically marginalized), to the corporate encouragement of humanity's addiction to fossil fuels, the exploitation of the earth's commons, and the all-too-common pattern of having the most vulnerable suffer its most immediate and severe consequences, climate change exemplifies the exploitative character of contemporary structures of power. The climate justice movement aims to right these wrongs, and to dismantle and transform the discriminatory and exploitative features of contemporary collective life. The quality and very viability of the future of life on earth may very well turn on its ability to do so.

The global climate justice movement is growing steadily, but it is still far too weak to lead the broader environmental movement, let alone mount a counterhegemonic challenge to the existing structures of power – at least for the moment. The next few years are thus crucial for its ability to scale up and transform the trajectory of climate change politics. In this period, it will be asked to mount irresistible pressure of all kinds on governments and on the corporations, banks, and all the institutions of neoliberal capitalism that they serve. It must *force* them to take decisive steps such as a fair and binding global climate treaty and a deeply sustainable post-capitalist society free of structured violence and run democratically by the ninety-nine percent. To rise to the challenge, the climate justice movement must be reimagined as a radical, revolutionary movement that aims ultimately at transforming the global capitalist system and its political, cultural, and economic coordinates. The status quo – characterized by private profit-making, unequal access to well-being, militarism, pervasive economic exploitation, and slow violence – needs to be confronted with an alternative vision, a "new political culture of resistance and creation" (Foran 2014c; Ellis *et al.* forthcoming). The global climate justice movement can usher in such a culture and encourage such transformation, but only if it is able to popularize and radicalize its activism. The movement has certainly demonstrated promise to date but it must deepen its commitments to radical social change if it is to marshal sufficient political power in the service of climate protection and social justice. By promoting horizontalism rather than hierarchy, active hope and joy rather than militant sadness, and – most importantly – justice rather than short-term benefits, the movement can reimagine a system that overcomes the ravages of global capitalism and achieves not only the minimal imperative of staying below 2° Celsius but our common dream of creating just, democratic societies. It seems evident that we will need to assemble the greatest social movement the world has ever seen to achieve these ends.

The need for a radical climate justice movement

The need to radicalize the global climate justice movement rests on three observations. First, most mitigation and adaptation measures to date deepen the injustices that wrack the world. They rely on existing states and corporations to make small regulatory or engineering adjustments that remain tone-deaf to rampant inequality, exploitation, militarism, and other structural injustices. Indeed, they involve doubling down in an incremental effort to fine-tune the engines of the production and culture of consumption so as, at best, to reduce greenhouse gas emissions. They leave untouched broader and deeper causes that give rise to climate intensification in the first place and fuel its acceleration. Conventional responses especially ignore the abuse of the weak and vulnerable who live on the frontlines of climate disruption; implicitly disrespect future generations who will experience climate change's increasingly disastrous effects; accelerate the mistreatment of the other-than-human world through extraction, pollution, and dwindling habitats; and in the end simply perpetuate the injustices that characterize present-day social life. In light of this, the climate justice movement adds a crucial missing dimension to climate mitigation and adaptation. To become more influential, however, the movement has to move even further away from those established mitigation and adaptation measures that more often than not support reforms compatible with existing socio-economic arrangements. The striving for compatibility and acceptance of current norms is precisely what hinders Climate Inc. efforts. The global climate justice movement must offer more.

Second, in December 2015, the United Nations Framework Convention on Climate Change (UNFCCC) convenes the COP 21 meetings (the Conference of the Parties, in this case the twenty-first annual UN climate summit) in Paris to finalize the global climate treaty it has been working on for several years. The stated objective has always been to find ways to prevent earth from warming more than 2° Celsius, a target set by climate scientists more than a decade ago and agreed to by the governments of the world at COP 15 in Copenhagen in 2009 (it is now increasingly realized that the even more difficult target of 1.5° Celsius should be the Rubicon that must not be passed; see Anderson 2012 on the gravity of the situation). The treaty under negotiation may therefore represent one of the last best chances to contain the disruptive climate change that is coming our way and to preserve some dignity for individuals and societies. But every year that passes without action closes the vise more tightly on efforts to avert business-as-usual climate scenarios. The reason states cannot agree on international measures is their inability to appreciate how dealing with climate change is not simply a collective action problem or a technical challenge but fundamentally a matter of justice. Instead, the power of the corporations, banks, and free market-oriented private sector in general, so evident at the November 2013 COP 19 in Warsaw, has become that much greater.[2] The intense conflict between the interests of the global North and global South – with economic powerhouses China, India, and Brazil now lodged in between – remains as sharp and intractable as ever in a stand-off that makes the chances of finding pathways to a less than 2° Celsius world look vanishingly small.

Third, the fact that historically the initial efforts to address climate change came out of a white, middle-class, Northern environmental movement means they share the conceptual and political baggage of a centuries-old process of development that has systematically undermined the possibilities for social justice. Inspired in the US by the rise of environmental justice movements, the climate justice movement initially appeared as an external critique aimed at pushing environmentalism toward greater sensitivity for the poor and underprivileged. More recently, mainstream activist groups, think tanks, and other elements of the broader environmental movement have embraced the term as a meaningful and inspiring goal. This is certainly to be welcomed but should also induce caution. The global climate justice movement must work against being coopted lest it see its core value of social justice diluted. The weight of white, middle-class environmentalism is heavy and not easily dismissed. The climate justice movement can do this by embracing further the energy and conceptual insights of youth, the voices of the global South and the marginalized populations of the global North, and the participation of women and other oppressed genders in its ongoing efforts. Such measures are requirements for both justice and political success.

Until very recently, the broader climate movement has not taken justice seriously enough. That is, many activists, scientists, policymakers, and much of the general public have been conceiving the problem as an economic, technological, ecological, or conventional political challenge rather than a moral and human one, and thus their best efforts have failed to address the root causes of climate change. The emergence of the climate justice movement provides a necessary corrective. By centering "justice," the fight against climate change can no longer be about environmental arguments, economic modeling, or the give and take of party politics, but must address the injustices at the center of our governmental, economic, technological, and cultural systems – injustices having to do with economic exploitation, racism, patriarchy, violence, and income inequality. The climate justice movement can reach out more successfully to environmentalism and pursue an agenda of genuine change to the degree that it embodies system change in the service of greater justice.

Of course, in doing this we must also ask about the deficits and blind spots of the climate justice movement. The challenge is not merely figuring out how to "scale-up" from local to global organizing of ever-increasing numbers. By asking if the climate justice movement is doing everything it can, or what it might do more lovingly to kindle the commitment of the larger climate movement to justice, we are looking for more creative ways to "reimagine" climate justice. This involves some serious playfulness with the various meanings and contextual applications of the idea of justice itself. Too often the movement merely invokes an ambiguous notion of justice assuming that it enjoys universal understanding and support. As such, justice appears as a mere call to make things nicer, fairer, more equal, and simply kinder. Such a generic, soft sense of justice can work against the movement since it lacks the ability to generate sufficient critical insight and momentum to actually transform societies. Put differently, the movement needs to clarify, intensify, and insist upon a commitment to eradicate the specific conditions that encourage exploitation, the exclusion of the under-privileged (including the more-than-human world), and gross moral blindness toward those on the receiving end of climate change.

The present moment: an earth in crisis

One way to think of the present moment and the foreseeable future is as a collision of three large entities: capitalism, climate change, and all the movements for social and climate justice. This clash is itself nested inside a *triple crisis* consisting of:

- economic uncertainty and increasingly unequal access to well-being (*el buen vivir*[3]) in the age of neoliberal capitalist globalization and profound economic crisis;
- despite this, and indeed because of it, there has been a corresponding waning of public confidence in political parties (the "democratic deficit");
- and because of both, we have economies and cultures saturated with militarism and endemic violence.

These are now bound together and exacerbated by the wild card of climate chaos, and all of this would seem to auger a perfect storm of crisis.

With climate change, we are faced with a "wicked" problem. Such problems are:

> difficult or impossible to solve because of incomplete, contradictory, and changing requirements that are often difficult to recognize ... Moreover, because of complex interdependencies, the effort to solve one aspect of a wicked problem may reveal or create other problems ... A problem whose solution requires a great number of people to change their mindsets and behavior is likely to be a wicked problem.
>
> (Wikipedia 2015, citing the Australian Public Service Commission 2007)[4]

For wicked theorists like Kelly Levin and her colleagues, many social problems present challenges in the above sense. Climate change, on the other hand, is a *super* wicked problem, characterized by four further features. Three of these are:

- time is running out;
- those seeking to end the problem (humans, and more precisely, global elites) are also causing it; and
- it is a global collective action problem overseen by at best a weak central authority (as anyone who has ever witnessed a UN climate summit can attest).

All of which lead to the fourth obstacle:

> Partly as a result of the above three features, super wicked problems generate a situation in which the public and decision makers, even in

the face of overwhelming evidence of the risks of significant or even catastrophic impacts from inaction, make decisions that disregard this information and reflect very short time horizons. It is this very feature that has frustrated so many climate policy advocates.

(Levin *et al.* 2012)

The interdependency of the several crises besetting us is significant; it means that we need to learn to connect the dots in confronting the climate crisis, and that the many intersecting struggles that call for justice must somehow be understood and acted upon together. The upside of dealing with such a complex crisis is that progress in any sphere of it can alter the balance of forces for the better in others, and that synergies among movements can emerge if they form strong alliances.

Another upside of wrestling with a super wicked problem is that one can identify centralized strands that animate the problem. The climate justice movement does this by focusing attention on how injustice courses through neoliberal capitalist globalization, the democratic deficit, and militarism and endemic violence. It provides, in other words, an interpretive frame to understand the triple crisis and uses this frame to explain and mobilize people on behalf of climate protection. Climate change is at once expression, symptom, cause, and accelerator of the triple crisis. The climate justice movement provides an activist articulation of this insight. In its more radical – and therefore promising – efforts, it aims not to diffuse or mitigate the crisis but to transform it. Ultimately, it seeks not the minimization of economic disruptions, undemocratic politics, or violence but their wholesale eradication. Nothing less will sufficiently address the climate crisis. As we shall see, this is the essential insight of Naomi Klein's key climate justice text, *This Changes Everything: Capitalism versus the Climate* (Klein 2014).

Humanity's future, then, looks increasingly set to be a race. On one hand, stand the perpetuation and acceleration of widespread injustice, bringing more intensified storms, higher temperatures, sea level rise, and every other ill associated with climate change. On the other, stand the efforts and ability of the climate justice movement to unpeel or "crack" (Holloway 2010) and eventually transform the structures that reproduce and drive the obscene levels of inequality, exploitation, and hierarchical abuse that generate climate change. To advance its prospects, the movement must, at a minimum, defeat the economic and political one percent at the ballot box, in the streets, at places of work and consumption, and in the very carbon-saturated culture and media in which we live, work, and dream. Beyond this, it must create more equal, compassionate, and fairer societies that take social and ecological interdependence seriously and work toward a more just, democratic future.

A sociology of the climate crisis

I'd like to make two observations that for me underpin the climate justice movement but have yet to become part of popular understanding: first, that the climate crisis is far more profound and daunting than most of us realize; and second, that the planet cannot stay below the bottom-line warming target of 2° (let alone 1.5°) Celsius under capitalism as we know it.

In his powerful essay "Global Warming's Terrifying New Math" (2012), prominent US climate activist Bill McKibben argues that to have a reasonable chance to stay under a 2° Celsius temperature rise in this century, we can only burn a given amount of fossil fuels (as he points out, in this case, "reasonable" means four chances in five, or "somewhat worse odds than playing Russian roulette with a six-shooter"). Science tells us that this means the world's largest fossil-fuel producing corporations and countries must be compelled to leave eighty percent of their proven reserves (worth as much as twenty-seven trillion dollars by some estimates,) in the ground. This is the inescapable physical and political economic logic of salvaging a livable planet for future generations.[5]

In 2012, McKibben estimated the cap for maximum future atmospheric CO_2 emissions at 565 gigatons as the upper limit for staying at or below a 2° Celsius temperature rise. With annual global emissions currently running around 34 gigatons a year, and rising about three percent per annum, this cap is roughly equal to a fourteen-year supply – till about 2026 – if business-as-usual trends of economic production and growth continue.[6]

Like McKibben, radical climate scientists Kevin Anderson and Alice Bows (now Bows-Larkin) are doing what more scientists need to do: they are not only analyzing the climate problem, but are mobilizing their knowledge to identify the larger political problem that underlies it (Anderson 2012; Anderson and Bows 2011, 2012). Their assessment is that emitting another 1,000 gigatons of CO_2, allowing for a 66 percent chance of staying under 2°, would mean that we have roughly twenty-one years at current rates of extraction before we exceed the limit (but now we would be playing Russian roulette with the planet with *two* bullets in the gun we're aiming at it). What makes Anderson and Bows true heroes within the climate science community is their bold articulation of the policy implications of our predicament. They argue that we need to avoid 4° *at all costs*, as even the World Bank (2012) now agrees – or as Hans Joachim Schellnhuber, director of the Potsdam Institute of Climate Impact Research, puts it: "The difference between two and four degrees is human civilization"[7] – and that the global North needs to cut 70 percent of its emissions *over the next decade*. As Anderson and Bows (2013) note, "we're not short of capital, just the initiative and courage." Even more damning are the political consequences that Anderson drew just before the COP 19 talks: "Today, after two decades of bluff and lies, the remaining 2° Celsius budget demands revolutionary change to the political and economic hegemony" (quoted in Clarke 2014a).

Following from this, the question the global climate justice movement confronts is: What are the corresponding *social and political* implications of McKibben's argument? In other words, just how *do* we keep warming in the 1.5–2° range, with the might of the world's largest corporations and richest governments united in a suicidal lockstep against us?

Here we come to the economic bedrock of the current situation named by Naomi Klein in the title of her landmark book, *This Changes Everything: Capitalism vs. the Climate* (2014). Neoliberal capitalism is undergoing multiple crises, mostly the effects of its "normal" operations. In the last twenty years, the rampant privatization of public goods and services has generated obscene inequality and unparalleled concentrations of wealth and power: while just ninety corporations and fossil-fuel exporting countries are responsible for fully two-thirds of all the carbon emissions discharged since the dawn of the industrial revolution, so the richest eighty-five individuals in the world now possess as much wealth as the poorest half of humanity – three and a half billion people (Weardon 2014; Oxfam 2014).[8] To this we may add what Rob Nixon (2011) refers to as the "slow violence" of resource depletion and the violence and militarism that accompany the attempt of the United States to secure its global primacy by massive spending to fight wars and maintain military bases all over the world. Combined, and with climate change now in the ascendant, we are entering the stage of the coming crisis of capitalism.

Because its economic logic is based on literally endless growth and places ever-rising demands on the planet's finite natural resources, life under capitalism will become unviable as resources are increasingly depleted, overworked, or made scarce by the impacts of climate change.[9] The problem in the medium-term future of capitalism (e.g. the next 25–50 years) is that the natural resource base necessary for producing what humans require to survive will no longer be dependable. Naomi Klein puts it this way:

> The bottom line is what matters here: our economic system and our planetary system are now at war. Or, more accurately, our economy is at war with many forms of life on earth, including human life. What the climate needs in order to avoid collapse is a contraction in humanity's use of resources; what our economic model demands to avoid collapse is unfettered expansion. Only one of these sets of rules can be changed, and it's not the laws of nature.
>
> (Klein 2014, 21)

It simply doesn't appear realistic to imagine that capitalism can be radically reformed, even with all the political will in the world (currently conspicuous by its absence) in the necessary time frame by 2050, by which point climate science tells us the vast majority of emissions must have ended.

While some excellent advocates of sustainable development, notably British ecological economist and University of Surrey professor Tim Jackson (2011), have advanced the important idea that an ecologically-guided "degrowth" economy is a solution to this contradiction, what's missing is a convincing case that this could be delivered under the political economy of capitalism as we know it. Australian journalist Renfrey Clarke (2014b) notes that in order to address climate change we require massive investments in renewable energy, possible only through determined state spending, and financed only by taxing the wealthy. He rightly asks: "Can anyone imagine the world's capitalist elites agreeing to such measures, except perhaps under the most extreme popular pressure?" and closes by quoting Noam Chomsky: "In the moral calculus of capitalism, greater profits in the next quarter outweigh the fate of your grandchildren" (he might have said even their own grandchildren).[10]

Both the depth of the current crisis, and the central role played by the climate disruption that exacerbates it, suggest that our activism around climate change may open a window to moving beyond capitalism in our lifetime. It seems increasingly evident that only *a strong and vigorous climate justice movement on a global scale* has the capacity to force governments to stand up to the economic and political forces of carbon capitalism. At the heart of such effort is a commitment to social justice. Capitalism provides so many of its own justifications. It can organize production, distribution, consumption, and all the rest for those with financial means and this, it must be admitted, is a remarkable feat. Its justifications fail mainly when one questions who benefits and who loses from a capitalist organization of the economy – who gains from capitalism's gifts and who suffers its violences. The global climate justice movement can only go up against capitalism if armed with such a critique. This is the basis of its conceptual and moral power to galvanize and mobilize that irresistible force.

The trajectory of the global climate justice movement

Let's consider the historical arc of this movement so far. One dividing line straddles the end of 2009, when the COP 15 climate summit met in Copenhagen amid great public fanfare and media attention in anticipation of a deal on climate. The global climate justice movement had announced its existence two years before,[11] at the 2007 COP 13 meeting in Bali, when the radical network Climate Justice Now! formed, forcefully criticizing the market-based solutions favored by many of the Northern negotiators and institutionalized environmental organizations as false. In their place, CJN! proposed that the only path toward a low-carbon, post-capitalist, democratic future would be an emissions reduction plan adequate to what climate science tells us to do.

In Copenhagen, climate justice advocates and activists had support inside the negotiation halls, as well as outside on the streets, where 100,000 people marched for the planet. Their allies included Mohamed Nasheed of the Maldives and much of the forty-plus member nations of the Alliance of Small Island States (AOSIS); Bolivian president Evo Morales, Venezuela's Hugo Chávez and the ALBA (Bolivarian Alliance) left-of-center countries of Latin America's Pink Tide; and a less radical but important part of the Global North, most notably the European Union, led by Gordon Brown in the UK, Germany, and some of the Scandinavian governments.

When the United States and China, the world's two biggest emitters of greenhouse gases, failed to find any common ground, the talks collapsed. In reality, neither they nor any of the other large emitting countries were willing to curb significantly the burning of fossil fuels on which their economies ran. With the economic collapse that triggered the Great Recession in the same year, the balance of forces shifted decisively away from the positions of AOSIS and ALBA, while the EU aligned itself more and more with the rest of the global North.

Building a radical climate justice movement

After the initial failure in Copenhagen, the global climate justice movement regrouped and built new momentum in Cochabamba, Bolivia in April 2010 to deliver its manifesto, the Universal Declaration of Rights of Mother Earth (Global Alliance for the Rights of Nature 2010). Meanwhile, some of the most active organizations, from 350.org to Friends of the Earth International and others withdrew energy and attention from what they saw as a hopelessly compromised process in the COPs, and focused instead on local and national-level campaigns building a network of global connections. These efforts have paid dividends in the struggles of recent years, from the many-sided battle over the construction of the Keystone XL pipeline to the ongoing movements against fracking gaining ground across the United States to community fights such as that waged to stop the expansion of the port in south Durban, South Africa.

Alongside these struggles a new front inside and around the COP has emerged in the form of a strengthened and increasingly vocal global *youth* climate justice movement, which has been equally active in many local campaigns (Ellis *et al.* 2014). They've mounted the fossil free divestment campaigns in the US and the UK, played an important role in the movement against the Keystone XL pipeline in Canada and the US by working alongside a revitalized Canadian indigenous movement in the form of Idle No More, and energized the anti-fracking movement in California and elsewhere. They have brought to the movement a new generation influenced by the moment of Occupy and other movements with a strong emphasis on consensus decision-making and non-hierarchical, horizontal organizational structures. Additionally, they've brought along some new ways of organizing that have real promise: PowerShifts (annual youth conferences across the world), social media of all kinds, and vast reserves of imagination, energy, openness, and hope.

   Meanwhile, parts of the radical left have turned their attention to climate change, while the more radical wing of the climate justice movement has begun to understand that its aims run parallel to other movements for social justice from #BlackLivesMatter in the US to the rise of Syriza in Greece and solidarity with immigrants' rights movements across the globe. At the same time, the Big Green environmental organizations (especially the Sierra Club), the mainstream global climate justice movement (such as CAN, the Climate Action Network, which publishes the indispensable *Eco* daily briefings at the COP), and the biggest climate social movement organization (350.org) are all moving in more radical directions. The same can be said of climate science in general (the increasingly certainty and implicit alarm of the IPCC's Fifth Assessment Report, among others), the Union of Concerned Scientists, and particular climate scientists such as Kevin Anderson, Alice Bows-Larkin, Michael Mann, and James Hansen. Finally, there is an enormous push coming up from young people, and from indigenous forces on all of these levels. As I see it, this evolution prefigures the kind of reimagining of climate justice that the movement so desperately needs to advance its promise.[12]

What now? Thinking forward

The question that the global climate justice movement is now asking is what are the prospects for synergy and movement building among all the forces fighting for the climate in one way or another? What are the ways forward?

   It's past time for the movement to engage all hands in a major rethink moving forward. As Paul Wapner has put it:

> The scarcest resource these days ... is the ability to unleash the mind, heart, and spirit to envision, entertain, and develop unorthodox possibilities ... Imagination, in this sense, is not a flight of fancy but closer to what C. Wright Mills understands as the ability to grasp a larger arc of collective experience and interpret its meaning for the choices we face. This involves disciplined inspiration, creativity, and ingenuity that can help us cognitively and emotionally enter into alternative futures.
> (Paul Wapner, personal communication, 23 June 2014)[13]

This is not to accuse anyone of lack of imagination – far from it. Rather, it as a call to mobilize our brilliant creativity and unleash our radical imaginations to work together with new resolve and joy in the service of deeper climate justice.

   We might consider a few of the many, many possibilities. For example, a major new campaign arose in the United States in 2014. The Global Climate Convergence (http://globalclimateconvergence.org) proclaims

"People, Planet, Peace over Profits" and is seeking to build "collaboration across national borders and fronts of struggle to harness the transformative power we already possess as a thousand separate movements springing up across the planet." The basic idea is to create a lasting collaboration between climate activism and other forms of social justice, including progressive labor, indigenous organizing, and the fledgling ecosocialist movement in the United States, and ultimately, no doubt, beyond, building up to some kind of a Global Climate Strike (Manksi and Stein 2014; Global Climate Convergence 2015). Co-convened by Jill Stein, 2012 presidential candidate of the Green Party of the United States, this call for a Global Climate Convergence resonates with the formation of the new US ecosocialist organization System Change Not Climate Change (http://systemchangenotclimatechange.org), which aims at shifting the momentum of the climate justice movement in an anti-capitalist direction by starting "a far-ranging discussion within society: can stopping climate change be compatible with an economic system that is flooded with fossil fuel profits? Can we create a safe and healthy planet for all human beings while simultaneously allowing ever-expanding resource extraction, endless growth, and the massive inequalities that come along with it?" In other words, can we genuinely address climate change without addressing widespread social injustice and the structure of capitalism itself?

Meanwhile, the faltering momentum for a UN-sponsored global climate deal received a strong new push at the unprecedented, massive, and diverse People's Climate March attended by as many as 400,000 people in New York City and 700,000 across the world on September 21, 2014. This event may well be seen in future histories as the turning point in the evolution of a strong North American climate justice movement (People's Climate Movement 2014; System Change Not Climate Change 2014; Foran 2014b). Multiple workshops, gatherings, and public events took place in the days leading up to the march, and a smaller, but more militant "Flood Wall Street" direct action took place the day after the march (Popular Resistance Staff 2014; Pantsios 2014; Holpuch 2014). Since the march, multiple initiatives have been embraced by thousands of people who saw their commitment grow and their possibilities for action widen as a result of their participation. The future is likely to witness repeated mass mobilizations and increasingly radical actions as global elites continue to double down on a failed business model and politics.

It may be that we also need to envision and create totally new and different kinds of political parties, responsive to the social movements out of which they will arise (Foran 2014c). We need to discover our own power and learn how to use it wisely to transcend the polarizing debate between adherents of the horizontalism of Occupy and those who favor efforts to transform societies by bringing progressive political forces to power. We have seen significant forerunners in countries as diverse as Ecuador, Bolivia, Venezuela, Iceland, Greece, and Spain; in sub-national areas within countries like Kerala in India, Chiapas in Mexico, and British Columbia in Canada; and in cities from Richmond, California, to Barcelona and Madrid, to Copenhagen, Denmark. It seems clear that we need to strengthen and make connections within and between such spaces.

Principles, practices, dreams, and hope: constructing vibrant political cultures of opposition and creation

None of the revolutions of the twentieth century was made without powerful political cultures of opposition capable of bringing diverse social groups to the side of a movement for deep social change, as happened in the Mexican, Russian, Chinese, Cuban, Nicaraguan, and Iranian revolutions (Foran 2005). These political cultures drew on people's experiences and emotions and were expressed in complex mixtures of popular, everyday ways of articulating grievances – whether in terms of fairness, justice, dignity, or freedom – and more consciously formulated radical ideologies such as socialism and liberation theology. The most effective revolutionary movements of history have found ways to tap into whatever political cultures emerge in their society, often through the creation of a clear common demand such as "the regime must step down" or "the foreign powers must leave." The forging of a strong and vibrant political culture of opposition is thus an accomplishment, carried through by the actions of many people, and, like revolutions themselves, such cultures are relatively rare in human history.

In the twenty-first century, the nature of movements for what we might now call radical social change (which I believe is a more apt term for this century's great social movements than revolution) has itself changed, as activists, reformers, dreamers, and revolutionaries globally have increasingly pursued nonviolent paths to a better world, intending to live and act as they would like that world to be. That is, the ends of justice are no longer held to justify the means of violence, but the means of non-violent resistance reflect and guarantee the ends that they seek. In this, they embody and illustrate the virtues of prefigurative politics and in particular horizontalist ways to realize them. We might call these positive, alternative visions "political cultures of *creation* (Foran 2014c; Ellis *et al.* forthcoming). Movements become even stronger when to a widely felt culture of opposition and resistance they add a positive vision of a better world, an alternative to strive for that could improve or replace what exists. In this sense, some of the differences between old and new movements for radical social change seem to include: the attempt to get away from the hierarchical organizations that made the great revolutions of the twentieth century and move in the direction of more horizontal, deeply democratic relations among participants; the expressive power of using popular idioms and memes more than ideological discourses; the growing use of civil disobedience and militant nonviolence; the building of coalitions as *networks* of movements and organizations that include diverse outlooks; and the salience of political cultures of creation alongside political cultures of opposition and resistance.

What might go into a radical political culture of climate justice? On the level of emotions, we would do well to cultivate what Gustavo Esteva has termed "joyful militancy":

> Joy means letting the world in and letting oneself into the world: being vulnerable, compassionate, experimental, creative, and embracing uncertainty. Sadness means creating boundaries, making distinctions, comparing, making plans, and so on ...
>
> All movements, spaces, collectives, and individuals have elements of joy and sadness: they're bound together, they help and hinder each other, and they're constantly shifting and changing. We often need good boundaries to create radical spaces in an oppressive world, we need to make plans [but we also need to] be open to changing them and changing ourselves ...
>
> We are arguing that "sad militancy" is hegemonic: that it predominates in many radical spaces today, squeezing out possibilities for conviviality and friendship. We're trying to offer up a conception of "joyful militancy" based on spaces, movements, thinkers, and doers who have inspired us, but there's no formula or guidebook. Even more importantly, we really don't want to suggest a new set of norms that should govern or police people into behaving a certain way: that would be an utter failure. We hope joyful militancy can remain loose and vague, while offering up some ideas that are inspiring and useful to think through.
>
> (Esteva 2014)

Similarly, it will be important to continue to cultivate new languages and ways of being together; one might think of the whole Occupy repertoire, so well captured in the book and website, Beautiful Trouble, followed by Beautiful Solutions, a project which "gathers the most promising and contagious strategies for building a more just, democratic and resilient world" (see https://solutions.thischangeseverything.org). Or the meme-based projects described in Patrick Reinsborough and Doyle Canning's 2010 handbook, *Re:imagining Change: An Introduction to Story-based Strategy*, followed by the brilliance of Occupy's "*We ... are ... the* 99 per*cent!*" And drawing from the history of our own movement, the simple yet profound slogan "System Change, Not Climate Change," so evocative and powerful (and very astutely chosen by the new North American ecosocialist network of the same name). In all of this, "artivism," creativity, and love are prominent, and youth movements everywhere are inventing and carrying the new political cultures of creation. As for new ideas about building alliances, one that many are finding illuminating is the "spectrum of allies and opponents" model (Figure 9.1).[14]

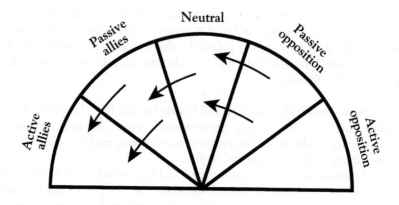

Figure 9.1 The spectrum of allies and opponents

Source: http://beautifultrouble.org/principle/shift-the-spectrum-of-allies (used with permission
from Joshua Russell Khan).

Veronika Libao explains the idea this way:

> The most important thing this movement has to realize in order to
> accomplish its goal is the fact that it can never convince everyone, and
> that is completely fine ... The "spectrum of allies" model avoids wast-
> ing valuable energy in convincing those in active opposition. Instead, it
> focuses on shifting those in a passive opposition to neutral, those in a
> neutral position to passive allies, and passive allies to active allies (as
> shown in the diagram). As disheartening as it is to know that there are
> those who openly choose to ignore climate change, there are plenty of
> others who devote their lives to ensuring that those people don't ruin
> the planet for all of us.
>
> (Libao 2014)

The key is to unlock ways to bring increasingly radical, broad forces
together to multiply our impact and networks exponentially, learn to build
the bridges, and generate the new ideas we need. As I have been suggesting
throughout, we can best do this by recommitting ourselves to fighting injustice as our core political project and creatively appropriating the language
of justice to speak to each other across our struggles. As the global climate
justice movement melds and finds solidarity with other movements, it
should cultivate such ties through a shared outrage at exploitation, abuse,
hierarchical corruption and mistreatment, and all assaults on human
dignity.

The briefest of conclusions

The forces of climate justice may seem weak, but this is the time for them to grow. What each of us brings to the table in the struggle for global climate justice has value. Our movements for climate justice around the world need all hands on deck, now and for as far as anyone can see into the future. That is the challenge the global climate justice movement now faces.

In this chapter, I have tried to reimagine the global climate justice movement. I have done so by identifying its core moral mission and calling for a scaling up and intensification of its efforts. Put differently, I have argued for radicalizing the movement. Climate change represents the most profound challenge humanity has ever faced. The forces behind it are powerful, ubiquitous, and ruthless. Undermining and eventually reversing them is not for the politically moderate since polite politics and negotiated compromise rarely survive hegemonic cooptation. Rather, we need to marshal new cultures of resistance and creation that focus on the deep causes of climate change as we imagine and realize anew a new post-capitalist world. The global climate justice movement represents our best hope for addressing climate change given its ability to identify root causes and mobilize on behalf of all life. It is up to all of us who care deeply about the future of life to nourish the climate justice movement with our support, actions, and visions for a better world. We can reradicalize the movement and further its promise by imaginative, open-hearted dialogue and determined action.

In the long run, the only real systemic "solution" to the crisis is a broad yet at the same time more radical climate justice movement willing to confront the root causes of the crisis, including capitalism, and strong enough to decisively cut emissions in a just way. This movement, or convergence and confluence of many movements, has to get there in the relatively medium term, say, the next twenty-five to fifty years, or by 2040 to 2065. In the short term from now out to ten to fifteen years, or from 2015 to 2025 or 2030, the task is to widen and radicalize climate justice movements everywhere we can, preparing ourselves and a new generation for the longer anti-capitalist project of deep social transformation in the direction of an ecologically sustainable, socially just, and deeply democratic global future.

Acknowledgements

My thanks to Corrie Ellis and Richard Widick for helpful comments on earlier drafts of this paper. I must also thank Paul Wapner and Anne Kantel for their detailed feedback on successive drafts of this chapter, which has contributed greatly to the argument and its exposition.

Notes

1   In 2007, Paul Hawken made the claim that the movement organizations already numbered in the thousands. For a partial, annotated list of some of the key climate justice movements and resources of which I am aware (see www.iicat.org).

2   See 350.org *et al.* (2013) for the open letter signed by dozens of climate organizations at the Warsaw COP 19.

3   *Buen vivir* (literally, "living well"), in its largest sense means living in harmony with other people and nature, and is often contrasted with the neoliberal notion of consuming more to live better. This Quechua and Aymara indigenous concept has been inscribed in the Ecuadoran constitution.

4   Wikipedia (2015), citing the Australian Public Service Commission (2007). The term apparently originated in social planning, and was first introduced by Rittel and Webber (1973).

5   McKibben (2012) notes that "John Fullerton, a former managing director at JP Morgan who now runs the Capital Institute, calculates that at today's market value, those 2,795 gigatons of carbon emissions are worth about $27 trillion."

6   My thanks to Eknath and Chetan Ghate, who calculated the 13.68 year supply (starting with 2012). The formula is

$$\sum_{t=1}^{x} (34 \times 1.03)^t = 565$$

where x is the number of years that it takes for the right-hand side to reach 565. The rate of increase in global CO_2 emissions in 2014 was zero, making this a crucial trend to watch.

7   Tim Radford (2014) sources the Schellnhuber quote to George Marshall (2014).

8   The original study is by Oxfam (2014). In 1999, the United Nations Development Program reported "The net worth of the world's 200 richest people increased from $440 billion to more than $1 trillion in just four years from 1994 to 1998. The assets of the three richest people were more than the combined GNP of the 48 least developed countries" (UNDP 1999, 36–37, quoted in Prasad 2014, 234).

9   The recently issued *Ecomodernist Manifesto* (Asafu-Adjaye *et al.* 2015) and the work of the Breakthrough Institute suggest that humans can "decouple" the environment and the economy through constant technological innovation, but this flies in the face of the first principles of ecology and is a profoundly a-sociological view of the world.

10 The original source for the Chomsky quote is Sethness (2014).

11 Some of the most visible signposts on the way to the climate justice movement include:

1991	People of Color Environmental Leadership Summit: US
2000	Climate Justice Summit at COP 6: The Hague, Netherlands
2002	Bali Principles for Climate Justice: UN World Summit on Sustainable Development: Johannesburg, South Africa
2002	Delhi Climate Justice Declaration: New Delhi, India
2004	Durban Group for Climate Justice is formed: Durban, South Africa

12 "Re-Imagining Climate Justice" is the name given to a gathering in Santa Barbara, California, in May 2014 in which I participated (see www.climatejusticeproject.com; see also Summer Gray's video at www.youtube.com/watch?v=GpJpbnMjiYs).

13 See also the burgeoning climate art, climate fiction, and other creative approaches to climate activism such as the Climate Justice Project at the University of California, Santa Barbara, which I participate in (see www.climatejusticeproject.com), or the Imagination and Climate Futures Initiative at Arizona State University (see https://climateimagination.asu.edu/about).

14 This image is from Joshua Khan Russell (2012). The "Spectrum of Allies" was presented to us by United Kingdom Youth Climate Coalition members Fatima Ibrahim and Louisa Casson.

References

350.org *et al.* 2013 Open letter calling for rules to protect the integrity of climate policy-making from vested corporate interests Corporate Europe Observatory, Warsaw 21 November (http://corporateeurope.org/blog/open-letter-calling-rules-protect-integrity-climate-policy-making-vested-corporate-interests) accessed 28 August 2015

Anderson K 2012 Climate change going beyond dangerous – brutal numbers and tenuous hope in Hällström N ed *What next? Climate, development and equity*, special issue of *Development Dialogue* 61 (www.whatnext.org/resources/Publications/Volume-III/Single-articles/wnv3_andersson_144.pdf) 16–40

Anderson K and Bows A 2011 Beyond "dangerous" climate change: emission scenarios for a new world *Philosophical Transactions of the Royal Society A* 369 20–44 (http://rsta.royalsocietypublishing.org/content/369/1934/20.full.pdf+html)

Anderson K and Bows A 2012 A new paradigm for climate change *Nature Climate Change* 2 639–40 (www.nature.com/nclimate/journal/v2/n9/full/nclimate1646.html?WT.ec_id=NCLIMATE-201209)

Anderson K and Bows A 2013 Global carbon budget 2013: rising emissions and a radical plan for 2 degrees Presentation at Conference of Parties (COP) 19 (side event), Warsaw

Asafu-Adjaye J, Blomqvist L, Brand S, Brook B, Defries R, Ellis E, Foreman C, Keith D, Lewis M, Lynas M, Nordhaus T, Pielke R Jr, Pritzker R, Roy J, Sagoff M, Shellenberger M, Stone R and Teague P 2015 *An Ecomodernist Manifesto* (www.ecomodernism.org/manifesto) accessed 28 August 2015

Australian Public Service Commission 2007 Archive: tackling wicked problems: a public policy perspective (www.apsc.gov.au/publications-and-media/archive/publications-archive/tackling-wicked-problems) accessed 28 August 2015

Clarke R 2014a The new revolutionaries: climate scientists demand radical change *Climate and Capitalism* 9 January (http://climateandcapitalism.com/2014/01/09/climate-scientists-become-revolutionaries) accessed 28 August 2015

Clarke R 2014b Climate change: evidence of the death-wish of capitalism *Green Left Weekly* 26 April (www.greenleft.org.au/node/56313) accessed 28 August 2015

Ellis C, Foran J and Gray S forthcoming Not yet the end of the world: political cultures of opposition and creation in the global youth climate justice movement

Esteva G 2014 The ecology of joy in our radical movements and spaces *Earthling Opinion* 31 July (http://earthlingopinion.wordpress.com/2014/07/31/the-ecology-of-joy-in-our-radical-movements-and-spaces) accessed 28 August 2015

Foran J 2005 *Taking Power: On the Origins of Social Revolutions in the Third World* Cambridge University Press, Cambridge

Foran J 2014a What now for climate justice? Re-imagining radical climate justice in Foran J and Widick R eds *What Now for Climate Justice: Social Movement Strategies for the Struggle over the Next Universal Climate Treaty* 20–38

Foran J 2014b John's journey (http://climatejusticeproject.com/johnsjourney) accessed 28 August 2015

Foran J 2014c Beyond insurgency to radical social change: the new situation *Studies in Social Justice* 8(1) 5–25 (http://brock.scholarsportal.info/journals/SSJ/article/view/1036/1006)

Global Alliance for the Rights of Nature 2010 Universal Declaration of Rights of Mother Earth April 22 World People's Conference on Climate Change and the Rights of Mother Earth Cochabamba (http://therightsofnature.org/universal-declaration) accessed 28 August 2015

Global Climate Convergence 2015 Climate strike! (http://globalclimateconvergence.org/climate-strike) accessed 28 August 2015

Hawken P 2007 *Blessed Unrest: How the Largest Movement in the World Came into Being and Why No One Saw it Coming* Viking, New York

Holloway J 2010 *Crack Capitalism* Pluto Press, London

Holpuch A 2014 Dozens arrested as police face off with Flood Wall Street protesters in New York *The Guardian* 22 September (www.theguardian.com/environment/2014/sep/22/flood-wall-street-protest-arrest-police-climate-change-new-york) accessed 28 August 2015

IPCC 2013 Summary for policymakers in Socker T F, Qin D, Plattner G-K, Tignor M, Allen S K, Boschung J, Nauels A, Xia Y, Bex V and Midgley P M eds *Climate Change 2013: The Physical Science Basis* Contribution of Working Group I to the Fifth Assessment Report of the Intergovernmental Panel on Climate Change, Cambridge University Press, Cambridge (www.climatechange2013.org/images/report/WG1AR5_SPM_FINAL.pdf) 1–28 accessed 28 August 2015

IPCC 2014 Summary for policymakers in Field C B, Barros V R, Dokken D J, Mach K J, Mastrandrea M D, Bilir T E, Chatterjee M, Ebi K L, Estrada Y O, Genova R C, Girma B, Kissel E S, Levy A N, MacCracken S, Mastrandrea P R and White L L eds *Climate Change 2014: Impacts, Adaptation, and Vulnerability* Contribution of Working Group II to the Fifth Assessment Report of the Intergovernmental Panel on Climate Change Cambridge University Press, Cambridge 1–44 (www.ipcc-wg2.gov/AR5/images/uploads/IPCC_WG2AR5_SPM_Approved.pdf) accessed 28 August 2015

Jackson T 2011 *Prosperity without Growth: Economics for a Finite Planet* Earthscan, London (www.ipu.org/splz-e/unga13/prosperity.pdf) accessed 28 August 2015

Klein N 2014 *This Changes Everything: Capitalism vs. the Climate* Simon & Schuster, New York

Levin K, Cashore B, Bernstein S and Auld G 2012 Overcoming the tragedy of super wicked problems: constraining our future selves to ameliorate global climate change *Policy Sciences* 45 123–52 (http://munkschool.utoronto.ca/egl/files/2015/01/Overcoming-the-tradegy-of-super-wicked-problems.pdf)

Libao V 2014 The cheapening of our lives: consumerism and its inevitable link to climate change Paper for Sociology 134GJ: Global Justice Movements Summer University of California, Santa Barbara, CA

Manski B and Stein J 2014 The global climate strike: why we can't wait 24 September (www.popularresistance.org/the-global-climate-strike-why-we-cant-wait)

Marshall G 2014 *Don't Even Think About It: Why Our Brains Are Wired to Ignore Climate Change* Bloomsbury, New York

McKibben B 2012 Global warming's terrifying new math: three simple numbers that add up to global catastrophe – and that make clear who the real enemy is *Rolling Stone* 19 July (www.rollingstone.com/politics/news/global-warmings-terrifying-new-math-20120719) accessed 28 August 2015

Nixon R 2011 *Slow Violence and the Environmentalism of the Poor* Harvard University Press, Cambridge MA

Oxfam 2014 *Working for the Few: Political Capture and Economic Inequality* Oxfam Briefing Paper 20 January Oxfam, Oxford (www.oxfam.org/en/research/working-few?utm_source=oxf.am&utm_medium=KHp&utm_content=redirect) accessed 28 August 2015

Pantsios A 2014 102 arrested at Flood Wall Street *EcoWatch* 23 September (http://ecowatch.com/2014/09/23/flood-wall-street-arrests-climate-change/?utm_source=EcoWatch+List&utm_campaign=553aab82ce-Top_News_9_23_2014&utm_medium=email&utm_term=0_49c7d43dc9-553aab82ce-85952877) accessed 28 August 2015

People's Climate Movement 2014 What is the People's Climate Movement? (http://peoplesclimate.org/about-us) accessed 30 August 2015

Popular Resistance Staff 2014 Flood Wall Street sit-in surrounds Wall Street bull, 100 arrests 22 September (www.popularresistance.org/flood-wall-steet-sit-in) accessed 28 August 2015

Prasad V 2014 *The Poorer Nations: A Possible History of the Global South* Verso, London

Radford T 2014 Why climate scientists receive death threats *EcoWatch* November (http://ecowatch.com/2014/11/10/climate-scientists-death-threats/?utm_source=EcoWatch+List&utm_campaign=aaf481d334-Top_News_11_10_2014&utm_medium=email&utm_term=0_49c7d43dc9-aaf481d334-85960137) accessed 28 August 2015

Reinsborough P and Canning D 2010 *Re:imagining Change: How to Use Story-Based Strategy to Win Campaigns, Build Movements, and Change the World* PM Press, Oakland CA (www.walkingbutterfly.com/wp.../smartMeme.ReImagining Change.pdf)

Rittel H and Webber M 1973 Dilemmas in a general theory of planning *Policy Sciences* 4 155–69

Russell J K 2012 Shift the spectrum of allies in Boyd A *et al Beautiful Trouble: A Toolbox for Revolution* (http://beautifultrouble.org/principle/shift-the-spectrum-of-allies) accessed 28 August 2015

Sethness J 2014 Noam Chomsky: ecology, ethics, anarchism *Truthout* 3 April (http://truth-out.org/news/item/22819-noam-chomsky-ecology-ethics-anarchism) accessed 28 August 2015

System Change Not Climate Change 2014 NYC climate convergence (http://system-changenotclimatechange.org/event/ny-sept-19-ny-climate-convergence-2014-09-19-211500) accessed 28 August 2015

UNDP 1999 *Human Development Report: Globalization with a Human Face* United Nations Development Programme, New York

Wearden G 2014 Oxfam: 85 richest people as wealthy as poorest half of the world *The Guardian* 20 January (www.theguardian.com/business/2014/jan/20/oxfam-85-richest-people-half-of-the-world) accessed 28 August 2015

Wikipedia 2015 Wicked problem (https://en.wikipedia.org/wiki/Wicked_problem) accessed 28 August 2015

World Bank 2012 *Turn Down the Heat: Why a 4° World Must Be Avoided* Report for the World Bank by the Potsdam Institute for Climate Impact Research and Climate Analytics (http://climatechange.worldbank.org/sites/default/files/Turn_Down_the_heat_Why_a_4_degree_centrigrade_warmer_world_must_be_avoided.pdf) accessed 28 August 2015

10 The promise of climate fiction

Imagination, storytelling, and the politics of the future

Manjana Milkoreit

Over the last two decades, climate change has risen on the global political agenda. Although attempts to create an effective international agreement have so far had a poor record of success, the range of climate-related discussions, decisions, actions and changes are proliferating around the world. Collectively, the human community has been devising an ever growing set of responses to the problem, ranging from grassroots mobilization and protests, to the creation of carbon markets, renewable energy policies, research programs, adaptation strategies, international funding mechanisms, and geoengineering technologies.

However, the multiple solutions that have been devised, deployed or conceptualized, so far have fallen short of producing any significant effect on the climate system. Observed processes of change have overtaken scientific predictions, occurring sooner than anticipated. One could argue that current mitigation and adaptation measures simply need more time – global energy infrastructures cannot be replaced within a decade or two, and renewable energy sources must evolve in terms of technological innovation and widespread deployment. Furthermore, nations need time to implement treaty obligations and voluntary measures, and cultures across the world similarly must go through phases in embracing post-carbon practices. Patience might be the order of the day. After all, we might take heart that greenhouse gas emissions remained stable in 2014 despite a growing economy, and this may be a harbinger for the future (IEA 2015). And yet, patience may also be the enemy of climate protection for, as I will argue and as this entire volume tries to make clear, the failure to address climate change effectively stems not from a lack of activity but of imagination. All of the change initiatives we are supposedly waiting for represent tweaks in a system that requires wholesale overhaul. They stand as various examples of Climate Inc. With the intensity and accelerating drumbeat of climate change, it is clear that we must move beyond the conceptual straightjacket of these strategies, and to do this we need to exercise the imagination. Imagination is essential not only for understanding and "seeing" climate change itself – a phenomenon no single human being can observe or experience in its entirety – but also for developing promising responses. The imagination can help us step away from and cast a critical eye toward existing institutions and practices, and envision radically different futures. This is the mental task put before us by climate change.

And we struggle with that task.

Our imagination is to a large extent bound to the systems we live in. The ideas represented and representable in the reality that surrounds us – the things we know – provide most of the source material for our thinking about alternative realities and different futures. In our minds, the universe of things that are is also the universe of things that could be. Given these constraints, it is not surprising that our future visions tend to look very much like the present, sometimes mixed with a little bit of the past. But the future will be nothing like the past thanks to the climate dynamics we have set in motion. The futures that have become possible due to climate change include a range of possibilities that are radically different from what we know, from what we have experienced, and from what we have read about in history books. An unprecedented problem like climate change requires – at least to some extent – unprecedented solutions. Our imagination needs to rise to this challenge of novelty.

Like with any new task or skill, mastery requires learning, work, and patience. Imagining climate futures, including the policies, technologies, behaviors, values and change processes that will take us there, is something that we – our brains and our social technologies of imagination – need to learn and practice. In that sense, it is a skill we need to attend to and develop, whether we make every-day decisions for our family, run a major corporation, strategize for an NGO, conduct science, or negotiate in the UNFCCC. We need to become proficient at imagining the previously unimaginable. To use the language of this volume, we need to find a way to free our minds from the constraints of Climate Inc.

In this chapter I explore the possibility of strengthening our imagination skills with the help of an unusual tool: climate fiction. Yes, books. To a large extent, the emerging literary genre of climate fiction (cli-fi) depicts stories set in a climatically changed world, describing the human experience of such fictional futures. With the help of some cognitive science, I argue that these stories might help us rethink Climate Inc. and open up new horizons of political, technological, economic, and cultural opportunity.

Beyond expanding our conceptualization of solutions, climate fiction has another, powerful effect: humanizing climate change. Cli-Fi stories invite readers to see themselves – in their humanness – in future, imagined conditions. Cli-Fi thus draws upon the full range of emotional, intellectual, philosophical, and spiritual capacities rather than appearing simply as a set of data points. This humanization allows us to feel, taste, smell, and think about climate change in a more personal way, creating meaning, relevance, and potentially the urgency currently absent from many political conversations.

I build the foundations for my argument with a brief discussion of the nature of imagination as both an individual cognitive-emotional process as well as a collective, social and political one. Treating imagination as a decision-making skill, I probe the question of whether and how works of climate fiction can affect climate politics, ideally making it more ambitious, creative, and productive. The second part of the chapter uses three novels that are paradigmatic of the climate fiction genre (Margaret Atwood's *MaddAddam* trilogy, Barbara Kingsolver's *Flight Behavior*, and George Turner's *The Sea and Summer*) to explore whether and how they might offer insights that help us reconceptualize our responses to climate change. I discuss potential problems when using fiction as a decision-aid – for example, the question how valid or correct the scientific base of fictional texts ought to be for them to be useful – and conclude by clarifying the prospects for integrating climate fiction in political processes.

Imagination and Climate Inc.

Climate change leaves a growing mark on modern societies, not only in terms of impacts but also on the social changes we devise in response to it – diplomats flying around the world to negotiate multiple times each year, governments devising policies and legislation, cities developing climate adaptation strategies, companies reporting on greenhouse gas emissions and participating in carbon markets, industries and infrastructure transforming the nature of energy production and consumption, civil society coming together to discuss, protest, shape and demand climate policy, and so forth.

Yet all this activity has so far not been able to make a significant dent into the global emissions curve, let alone slow the phenomenon we refer to as climate change. Remaining firmly rooted in the very systems that have brought about anthropogenic climate change – sovereign statehood, neoliberalism and capitalism, individualism and consumerism – the solution set we have so far collectively devised is unlikely to succeed. Climate Inc. might be able to tinker at the margins, reorganize the pieces of the current system, and give some of these pieces a new coat of paint, but its purpose is to allow the existing system to prevail. It draws in amazingly creative ways on current patterns of thinking and acting that have been applied successfully to past problems, uses well-known categories and frameworks – states, markets, science, incentives, supply and demand, risk and planning – and builds on skills we have mastered to try to address the engines of climate intensification. Conducting international negotiations is one such skill that we believe to be fairly good at. After all, that is how we solved the ozone issue! Devising artificial markets is another such skill, so is making devices and systems more efficient to reduce energy and material consumption. But in the end, all these efforts are system-internal fixes, reorganizing its pieces while leaving its fundamental principles and mechanisms intact.

But what if our current ways of thinking and acting, our skills and abilities simply will not do when it comes to climate change? What if the solutions needed to address this problem lay beyond the possibilities and categories of the systems we live in? How do we break free of the constraints created by our own reality? How can we begin to imagine a post-Climate Inc. reality, or a non-Climate Inc. reality?

Imagining alternative ways of thinking, acting, producing, solving, governing or simply living that are outside of our collective experience might be the toughest part of the climate challenge. Once the ideas are there and enough people can get excited about them, human ingenuity might allow us to create an alternative future. But it seems, we are stuck at the imagination stage.

Imagination

Imagination is both an individual-cognitive process, taking place in the brain, and a collective-social process that relies on communication and interaction between people but also between people and nature.

From a cognitive perspective, imagination concerns the ability of the human mind to create mental representations of things that are not currently present or things that can simply not be experienced with the human senses. Some researchers define it as "the vehicle of active creativity … which enables people to go beyond actual experience and construct alternative possibilities in which a fragmented situation becomes a meaningful whole" (Liang *et al.* 2013, 1038). Others focus more broadly on imagination as "possibility thinking" (Greene 1995), on its role in learning (Heath 2008), or forming intentions (Anderson 1983).

Imagination is often related to the ability to create mental images (Pelaprat and Cole 2011), but concepts and ideas, smells, sounds, stories, processes, and emotions are also features of imagination (O'Connor and Aardema 2005). We are not only able to see places in our mind (e.g., a fictional planet), we can also conjure mental states and feel emotions such as fear, jealousy, or happiness in fictional characters. Furthermore, we can hear the sounds of a jungle we have never visited or the smell of a landfill that is being planned close to our community.

Imagining the future and remembering the past, also known as episodic mental time travel, share the same cognitive anatomy – they take place in the same parts of the brain (Weiler *et al.* 2010a, 2010b), which indicates that they might be linked in important ways. Buckner and Carroll argue that "past experiences are used adaptively to imagine perspectives and events beyond those that emerge from the immediate environment" (Buckner and Carroll 2007, 49).

Imagination is also a social activity, shaped by communication, symbolism, shared patterns of behavior, and all the emotions wound up in the universe of collective life. Our brain is an open system, constantly receiving input from its surroundings and providing feedback to those surroundings through decisions and actions. This social environment includes all other people we interact with, but also institutions like states, borders, markets, companies, artwork, music, and mass media. Technology plays a major role in these social interactions, shaping what kind of information is available to the senses, and how and when it is transmitted and interpreted. Telescopes, microscopes, television, the Internet, bullet trains – all of these technologies reveal different elements of reality to us from the color of stars and planets to the shape of viruses or the nature of speed. Those social and technological structures to a large extent determine the reality that we are able to experience and therefore impose certain ideas about reality, possibility, and probability.

Not only social but also non-human environments – nature – can influence the imagination (and obviously, be affected by the imagination). And more often than not, our interactions with nature are surprisingly emotional, filling us with joy, happiness, fear, sadness, a sense of fulfillment, freedom or loss (Cervinka *et al.* 2012; Zelenski and Nisbet 2014).

The political imagination and climate change

Not all kinds of imagination are equally relevant for the political imagination related to climate change. The faculty to create mental representations of what is not *yet* present – the future affected by changing climatic conditions – seems particularly important, as does the link between memory (the past) and anticipation (of the future). Even making scientific information meaningful requires imagination, because many scientific concepts (e.g., global average temperature change, atmospheric greenhouse gas concentrations, ocean acidification) are abstract and not perceivable with the human senses. Merging these two categories – science and the future – climate-related imagination has to capture anticipated changes in the biophysical system (the story told by climate science), future social system change, and the complex interactions between natural and social systems over time. The role of imagination in creativity is significant for developing effective solutions to climate challenges. We have to imagine "alternatives to our current path of ever-escalating greenhouse gas emissions and economic growth" (Wright *et al.* 2013, 647). And the ability to think of something – some place, ecosystem, company or community – as possibly being different than it is today is absolutely necessary to provide us with the mental source material and motivation for creating change.

Even if we can think and talk about future climate impacts using scientific data, it is our ability to connect with the future emotionally that personalizes it and allows us to value its inhabitants, places and possibilities, to feel and experience what it is we are talking about, show us the things we might lose in a way that registers in our minds and bodies. In short, imagination can serve as cognitive-emotional time machine that can make the future matter by humanizing climate change.

Beyond making sense of and humanizing the problem, rendering the future meaningful, and getting creative about solutions, *what are the more general political functions of climate imagination?* Yusoff and Gabrys suggest that imagination is "a way of seeing, sensing, thinking, and dreaming that creates the conditions for material interventions in and political sensibilities of the world" (Yusoff and Gabrys 2011, 516). In other words, we need imagination to act upon problems. The mental process of imagining is a pre-condition for decision-making and political behavior – it is a political act. Along similar lines, Skrimshire raises the following questions: "how can one know and grasp meaningfully [a far future], let alone relate ethically and politically to it? Can one imagine, believe in, empathize with the future of the human at all?" (Skrimshire 2010, 2). Making decisions with a view to the future demands not only that we imagine not-yet real worlds, but also that we are able to relate to them in ethical and political ways. For example, do we experience a moral obligation towards humans that are not yet born? Or how do we acknowledge today the rights of communities who will be forced to relocate due to climate change in 2067? This political and relational function of imagination applies not only to political communities, like states party to the UNFCCC or politicians debating national climate policies, but also to corporations, universities, civil society groups, or other organizations. Lê, for example, establishes clear linkages between decision-makers' different mental constructions of the future, and the strategies and actions they pursue in the present (Lê 2013).

In essence, our imagination relates planning, decision-making, behavior, and action today to goals and outcomes in the future. It is this connecting function that facilitates and gives meaning to political decisions and actions.

Imagination, as I have outlined it, is a pervasive, necessary component of all political processes related to climate change. What makes this observation interesting is the fact that currently these imagination processes are in important ways constrained and insufficient to generate the solutions needed to take us into a preferred livable future.

Climate fiction – an imagination tool?

The literary genre of climate fiction deals with climate change either by making an altered climate the backdrop of a story, or creating a plot centered on the challenge of climate change. Scholars, authors, and media voices are debating whether climate fiction is truly a new phenomenon – after all, stories about the weather are as old as storytelling itself. Assuming that this modern wave of climate fiction is a creative response to the recognition that humans are now collectively changing the planet's climate system, Ballard's *The Drowned World* (1962) and Turner's *The Sea and Summer* (1987) have been identified as strong candidates for origin novels (Tait 2014).

The emergence of cli-fi is part of a larger cultural trend that uses artistic means and tools to explore the meaning of climate change for contemporary societies, often with the goal of creating greater public engagement. These activities include a growing number of movies (e.g., *Interstellar*, 2014) and documentaries such as *Chasing Ice* (2012), the creation of organizations like Cape Farewell, art exhibits, writing contests, and the screening of films like *Glacial Balance*[1] on the sidelines of COP20 in Lima. Even international organizations like the World Bank[2] and the World Meteorological Organization (WMO 2015; YouTube 2015) are beginning to use artistic means to communicate about climate change.

The emergence of climate fiction has been accompanied by many excited claims about the power of climate change novels to "save the planet" (Holmes 2014; L. Miller 2014) and help coax humanity into action. The *New York Times* asked in July 2014, "Will fiction influence how we react to climate change?" (New York Times 2014) The *Guardian* has been running a series of cli-fi articles since 2012, and *The New Yorker* published "Scenes from a melting planet: on the climate change novel" in 2013 (Kormann 2013). All of these pieces imply that climate fiction has a role to play in shaping societies' responses to climate change.

Of course, such a suggestion is pure speculation, fueled by hope rather than observation. Novels are unlikely to change readers' minds on climate science or policy. But climate fiction could be very important in more subtle ways: shaping our collective imaginations of possible, plausible, desirable, and undesirable futures, thereby helping us reflect not only on the nature of climate change, but on the meaning of human life and social existence in a changing climate.

The key reason why climate fiction can exert this subtle influence is the power of story. Storytelling and narratives are central components of the human toolkit for making sense of and interacting with the increasingly complex world we inhabit (Gottschall 2013). Our brains have evolved to be great story-identifiers and story-developers (Boyd 2010) – we constantly scan our environment for stories that render the world meaningful (Hanne 1996, 8). Information presented in a story format thus has a much easier time to be picked up, memorized and be integrated into our minds than information presented in other ways.

Over the last decade, narrative instruments have become increasingly popular in participatory policy processes (Hampton 2009) on topics like energy transitions (C. A. Miller *et al.* 2015), nanotechnology (Macnaghten 2010), and climate adaptation (Paschen and Ison 2014). The benefits of using narrative strategies to address complex policy issues include the strengthening of public engagement in an otherwise expert-driven policy process, allowing participants to construct meaningful stories about the challenges they face, mentally inhabiting multiple, alternative future worlds, exploring the meanings of alternative futures for one's own life, identity and values (C. A. Miller *et al.* 2015). Stories as a basic human communication tool and organizing principle of human cognition (Paschen and Ison 2014) can expose differences in values and beliefs in a community and provide opportunities for creating shared visions of the future (van der Helm 2009; C. A. Miller *et al.* 2015).

Exploring the link between environmental storytelling and culture, Buell argues that nature writing exercises "however unconsciously, an influence upon the emerging culture of environmental concern. ... How we image a thing, true or false, affects our conduct towards it, the conduct of nations as well as persons" (Buell 1996, 3). In Buell's view, literature is one of society's ways to reflect on its cultural identity and relationship with nature. Going beyond critical reflections of what is, environmental fiction can also show us realities that could be – the alternative futures mentioned by Miller and others – and raise questions concerning our actions and choices today. Linking future possibilities (however desirable or undesirable) with present realities, fictional worlds can make obvious the need for change and create the accompanying desire to act. Future-oriented fiction can inspire its readers to work towards desirable change; it can also shock and horrify them, creating motivation to prevent certain futures. Therefore climate fiction is not just a form of storytelling, but possibly an anticipatory governance instrument.

The nature of storytelling (Gottschall 2013) offers an easy-to-use framework for thinking about the future. This framework has at least four components: characters, places, plot lines, and time.

Most importantly, stories introduce us to characters – heroes, villains, victims, and so forth – that allow us to experience a future world through their bodies, their thoughts, their actions and emotions. When we identify with a fictional character, we actually live in the future for a few hours. We get to taste the protagonist's food, drink her wine, listen to her environment, feel her pain.

Stories also put us into future places and show us around – what does a city, a house or a farm look like? What does it take to move around? Is there a form of public transport? Through the books' characters, readers get attached to places in a fictional world, love or despise its inhabitants, feel its heat or wind, thirst for its scarce water or mourn its lack of creatures and plants. Stories don't talk about technology or climate; they let us interact with technology and experience weather.

All stories have a plot or trajectory – they move through a period of time, in which things change, often involving the resolution of conflict or overcoming obstacles. The plot line gives readers a glimpse into what scientists call causality or system dynamics, helping them imagine how and why change can unfold, especially how and why decisions often have unexpected consequences.

Introducing time – often through the memories of characters – climate-related stories give us a sense that climate change has a past, present, and future, and that these time periods can be radically different. For example, when a character's memories or encounters with remnants of past societies bring up events closer to a reader's present and lived reality, that reality can take on new meanings. What will our present actions and omissions one day mean to people who contemplate their history? How am I connected to these future human beings? What will they think of me? And why should I care about people's judgments of me after my death?

This cognitive-emotional exploration of fictional future worlds mixes in complex and interesting ways with our experience of the present. Our imagination turns our current attachment to a place into a future feeling of sadness about its changed character or disappearance. Through this intermingling of present reality and future possibility, our minds begin to grapple with the meaning of anthropogenic climate change and the meaning of being human on a changing planet.

But with more meaning also comes more complexity, cognitive dissonance and dislocation. The diverse storylines of climate fiction make it impossible to think about the future in the singular way.

Another way of describing these effects of climate fiction is humanization – rendering climate change a thoroughly human and social experience rather than an environmental problem. Cli-fi places the reader in plausible, emotionally wrought, complex situations in which social, technological, and natural systems condition one's experience. All of a sudden, climate change becomes viscerally more "real" than it appears in a scientific discourse. With this deeper, more intuitive understanding, different kinds of questions can be asked, for example, concerning a community's coping mechanisms in periods of disruptive change, or the ability of the international system to maintain its functionality if and when globalization goes into reverse. It also broadens the set of issues that seem relevant for climate policy, focusing the mind on human and social dimensions of what is currently seen as an economic-technological problem. Most of the climate-related challenges faced by the characters in a climate fiction story have little to do with renewable energy technologies or the price of carbon. This humanizing function of climate fiction has the potential reshape the political climate discourse and agenda (Hanne 1996).

Some of this mental future making requires the integration of climate science into the story and the daily life and history of a fictional world. It is debatable whether climate fiction can and should serve as a science lesson, and whether cli-fi authors have a responsibility to make their stories scientifically credible or at least plausible. Given that people learn facts from fiction (Marsh *et al.* 2003) and narratives (McQuiggan *et al.* 2008), including wrong facts (Barnett *et al.* 2006), this is at least something that authors have to grapple with. Authors like Atwood, Kingsolver, and Turner have made major efforts to get their science right, which makes their books interesting illustrations of what kinds of scientific learning the genre might enable. Among the most valuable science lessons the books provide is the insight that the world consists of systems that interact with each other in complex and often surprising ways. Changes in the natural world can be felt in small and big ways in the social world, and vice versa. Technology often plays a significant role in mediation or amplifying these interactions. By helping readers to think in systems, look for connections and recognize that change can happen abruptly rather than in a predictable linear fashion, climate fiction might convey some central scientific lessons without ever using a graph, number, or equation.

For the much older literary genre of science fiction, some of these effects have been researched and well documented. Works of sci-fi have inspired technological changes and even shaped world history (Parrinder 1995; Rhodes 2012). Conceptualizing this link between fiction writing and social decision-making, Miller and Bennett argue that science fiction can serve as a tremendously useful tool for "thinking longer-term about technology" (C. A. Miller and Bennett 2008, 597). Due to the stories' focus on people and social life, their futurity, and their ability to link changes in different systems – economic, political, technological and environmental – in a dynamic, and often non-linear manner, sci-fi can help the human mind explore the future in ways that science cannot.

Climate fiction is too young to benefit from a similar track record of studies that can document the link between works of fiction and reality. But Miller and Bennett's argument about long-term thinking is just as relevant for cli-fi as it is for sci-fi. Climate fiction can serve as a cognitive-emotional simulator of future worlds – a mental time machine if you will. The novels take their readers into futures that are not only climatically altered, but reveal in multiple ways the interactive changes between the climate system, societal institutions, culture, technology, identity, and the human experience. In these complex fictional worlds, climate change is often merely the backdrop for a story of humans grappling with change, loss, love, possibility, morality and conflict.

What makes climate fiction a potentially powerful tool for shaping the politics of climate change is not only its ability to expand the climate imagination of individual readers in specific places, but to reach potentially millions of readers around the world, irrespective of nationality, ideology, party affiliation, or vulnerability to climate change. The stories can turn into a shared cognitive-emotional experience that connects readers regardless of various differences. It becomes an entry point for conversations about the future people want to pursue. By opening space for conversations about the future, the stories can affect multiple deliberative systems (Dryzek 2009; Dryzek and Stevenson 2011) at local, regional, national, trans- and international scales through its readers, who are not only citizens but also teachers, NGO workers, public officials, company owners, market analysts, or diplomats.

In sum, playing out utopian or dystopian impulses, climate fiction novels create political imaginaries (Strauss 2014) that can inform and guide our future-oriented decisions.

What can be learned from climate fiction?

The number and variety of climate fiction novels grows by the week, and the works I have selected for this analysis only capture a small share of the rich stories and the diversity of insights and lessons to be gained. Nonetheless, they offer a useful starting point for both the exploration of the nature of cli-fi and the type of imagination support climate fiction can provide.

Barbara Kingsolver: Flight Behavior

Kingsolver's *Flight Behavior* (2012) is not set in the future, but present rural Tennessee. It tells the story of young mother of two, caught in an unhappy marriage on a failing farm. The heroine makes a discovery that upends her life and throws the whole town into a period of disarray: millions of Monarch butterflies have appeared in a valley behind her farm, turning the forest into what looks to her like a lake of fire "blazing with its own internal flame." Her discovery creates an uproar in the community, putting her in the center of events unfolding between different characters – stakeholders in the climate change debate – including her in-laws, a religious community, a team of scientists studying the phenomenon, and even the national media. Initially the appearance of the butterflies is seen as divine intervention and calls for religious interpretation as well as a personal search for meaning and identity among the members of the community. Soon there are arguments over the use of the property – monarch sightseeing competes with selling the wood to paying off farm-related debt. The appearance of the scientists confronts the town with a whole new set of questions, challenging not just daily routines but deeply rooted ideological and religious values. The story lays bare how and why climate change presents a puzzle for conservative America, its loyalties, convictions, and ways of life.

The story of Dellarobia Turnbow does not involve mental time travel into the future, and hardly touches on what we would today consider a solution to climate change. There is no role for renewable energy sources, carbon pricing, or the green economy in this story. Instead, the novel offers lessons about the social realities that have created America's political culture around climate change today. It describes and brings to life some of the conservative forces that hold the country fixed in its current place, and that need to be wrestled with if any progress is to be made. Therefore, the first big lesson from *Flight Behavior* is the fact that the solutions we have developed – from carbon accounting and reduction to renewable power, feed-in tariffs and carbon markets – remain completely oblivious to the social dimensions of and roots of resistance to change: family loyalties, identity commitments, value and belief systems, human motivations, and systemic constraints of human behavior, including poverty, lack of education and choice. The novel offers the suggestion that, as long as existing solution sets do not pay attention to these features of social life, they will continue to face skepticism, and struggle to scale-up. Put more simply, solution sets need to account for human experience and structural constraints.

In terms of climate science, *Flight Behavior* carefully develops a storyline around monarch migration that is not true but plausible. Through the character of the scientist, Ovid Byron, and Dellarobia's own curiosity and online searches, the reader learns about the complexities of butterfly migration across multiple countries, especially the diverse ecosystems, weather patterns, and distinct temperature ranges they depend on. Kingsolver connects ecological calamity and social tragedy (mud slides) in Mexico with patterns of plant growth and changing precipitation in the Southern United States to illustrate the complexity and interdependence of multiple ecological systems, but also the mesmerizing beauty of nature and the wonder it can inspire. The story brings climate change home for Americans today, making it relevant for small-town life in Tennessee rather some distant island state or village in Africa. It also suggests that climate change can show up in unexpected ways that have very little to do with warmer temperatures. In fact, the characters in *Flight Behavior* suffer from a strange pattern of extended periods of rain, replacing formerly distinct seasons.

The plot also invites the reader to reflect on the role of science in society and in particular its fraught relationship with the media. Dellarobia gains insight into the scientific method – the slow, tedious, and detail-oriented process of data gathering – and also learns how far removed this process is from developing and implementing solutions to the problem of climate change. The lesson that science is both necessary yet insufficient, powerful yet impotent, is troubling but important for the heroine, who ends up pursuing a college degree and a career as a scientist.

Margaret Atwood: MaddAddam Trilogy

Atwood's *MaddAddam* trilogy – *Oryx and Crake* (Atwood 2003), *The Year of the Flood* (Atwood 2009), *MaddAddam* (Atwood 2013) – is set towards the end of the twenty-first century at the US northeast coast, although the reader would find it hard to find that information on a specific page in the book. Climate change has drastically changed not simply the geography of Back Bay, but also the daily weather patterns experienced by the book's characters (e.g., blistering mid-day heat and violent afternoon storms), and other aspects of life such as the kind of food available and how it is produced. But climate change is merely a background condition – the scene – for the story. Atwood's protagonists are a small group of individuals whose lives intersect while they individually survive the waterless flood – a bio-engineered plague that wipes out most of humanity. Atwood's pre-plague fictional North America of the late twenty-first century is a society divided between an elite that lives in guarded and luxurious compounds, and the rest of the population, struggling to make a living in run-down and often dangerous "plebelands" – city slums. In the post-plague world without any of the social and material infrastructure of modern life, survivors struggle to find or grow food, keep safe from roaming hybrid animals and each other. Most elements of this fictional world, including climate change impacts, hybrid and bio-engineered animals to grow human tissue, organs or hair, brainless chickens bred for meat production, and most importantly, a genetically engineered post-human species, are mere extrapolations from current scientific and technological developments. Atwood's work falls into a category she calls speculative fiction (Atwood 2011) – it is plausible, and therefore all the more disconcerting.

Given the trilogy's dystopian tendencies – the destruction of civilization as we know it in the waterless flood – there seem to be no obvious lessons at first glance. Even if you imagine being one of the few survivors of a catastrophe that wipes out most of humanity, what could you learn for climate governance today from a small group's efforts to reboot social life post-apocalypse? But the lessons here are not in the detail but in the gestalt. I would like to point to two.

Both Atwood's pre- and post-plague worlds present futures, subtly influenced by climate change, that appall. The reader is confronted with the possibility of living in these worlds and the stark ethical questions they raise. What would it be like to live in a society starkly divided between elites living a claustrophobic life in enclosed compounds and impoverished, crime-ridden plebelands, kept apart and held together by powerful corporate security providers? Would we eat secret burgers ("because everyone loves a secret" when it comes to your burger meat) or Chickienobs – meat from a transgenic organism that resembles a chicken but has only a "nutrient opening" instead of a head and brain? And how would we feel about having to kill a creature with human brain tissue for our breakfast bacon? Those solutions to the climate-induced food shortage might meet the nutritional needs of future societies, but probably fail from a number of ethical and value perspectives. Most of us would probably not think about the daily struggles of people in the plebelands as a desirable future, and even life in the elite compounds might seem unappealing, superficial, often unethical and disturbingly unsociable. These worlds offer almost no room for true social connections, morality, love and lightheartedness. Could we ever end up there? And if so, how?

The genius of Atwood's storytelling is the insight that we could end up there. This larger message serves as a clarion call – we have all the technologies and all the human tendencies to move closer to this kind of future, in which producing food naturally becomes increasingly challenging, and weather conditions make outdoor experiences more and more unpleasant, even dangerous. And although the author does not tell us how the US turned into a corporatist, class-divided and artificially fed country, there is lots of room to imagine how things might have gone wrong; how the decision-tree of history has taken the country and its people down to this branch with the interactive help of climate change and technology. Simulating a reality that the reader finds in many ways objectionable inevitably raises the question how such a future can be avoided.

And therein lies the second lesson: climate change needs to be understood in context. It is not the only system that is in the process of changing and will change – potentially dramatically – in the future. Not only does the climate interact with many other natural systems, most importantly the ocean and the planet's hydrology. Social-economic-political systems can undergo rapid transformation, often aided by developments in science and technology, sometimes simply by the force of human will, moral outrage, or dreams of a better future. If we want to get a glimpse into our climate futures – including the plausible, desirable, and abhorrent – we need to look at all of these elements and the change dynamics produced by their complex interactions over long periods of time. Most importantly, we need to understand human agency within these multiple, interdependent, complex systems, interacting in surprising ways. What elements of the system can we control, shape, or nudge, either through individual or collective action, institutional design, technological interventions or policy? Which ones do we affect indirectly (e.g., through our consumption choices)? Which ones are simply uncontrollable, but could respond in unpredictable ways to our collective behavior? Where are our leverage points? When do we expect major branches in humanity's collective decision tree? Atwood's dystopia encourages us to ask such questions.

Looking at climate change through the complex-systems lens and keeping in mind Kingsolver's lessons, Atwood's books teach us that solutions to climate change lie not only in mitigation technologies like renewable energy sources, or adaptation technologies like sea-walls and salt water desalination. They will have to come in the form of new social technologies (e.g., how to deal with poverty, provide security, offer education, communicate, run a country, or design clothing), including the development of new kinds of belief systems (e.g., religions, ideologies) that will not only fit the circumstances, but help people thrive and lead meaningful lives by orienting their decisions through a set of values and social practices. In the *MaddAddam* trilogy, one such new belief system is the religion of the God's Gardeners, an anti-technology, rooftop-gardening eco-cult promoting communal life and a small ecological footprint. Another belief system and associated organization in Atwood's story is the Church of PetrOleum, which worships oil and money. These stand as alternatives to the dominant world Atwood draws and thus joggle the imagination by producing tension between alternative futures.

George Turner: The Sea and Summer

The Sea and Summer (Turner 1987) is set in Melbourne, Australia. The book's central story takes place in the middle of the twenty-first century, when the overpopulated coastal city struggles with sea-level-rise, flooding, and heat. Not only the weather has changed, but Australia's society, economy, and mode of government look nothing like they do today. The society is starkly divided between a productive and well-off elite living in the city center ("Sweet") and a non-working, poor majority ("Swill"), depending on government hand-outs and living in densely packed run-down apartment towers that are slowly being submerged by the rising sea. Due to overpopulation, food shortages, and other factors, the international financial system has collapsed, money has disappeared, and globalization is drastically reversed. This narrative is framed by a second story set a couple centuries later when the "Autumn People" are looking back at the "Greenhouse Culture" through a historical-scholarly lens, seeking to understand why the Greenhouse Culture allowed climate change to unfold despite their scientific knowledge and awareness of the slow undoing of their world in front of their eyes.

Similar to Atwood's novels, Turner presents a dystopian future with a deep divide – social and spatial – between the rich and poor. The effects of climate change in the Greenhouse Culture go far beyond environmental changes – they have undone an entire society and its social-economic organization. As Graham Sleight notes in his introduction to the 2012 reprint of the book, "*The Sea and Summer* isn't just about environmental issues, though. It has far broader political concerns, and – moreover – a sense of how all the influences on a society interact and affect individuals" (xi–xii). These two insights – (i) the interaction of various influences on a society and (ii) the impact of these interactions on individuals – offer distinct lessons for the reader.

Turner is able to tell a plausible story about the systemic linkages between the climate, food, economy, society, and government, offering similar lessons in systems thinking like Atwood. But some features of his storytelling are also markedly different than Atwood's. For example, he creates a cohesive history of Greenhouse Culture through the memories of the protagonists (e.g., the dynamics that lead to the collapse of the international trading and monetary systems, along with parts of the present global governance infrastructure), which allows the reader to understand how things came to be the way they are. He also offers a much more comprehensive articulation of the governance logic and the belief systems of public officials in his fictional world. This macro perspective, both in terms of time and governance, is absent in Atwood's work, leaving the reader with more questions and room for imagination. Turner tells us how and when things went wrong.

Turner's writing does not just add a macro-scale perspective on social-environmental change, but artfully weaves in details about the impacts of such systemic changes at the individual, family, and community levels. Focusing, for example, on personal and professional identities, *The Sea and Summer* details the kinds of career profiles, family relationships, or educational pathways available to and practiced by the inhabitants of a fictional Melbourne around 2050. Going even further, Turner offers the reader a journey into the emotional world of these future Australians, who struggle not only with their own destiny in society's two-class system and its dead-ends, but also with the loss of nature experiences (e.g., going to the beach, love of the ocean) and associated sadness, life in constantly crowded and noisy spaces, and uncertainty and anxiety over access to food. Taking the reader into the partly submerged apartment towers of the Swill or a frequently flooded family home, the author turns a slow and hard-to-perceive phenomenon like sea-level rise into a stark and imaginable, almost visceral mental and emotional reality.

Although Turner has created an incredibly detailed fictional world, he is skeptical about the predictive power of science (or climate) fiction. In the postscript to *The Sea and Summer* he writes: "This novel cannot be regarded as prophetic; it is not offered as a dire warning. Its purpose is simply to highlight a number of possibilities that deserve urgent thought." Rather than sending a warning – shaking people out of their lethargy – he merely hopes to make his readers think about the issues at the center of his novel. Nevertheless, the reader can't help but wonder – as Sleight does in his introduction – "It is not in any sense predestined that things have to be this way; so how might they be otherwise? How could a different world be built?"

Cli-fi lessons and challenges

The cli-fi lessons I have discussed are maybe not the ones the reader had hoped for. They do not offer specific decision advice, present a novel solution, or answer the question whether a carbon tax or a renewable energy policy is a better measure in a specific political context. Neither do they help decide whether the stabilization of global warming around 2°C is a reasonable and worthwhile goal of global climate governance.

Instead, the three stories offer more diffuse and complicated lessons concerning the nature of the problem we are dealing with, and the many ways in which our current approaches to climate policy are too constrained, narrow, and unimaginative. These books point to the fact that climate change is not a scientific, technological, or economic problem, although it is all of these things. It is primarily a challenge to the values and ideas embedded in all parts of our lives, from our commute to work, to the products we produce and buy, the vacations we take, the institutions we are part of, and the governments we vote into power.

Devising solutions to climate change requires first and foremost the ability to see the world through a systems lens, identifying its patterns, linkages, and potentially surprising and non-linear change dynamics. Seeing the connections between the nature, society, and what has been termed the Technosphere is a first step towards creating systemic change.

Whether it is Dellarobia Turnbow in Tennessee, Toby and Zeb in what used to be Boston, or Francis Conway in Melbourne, each story allows the reader to viscerally connect through its characters with the reality of climate change and the future – using our emotions to unsettle our perceptions and lives. Suddenly climate change is no longer a technical issue to be solved by bureaucrats, energy companies, and politicians, nor a phenomenon to be suffered by people distant in place or time. It is something that makes the reader feel discomfort, potential loss and sadness, frustration, and a desire for a better world than those created by Atwood or Turner.

These multiple plot lines render a complex and intriguing context for understanding climate change – at once more human and intensely social, but also a lot messier. None of the stories allows its readers to draw a single conclusion or see the world in black-and-white. Very much like our reality, these fictional depictions present opposites and irreconcilable contradictions. Each world contains good and bad elements – love and cruelty, happiness and suffering, loss and novelty. But the balance between those elements can differ remarkably, sensitizing the reader to difficult questions about trade-offs, uncertainties and unavoidable downsides involved in climate decision-making, and maybe even more so in times of involuntary transformation.

Along with those insights, the reader has learned a thing or two about ecosystems, the role of science in society, and the dark as well as bright sides of human nature. One has also been confronted with a number of unavoidable ethical dilemmas embedded in the climate-related choices that line our collective path into the future.

Notwithstanding these benefits, it is important to recognize some of the challenges associated with the proposition that works of fiction could and should have an effect on political life.

First, different people might learn very different things from these books. The novels are complex and multilayered works of art that require and invite interpretation. The worldviews, values, and identities of readers will serve as lenses through which they understand the story and which allows them to create meaningful relations between self, story, and reality.

Second, there are risks involved in using fiction as a source of lessons for climate governance. Artists do not have an obligation to be true to science, only to their own imagination. They are free to create fictional worlds that are unconstrained by the laws of physics or existing knowledge about climate change. Even if they build on existing scientific knowledge – which is the case for all three authors featured here – their scientific understanding might be wholly inaccurate and certainly, at times, at odds with that of the reader. While authors have to struggle with the issue of scientific plausibility – this is part of their ethical-professional challenge – one could also argue that there is no need for climate fiction stories to "get the science right." It is simply not the function of storytelling to provide lessons in climate science. In fact, the decision to cross the boundary between reality and fiction might be a useful creative device to strengthen the story, raise a certain question or make a point.

Further, by creating some future scenarios in great detail in our minds, the novels might hide and obscure other possible futures. Highlighting some pathways into the future might make it a lot harder for the reader to imagine alternatives. This phenomenon is particularly relevant when considering that most climate fiction to date has a strong dystopian tendency, which might create challenges for readers to imagine and work towards utopias – desirable futures, focusing on climate solutions and their effects on social and economic organization or cultural developments.

Conclusion

Political decision-making on climate change faces major imagination challenges – envisioning possible and desirable futures based on available scientific data, understanding possible pathways of change in interacting social-environmental systems, and understanding how today's decisions might affect different pathways of change and ultimately the future humans will experience. Such imaginations are not only hard, they also hardly ever happen in the minds of political decision-makers today. It is a cognitive-emotional skill that needs to learned and practiced.

This chapter has explored the potential power of climate fiction – a growing literary genre that deals with climate change – to stimulate, aid, and enrich the political imagination.

I have argued that rather than offering novel solutions, climate fiction stories provide subtle and complex lessons concerning the intricate relationship between climate, society, economics, and politics. There are six possible effects of reading climate fiction on the individual and collective imagination regarding climate change:

1   meaning-making and learning;
2   mental simulation of (novel) solutions;
3   exploring values and ethical dimensions of climate change;
4   emotional time travel;
5   complex systems thinking; and
6   reaching diverse mass audiences.

My discussion of three specific works of climate fiction – Kingsolver's *Flight Behavior*, Atwood's *MaddAddam* triology and Turner's *The Sea and Sumer* – touched on some these, especially (1) and (5).

None of the novels selected for this analysis has a happy ending, which raises important questions concerning the impacts of dystopian versus utopian writing. Dystopian novels might make it more challenging for the reader to envision positive and desirable futures. They can also generate a host of difficult, negative emotions, reinforcing the scientific doomsday messages that have had, at best, a mixed record in mobilizing people for change. At the same time, dystopian stories can offer valuable reflections concerning today's social challenges and the long-term implications of the decisions we make, both individually and collectively. At the very least they can help us understand what kinds of futures we want to prevent, motivating us to contemplate steps in more desirable directions.

The ideas I have explored in this chapter are an invitation to scholars working at the boundary between social science, arts, and humanities to start exploring the phenomenon of imagination and the impact of climate fiction on climate politics empirically. Beyond this research awaits the question whether and how insights about imagination and climate fiction can be used to design or improve existing decision-making and governance processes, maybe through participatory methods or targeted interventions into a deliberative system.

At the very least, I hope that this foray into cli-fi demonstrates the benefits of using the imagination in artistic ways to shake-up habitual thinking and create room for novel explorations into how to respond to climate change. Naomi Klein has recently argued that addressing climate change requires changing everything – our economic, technological, governmental, and cultural systems. If she is even half right, we need to move beyond Climate Inc. strategies. Cultivating an appreciation for cli-fi and mining cli-fi's insights for lessons and inspiration supports such an exploration. It allows us to get out of the bind that Einstein defined when he supposedly said, "We cannot solve our problems with the same thinking we used when we created them."

Notes

1   See www.glacialbalance.com.
2   In April 2014 the World Bank supported the launch of Cameron's documentary TV series *Years of Living Dangerously* with a panel event (Murphy 2014).

References

Anderson C A 1983 Imagination and expectation: the effect of imagining behavioral scripts on personal intentions *Journal of Personality and Social Psychology* 45(2) 293–305

Atwood M 2003 *Oryx and Crake* Nan A. Talese, New York

Atwood M 2009 *The Year of the Flood* Anchor, New York

Atwood M 2011 *In Other Worlds: SF and the Human Imagination* Anchor, New York

Atwood M 2013 *MaddAddam* Anchor, New York

Ballard J G 1962 *The Drowned World: A Novel* Liveright, New York

Barnett M, Wagner H, Gatling A, Anderson J, Houle M and Kafka A 2006 The impact of science fiction film on student understanding of science *Journal of Science Education and Technology* 15(2) 179–91

Boyd B 2010 *On the Origin of Stories: Evolution, Cognition, and Fiction* Belknap Press, Cambridge MA

Buckner R L and Carroll D C 2007 Self-projection and the brain. *Trends in Cognitive Sciences* 11(2) 49–57

Buell L 1996 *The Environmental Imagination: Thoreau, Nature Writing, and the Formation of American Culture* Harvard University Press, Boston MA

Cervinka R, Röderer K and Hefler E 2012 Are nature lovers happy? On various indicators of well-being and connectedness with nature *Journal of Health Psychology* 17(3) 379–88

Dryzek J S 2009 Democratization as deliberative capacity building *Comparative Political Studies* 42(11) 1379–1402

Dryzek J S and Stevenson H 2011 Global democracy and earth system governance *Ecological Economics* 70(11) 1865–74

Gottschall J 2013 *The Storytelling Animal: How Stories Make Us Human* Mariner Books, Boston MA

Greene M 1995 Art and imagination: reclaiming the sense of possibility *The Phi Delta Kappan* 76(5) 378–82

Hampton G 2009 Narrative policy analysis and the integration of public involvement in decision making *Policy Sciences* 42(3) 227–42

Hanne M 1996 *The Power of the Story: Fiction and Political Change* Berghahn Books, New York

Heath G 2008 Exploring the imagination to establish frameworks for learning *Studies in Philosophy and Education* 27(2–3) 115–23

Holmes D 2014 'Cli-fi': could a literary genre help save the planet? *The Conversation* February 20 (http://theconversation.com/cli-fi-could-a-literary-genre-help-save-the-planet-23478) accessed 30 August 2015

IEA 2015 Global energy-related emissions of carbon dioxide stalled in 2014 13 March (www.iea.org/newsroomandevents/news/2015/march/global-energy-related-emissions-of-carbon-dioxide-stalled-in-2014.html) accessed 10 April 2015

Kingsolver B 2012 *Flight Behavior: A Novel* Harper, New York

Kormann C 2013 Scenes from a melting planet – on the climate change novel *The New Yorker* 3 July (www.newyorker.com/books/page-turner/scenes-from-a-melting-planet-on-the-climate-change-novel) accessed 30 August 2015

Lê J K 2013 How constructions of the future shape organizational responses: climate change and the Canadian oil sands *Organization* 20(5) 722–42

Liang C, Hsu Y, Chang C-C and Lin L-J 2013 In search of an index of imagination for virtual experience designers *International Journal of Technology and Design Education* 23(4) 1037–46

Macnaghten P 2010 Researching technoscientific concerns in the making: narrative structures, public responses, and emerging nanotechnologies *Environment and Planning A* 42(1) 23–37

Marsh E J, Meade M L and Roediger III H L 2003 Learning facts from fiction *Journal of Memory and Language* 49(4) 519–36

McQuiggan S W, Rowe J P, Lee S and Lester J C 2008 Story-based learning: the impact of narrative on learning experiences and outcomes in Woolf B P, Aïmeur E, Nkambou R and Lajoie S eds *Intelligent Tutoring Systems* Lecture Notes in Computer Science Springer, Berlin 530–39 (http://link.springer.com/chapter/10.1007/978-3-540-69132-7_56) accessed 25 February 2014

Miller C A and Bennett I 2008 Thinking longer term about technology: is there value in science fiction-inspired approaches to constructing futures? *Science and Public Policy* 35(8) 597–606

Miller C A, O'Leary J, Graffy E, Stechel E B and Dirks G 2015 Narrative futures and the governance of energy transitions *Futures* 70 65–74

Miller L 2014 Can "cli-fi" movies save the planet? October 23 *USA Today Live* (http://entertainthis.usatoday.com/2014/10/23/climate-fiction-cliffies-awards-movies) accessed 30 August 2015

Murphy C 2014 Years of living dangerously launch at World Bank *Connect4 Climate* 12 April (www.connect4climate.org/blog/video-years-of-living-danger-ously-preview-at-the-world-bank) accessed 30 August 2015

New York Times 2014 Room for debate *New York Times* 29 July (www.nytimes.com/roomfordebate/2014/07/29/will-fiction-influence-how-we-react-to-climate-change) accessed 30 August 2015

O'Connor K P and Aardema F 2005 The imagination: cognitive, pre-cognitive, and meta-cognitive aspects *Consciousness and Cognition* 14(2) 233–56

Parrinder P 1995 *Shadows of the Future: H G Wells, Science Fiction, and Prophecy* Syracuse University Press, Syracuse NY

Paschen J A and Ison R 2014 Narrative research in climate change adaptation – exploring a complementary paradigm for research and governance *Research Policy* 43(6) 1083–92

Pelaprat E and Cole M 2011 "Minding the gap": imagination, creativity and human cognition *Integrative Psychological and Behavioral Science* 45(4) 397–418

Rhodes R 2012 *Making of the Atomic Bomb* Simon & Schuster, New York

Skrimshire S 2010 *Future Ethics Climate Change and Apocalyptic Imagination* Continuum, London

Strauss K 2014 These overheating worlds *Annals of the Association of American Geographers* 105(2) 342

Tait A 2014 Nature reclaims her own: J G Ballard's *The Drowned World Australian Humanities Review* 57 25–41

Turner G 1987 *The Sea and Summer* Gollancz, London

Van der Helm R 2009 The vision phenomenon: towards a theoretical underpinning of visions of the future and the process of envisioning *Futures* 41(2) 96–104

Weiler J A, Suchan B and Daum I 2010a Foreseeing the future: occurrence proba-bility of imagined future events modulates hippocampal activation *Hippocampus* 20(6) 685–90

Weiler J A, Suchan B and Daum I 2010b When the future becomes the past: differ-ences in brain activation patterns for episodic memory and episodic future thinking *Behavioural Brain Research* 212(2) 196–203

WMO 2015 Weather reports from the future World Meteorological Organization Media Center (www.wmo.int/media/content/weather-reports-future-0) accessed 8 July 2015

Wright C, De Cock C, Nyberg D and Whiteman G 2013 Future imaginings: organ-izing in response to climate change *Organization* 20(5) 647–58

You Tube 2015 WMO weather reports 2050 (www.youtube.com/playlist?list=PLNaX-uTWSWrHU3ADBXLCwSs13IqF2gTIm) accessed 8 July 2015

Yusoff K and Gabrys J 2011 Climate change and the imagination *Wiley Interdisciplinary Reviews: Climate Change* 2(4) 516–34

Zelenski J M and Nisbet E K 2014 Happiness and feeling connected: the distinct role of nature relatedness *Environment and Behavior* 46(1) 3–23

Index

350.org (organization) 160

Abu Dhabi *see* United Arab Emirates (UAE)
adaptation strategy: avoidance of 94; and climate engineering 125, 126; climate regime ('Climate Inc.') 12, 70, 81; and climate suffering 131–2, 134, 137, 141; costs 64 n3; and human rights 103, 104; limitations of 10, 11, 50, 55, 88, 146; as 'moral hazard' 131; and 'radical resilience' 143–4
Africa: Chinese land acquisitions 145; food insecurity 90; harm from climate change 51; local farming methods, resilience of 99; sustainable farming 95
agriculture *see also* food security: agroecology 94–9; 'agro-pessimism' 92; author's analysis summarized 9–10; climate smart agriculture (CSA) 94–5; emissions from 91–2; genetically modified crops (GMCs) 92–4; local farming methods, resilience of 98–9; methane emissions from early agriculture 34–5; reform of global agriculture and food system 94–104; traditional farming methods, resilience of 96–8; water consumption 91
ALBA (Bolivarian Alliance) 159
Alliance of Small Island States (AOSIS) 159
Anderson, Kevin 156–7, 160
'Anthropocene' epoch: author's analysis summarized 7–8; beginning of 33; carbon, impact of 33–4; climate security, new perspective on 31–3, and territorial sovereignty 37–40, urbanization and 37–40; concept of 29–31; Gaia hypothesis 43–5; humanity as geological scale actor 45–6; methane, impact of 34–6; territorial sovereignty and climate security 40–3; urbanization, and climate security 37–40, impact of 36–7
Arab Spring 66 n19, 90
Arabian Peninsula *see* Gulf Cooperation Council (GCC) states
Atwood, Margaret 173, 179, 182, 188

Bahamas, water scarcity 75
Bahrain: carbon dioxide emissions, per capita 83 n14; water scarcity 73, 75
Ballard, J. G. 176
Bangladesh, Indian border wall 145
Barbara Kingsolver 173, 179, 181, 188
Beautiful Solutions project 163
Beck, Ulrich 120
Beddington Zero Energy Development (BedZed) 23
Bell, Michael Mayerfeld 120
Bennett, Ira 180
bioengineering 92
#BlackLivesMatter (organization) 160
'black swan' concept of historical change 66 n19
Bows-Larkin, Alice 156, 160
Breakthrough Institute 30, 121
Brown, Gordon 159
Buckner, Randy L. 174
Buell, Lawrence 178
buen vivir 154, 166 n3
Byrd–Hagel resolution (US) 23

Cairns, Rose 121, 123

movement 159; genetically modified crops (GMCs) 93; local farming methods, resilience of 99
Soviet Union, collapse of 66 n19
Sowers, Jeannie 83 n6, 83 n14
spatial perspective: author's analysis summarized 8; climate change as challenge to 51–2; of political imagination 49–51; and precautionary principle 54–5, 60–2; territorial sovereignty and climate security 37–40
steam engine, invention of 33
Stein, Jill 161
Stern, Nicholas 64 n7
Stockholm Declaration on the Human Environment 54, 64 n6
storms, climate change as cause 53
Sudan, droughts in Darfur 53
suffering *see* climate suffering
Syria, droughts 53
System Change Not Climate Change (organization) 161

Taleb, Nassim 137
Taylor, Peter 37, 38, 40, 41
temperature increase since 1997 1
territorial sovereignty *see* spatial perspective
Thompson, E.P. 57
Thucydides 56
time perspective *see also* 'Anthropocene' epoch: ancient societies 64 n1; coping with the future 52–7; indigenous peoples 64 n1; *kairos*, concept of 61–3; linear approach 61; negative temporality 50, 65 n12; nuclear weaponry analogy with climate change 56–7; positive temporality 50; ruptures in flow of time 61–2; science and 52–7
towns *see* urbanization
Transition Towns network 20, 24, 145
Turner, George 173, 176, 179, 184, 188

Union of Concerned Scientists 160
United Arab Emirates (UAE): Abu Dhabi Future Energy Company (ADFEC) 79; carbon dioxide emissions, per capita 83 n14; ecological footprint 83 n19; Masdar Initiative (Abu Dhabi) 78–81; Masdar Institute of Science and Technology (MIST) 78, 80; oil and gas consumption, per capita 73; urban development schemes (Dubai) 73; water scarcity 73, 75; zero-carbon city project 71
United Kingdom (UK): solar panel take-up 25; Transition Towns network 24, 145
United Nations Climate Summit 2014 95
United Nations Conference on Sustainable Development, Zero Hunger Challenge 103
United Nations Food and Agricultural Organization (FAO): climate smart agriculture (CSA) concept 94–5; food crises warnings 87
United Nations Framework Convention on Climate Change (UNFCCC): COP 15 *see* Copenhagen Accord; COP 19 152; COP 21 104, 133, 152; food security issues 87, 95; greenhouse gas stabilization objective 19; human rights issues 103, 104; Kyoto Protocol *see* Kyoto Protocol; and normative sensitivity 59; signatories 51
United Nations Human Rights Council 104
United States (US): bilateral emissions agreement with China 61; Byrd–Hagel resolution 23; carbon dioxide emissions, per capita 83 n14; climate justice movement 159–61; diet and health 101–2; droughts 90; farmland-mapping projects 100–1; food loss and waste 102; food security issues 90; genetically modified crops (GMCs) 93; Keystone XL pipeline 159; Kyoto Protocol 23, 52, 60; and law of the seas 64 n3; local food sourcing 101; plant-based diet, shift to 101; severe storms 53; state carbon emission regulations 64 n2; Transition Towns network 145
Universal Declaration of Human Rights 66 n16
Universal Declaration of Rights of Mother Earth 159
urbanization: and climate security 37–40; impact of 36–7